The Name Below the Title

65 Classic Movie Character Actors From Hollywood's Golden Age

RUPERT ALISTAIR

Table of Contents

That Fabulous Face!

During its glory days, Metro-Goldwyn-Mayer claimed its roster of leading men and women ranked "more stars than there are in the heavens." Movie actors were the fuel that made the picture machine go 'round. They exuded glamour and grace, sophistication and clever wit. Handsome men and beautiful women filled the studio lots, not only at MGM, but at every film organization in Hollywood. However, no matter how big the star who appeared in a classic favorite, no man (or woman) is an island. Where would Humphrey Bogart be in *The Maltese Falcon* without Sydney Greenstreet or Peter Lorre? How would Shearer, Crawford, Russell and Goddard fare in *The Women* without Butterfly McQueen, Marjorie Main or Lucile Watson? Sure, they would still be terrific, but the nuanced performances that these and other character actors and supporting players add to great classic movies make all the difference in the world. These are the folk whose lines are repeated over and over again and whose faces we could never forget.

They are gum-chewers, cigar-chompers and eyelash-batters. They are cops on the beat, and beauty pageant contestants on parade. They have voices as brusque and booming as they have the twittery laugh of a bird. Some of them can be anything they want to be (or the studio pays them to be) but some can only be the same thing they were in the last picture, just with a different name, under a different circumstance. That's okay for them though, because those who are the same sort of person are someone the audience recognizes and warms to (or is repelled by).

Hollywood character actors are often scene stealers and always star supporters. We recognize them from their facial expressions, their comic timing or the way they saunter down the sidewalk. You don't always know their name, but you always remember their face. Some of these actors had no more than a glorified bit part (though in most cases they made the most of it), but some had substantial supporting roles and even a second lead in a movie, meaning a part that was integral to the story but not as important as the main stars. They did, however, have more job security than the sequined sirens and glamour boys whose names landed above the title on the movie house marquee.

During the golden age of the '30s and '40s, female stars of "a certain age" often saw a career decline as their leading lady status was concerned. Both Norma Shearer and Greta Garbo, queens of MGM in their day, made their last movie before they reached their fortieth birthday. Fox musical star Betty Grable made her film finale at thirty-nine and her blonde predecessor, Alice Faye quit Hollywood at thirty, when Fox promoted its current cutie Linda Darnell over her in *Fallen Angel*. This "limited shelf life," whether dictated by the studios or the stars themselves, didn't affect the career lifespan of the versatile and flexible character actor, and in many cases supporting players were just getting started long after the age that their more glamorous counterparts had exited the studio gates.

Screen goddesses weren't the only ones to fall prey to the ravages of time and gravity. Leading men may lose their hair or gain a paunch. Their lusty lothario onscreen could be replaced by the latest mustachioed beefcake who had just signed on the dotted line. The character actor didn't have these problems, in fact, a few more hairs in their bathroom sink or a deeper crevice between their eyes could give them even more character. Many, if not most, whose film careers lent support to numerous motion pictures, went on to successful periods in television, which was a perfect medium for their skills and experience. In some cases, stars who had headed a cast in their more youthful years fell into character parts as they aged. For the audience, this was not a bad thing, for it offered the picture a familiarity and security that might have lacked in lesser hands.

The contribution of classic movie supporting players often goes unacknowledged or, though perhaps not forgotten, underappreciated; the unsung heroes. Studios had large stables of contract and stock talent from all walks of life and in all shapes, sizes and ages. This great population of personalities formed the league of character actors. They played the sidekicks and best friends of the stars who headlined the movies in which they appeared. They also portrayed parents, grandparents, oddball relatives, wise-cracking neighbors, smart aleck store clerks and loveable barkeeps. Lest we forget the sinister side of this society, villains also claimed a stake in this assembly of saints, sinners and every type in between. These colorful personalities were usually one-dimensional, someone to whom the star could confide secrets or vent frustrations. In many cases they carried the same persona over from one film to the next, perfecting their stereotype so that audiences knew what to expect from them in a positive and affectionate way, collecting their beloved favorites over the years.

During Hollywood's glorious heyday, the studio system was the name of the game. MGM, Warner Brothers, Paramount, 20th Century-Fox, RKO and on a lesser scale smaller outfits like Republic pumped out dozens of movies every month. Their roster of top tier stars headlined these films, but leading roles only counted two, possibly three per picture. The supporting cast, however, was numerous, and there was always work for a good, solid character actor or actress. They were prolific to say the least and their skill was essential to the picture's success. Many of these players made dozens, in some cases well over a hundred movies during their career. This was a boon, not only to their personal movie resumes but to viewers, who could see and enjoy even more of their great performances. Whereas a bona fide film star during the golden age might make three or four films on average per year, a well-known and professional supporting player, whether under contract to a major studio or as an independent, might appear in double or triple that number. As much as we may love our classic stars, they are sometimes lofty and unattainable (in some instances that is why we like them so much), but with a solid character player beside them, the star, and often the situation they are in, are brought back down to earth and often humanize the film's story. We can relate. We care about and are interested in them.

Some of these people were star material who just couldn't crack the big time. Virginia Grey, Lynn Bari, or Glenn Langan had the looks and the talent but, for whatever reason, just couldn't catch that big break. Some strong supporting players were, at some point in their careers, stars in their own right (Walter Huston or Betty Field for example) before they grew into their character stage and wore it like a well-used, comfortable glove. Also, on a rare occasion, the character actor became so popular, usually by way of a signature role, that he or she became a star, after working a long apprenticeship as a secondary player. A perfect example is Edmund Gwenn after his success in *Miracle on 34th Street*.

In most cases, these professionals were personalities more than actors, you knew them like you did your neighbor down the street, and you knew what to expect from them and the role they played. If Barton

MacLane showed up, it was a given that he was going to be the muscle that pushed people around (until the cops or the leading man pushed back). C. Aubrey Smith brought with him the air of old world elegant grace and sophistication wrapped in the ultimate grandfatherly package and when Joan Davis entered the camera's lens, silly shenanigans were only seconds away. But having that comfort level with these personas, and the sense of knowing how they would play the role, wasn't a bad thing. Instead, it offered a sense of satisfaction, of knowing that they were perfect for the part and they would do it justice, to give just the right response to the given situation.

Dialogue was a key feature to the character actor's popularity, as well. Just as classic film quotes were delivered by leading men and women, the supporting cast could and would toss off a line that would be repeated over and over again with great relish by their fans. *The Women* (1939) is one picture that has a plethora of fun and memorable dialogue, and a superb cast to take it to the humorous level for which it was meant. Any fan of the film can quote the daffy and love-struck Countess de Lave (played with great gusto by character great Mary Boland), whose hysterical response to discovering her much younger husband's infidelity with Joan Crawford's Crystal Allen is: "Get me a bromide (and after a short pause) and put some gin in it." Another great dialogue driven script is Joseph L. Mankiewicz's *A Letter to Three Wives* (1949). It featured some of the best supporting talent of the late 1940s, including Thelma Ritter and Florence Bates. When radio mogul Bates asks housekeeper/cook Ritter about her radio listening habits the result is the following:

> Bates: Tell me, uh, what are your favorite programs?
> Ritter: During the day, anything.
> Bates: Anything?
> Ritter: Anything that keeps my mind off my feet.
> Bates: I see. And at night?
> Ritter: In bed, I listen to the police calls.
> Bates: But you can't understand them, they're in code!
> Ritter: I sleep like a baby.

It is a beauteous thing when two or more character greats get together in a scene.

They came in all ages but some of the most seasoned were middle-aged to elderly. Many in this age range had extensive stage experience before trying their hand at screen acting. Harry Davenport, Fay Bainter and Monty Woolley honed their craft on the boards, then went on to create some of the most memorable roles in film. These and other supporting players were ultimate professionals, efficient and skillful in their delivery. They made it look extremely easy to light up screens with their trademark quirks and unique looks. They eventually became so popular and their contributions gained such importance to the movies in which they were cast, that the Academy of Motion Picture Arts and Sciences created categories for them as part of their annual award ceremonies: Best Supporting Actor and Actress.

Many of these second-string celebrities were quickly and easily associated with a specific studio. Warner Brothers showcased the talents of Alan Hale, Sr., Nat Pendleton, Dolores Moran, Faye Emerson and Patrick Knowles among dozens upon dozens more of its varied personnel. Twentieth Century-Fox cast Carole Landis, John Russell, Betty Lynn, Barbara Lawrence and Cesar Romero as lively support in both its large-scale and "B" unit productions. Other character stars were independent, working for different studios and with different leading actors. In some cases, directors would form their own stock players, actors hired regularly and becoming signature cast members in the director's best-known films. John Ford and Preston Sturges were two such filmmakers who followed this pattern. Famed director Frank Capra gave a loving and lovely description of casting his films with both stars and character players. "On the top of my table, which is bright and shiny, I have these lovely dolls that are my leading actors and actresses. But it is not a table until I put legs under it, and those are my character people. That's what holds my picture up." Capra gives a very apt illustration of the hierarchy and strengths of the entire cast.

Some actors starred in leading roles on occasion, often heading timeless or very popular movies, such as Walter Huston in *Dodsworth* or Jack Carson in *Romance on the High Seas*, but these were mere forays into an anchoring position, shifting away from the place where they really shone; creating the wonderful characters for which they would be best-known. Just as many older supporting actors came from the stage, they also shifted their attention to television in the 1950s as work became less available on the large screen. The movie audience's loss was the TV audience's gain. The experience and polish of these great actors and actresses was still in demand with the growing variety of the newer medium. Just as these stars found their niche in the '30s and '40s, they often could play these same kinds of characters in drama and comedy series.

The players featured here are by no means the only ones who are worthy of being showcased, on the contrary, there are hundreds of talented and deserving actors and actresses who could easily have found their way into these pages. Those chosen to be featured here are, however, a good sampling of what Hollywood had to offer during the classic days of the 1930s, 1940s and early 1950s. They are all strong performers; personalities able to hold their own when called upon to do so or be subtle enough to offer the kind of support necessary for more delicate roles. You may not know all their names, but you probably recognize their indelible faces instantly.

Judith Anderson

Sending chills down the spines of audiences as the icy cold and sinister Mrs. Danvers in Alfred Hitchcock's *Rebecca* (1940) cemented Judith Anderson's place as one of the great character actresses of her day and thereafter. It also opened doors in Hollywood for her to flourish throughout the 1940s in roles as powerful, aloof women, often with a mysterious or unsavory past. Establishing herself on stage early on in Shakespearean roles, she eventually honed her craft on-screen in heavy dramas, mysteries and film noir. Of her portrayals, Anderson said: "I may play demons, but I've never played a wimp!" And true it was.

She was born Frances Margaret Anderson in Adelaide, South Australia on February 10, 1897. As Francee Anderson, the young thespian made her professional stage debut in 1915 while still in her teens, playing Stephanie in *A Royal Divorce* at Australia's oldest and most prestigious dramatic venue, the Theatre Royal, Sydney. At this point, Anderson was encouraged by the head of the company, Julius Knight, a Scottish actor who had become an extremely popular matinee idol while touring Australia. On Knight's advice, as well as that of other actors who hailed from the United States, Frances was convinced to make her way to America. Her first stop in Hollywood met with little to no success, and this failure was duplicated when trying her hand in New York. After touring with several stock companies, changing her stage name to Judith and making her Broadway debut, the actress finally found success opposite actor Louis Calhern in a production called *Cobra* in 1924.

The actress continued to establish a firm reputation on the stage into the early 1930s and she made her film debut in 1933's *Blood Money*, a crime drama which failed to impress and caused *New York Times* critic Mordaunt Hall to note that Anderson plays a part "which does not give her any great opportunity to display her real ability." She continued her successful ascent on the New York stage, becoming a major Broadway star and appearing in Eugene O'Neill's *Mourning Becomes Electra*, Zoe Atkins' *The Old Maid* (which would be filmed in 1939 with Bette Davis and Miriam Hopkins) and as Gertrude opposite John Gielgud's *Hamlet* in 1936.

The role for which she would be most-remembered, however, is as Mrs. Danvers in the classic gothic romance, *Rebecca*, written by Daphne du Maurier and brought most majestically to the screen by Alfred Hitchcock and David O. Selznick. Before she was cast, consideration was given to British actress Flora Robson and Russian-born silent film star, Alla Nazimova. The latter had expressed an interest in the part through director George Cukor, who had currently finished his association with Selznick on the set of *Gone with the Wind*. At Katherine Brown's suggestion, Anderson was considered and hired as Mrs. Danvers in the upcoming production. Brown was a key Selznick employee, the one who pushed hard for the producer to purchase the film rights to *Gone with the Wind* and a valued and trusted associate of the filmmaker. Anderson's confidence was overwhelming for a stage actress, albeit an acclaimed one, who had one, not very successful film on her resume. She demanded transportation from New York to California, a thousand dollars a week, plus all other expenses paid and a "written guarantee" that Hitchcock would direct her screen test. An egomaniac by nature, producer David Selznick railed, "Just who the hell does she think she is dealing with?"

Regardless of the slight she cast upon Mr. Selznick, Anderson was nominated for an Oscar for her wicked portrayal.

She went on to co-star in some of the most memorable movies of the 1940s, particularly thriving with artistic and successful European directors of the day. Under the direction of Otto Preminger, Anderson appeared in *Laura* (1944), a stylish and sophisticated film noir in which the actress played the aloof socialite aunt of Gene Tierney. In *And Then There Were None* (1945), directed by René Clair, she joined an ensemble cast to recreate the classic whodunit based on Agatha Christie's novel (also known as *Ten Little Indians*) and *Diary of a Chambermaid* (1946), was an American film with a very European feel, thanks to French director Jean Renoir. Throughout the 1950s the actress graced the big screen less frequently but made a very notable if not surprising appearance in 1958's *Cat on a Hot Tin Roof*. Though she was not the likely choice to play family matriarch Big Mama Pollitt in Tennessee Williams' sexy, Southern potboiler, Anderson was fun to watch as Burl Ives loud and crass better half.

Her preference for the stage led her back to Broadway throughout the '40s and '50s where she won a Tony Award for the title role in *Medea* (1948), one of the more famous modern versions of the ancient Greek tragedy. In addition to her theatrical work, Judith made several television appearances throughout the '50s and the subsequent decades until her death. She veered far from her Shakespearean roots in her last roles, first as Vulcan High Priestess T'Lar in *Star Trek III: The Search for Spock* in 1984 and as Minx Lockridge in the daytime soap opera *Santa Barbara* from 1984 thru 1987, a role for which she was nominated for a Daytime Emmy Award.

Ironically, Anderson lived in Santa Barbara off-screen as well, and it was there that she died on January 3, 1992 of pneumonia at the age of ninety-four. A great lady of both stage and screen, the actress hailed numerous honors included being created a Dame Commander of the Order of the British Empire in the 1960 Queen's New Year's Honours List and later awarded Companion of the Order of Australia in the 1991 Queen's Birthday Honours List, like the earlier acclamation, for her accomplishments in the performing arts. Her varied career was summed up when she stated: "I am inspired by many mediums and use them to express varied aspects of my philosophies and life observations."

Eve Arden

"Personally, Veda's convinced me that alligators have the right idea. They eat their young." That quote from 1945's *Mildred Pierce* is the kind of line tossed off so easily and deliciously by Eve Arden, the actress whose biting wit and razor-sharp delivery was demonstrated in dozens of classic motion pictures including *Pierce*. Glamorous and chic, Arden was the eternal wisecracking best friend of the star or the sassy personal assistant to the main character. Although rarely receiving top billing, her impeccable comic timing garnered her roles in more than 100 movies including some of Hollywood's most remembered classics.

Hailing from Mill Valley, California, a coastal town just 14 miles from San Francisco, Arden was born Eunice Mary Quedens on April 30, 1908. She appeared in a high school play, then after graduating, joined a stock theater company. She proved herself in small roles and was eventually cast in featured parts, which caught the attention of Columbia

Studios. She made her film debut in 1929, but didn't appear on the screen again until 1933, with a small part in the Joan Crawford vehicle, *Dancing Lady*. There was little success for her in pictures, so she took to the New York stage, unfortunately achieving the same slim results. Arden eventually landed a comedy sketch in the *Ziegfeld Follies* in 1934, making $100 a week (not bad in Depression dollars). She shared the stage with *Follies* stars Fanny Brice, Buddy Ebsen and singer Jane Froman. Then it was back to the movies in the late '30s, finally breaking through with a supporting appearance in RKO's *Stage Door*, so impressing director Gregory La Cava, that he expanded her original small role to a featured one. From that point the size of her parts increased and her persona as a seasoned career woman, spouting sardonic wit and rarely getting the man, blossomed. After adding fine and fun support to the Marx Brothers in *At the Circus* (one of seven film appearances in 1939), Arden's film career flourished in the 1940s. Her statuesque frame (she was 5' 7 ½) accentuated with the shoulder pads and tall hats of the decade, gave her self-confident dialogue even more presence. She earned an Oscar nomination in the Best Supporting Actress category for her role in *Mildred Pierce*. Arden's Ida was Mildred's best friend, a sophisticated, single gal who told it like it was with extra pizzazz and one-liners were her bread and butter. When Jack Carson's Wally Fay ogles her as she adjusts her skirt, she knowingly tells him: "Leave something on me – I might catch cold." She also played fun parts in *Cover Girl* (1944), *The Kid from Brooklyn* (1946) and *Tea for Two* (1950) with Doris Day.

Admittedly, Arden would like to have expanded her acting repertoire and play more three-dimensional roles. In a 1991 interview for the *Toronto Star*, she told journalist Jim Bawden: "I wanted to play the kind of parts offered Irene Dunne and Rosalind Russell. Instead, Mr. [Jack] Warner used me as what he called his backdoor insurance. I was always in the back of the picture and whenever it got boring I'd come forward with a few wisecracks." Still, she had a variety of characters on her resume, though the lighthearted, tough-girls always come first to mind.

In 1946, Arden became a regular on the Danny Kaye radio program, which lasted only one season but her flair for the medium paved the way for her own show. In 1948, she debuted as high school teacher Connie Brooks in *Our Miss Brooks*, a role perfectly suited to her comic timing, and as a testament to her persistence in the entertainment industry, as well as her popularity with her audience, Arden won a radio listeners' poll taken by *Radio Mirror* magazine as the top-ranking comedienne of 1948-49. The program was a bona fide hit, running on the air until 1957 and simultaneously spinning off a television version from 1952 through 1956, becoming one of the first highly successful TV shows of the '50s. *Our Miss Brooks* was so popular that a movie version was adapted in 1956, also starring Arden.

As the 1960s and 1970s came and went, Eve Arden, like so many of her contemporaries, played famed stage roles, taking her turn in *Hello, Dolly!* and *Auntie Mame*. She made new movie fans in 1978 with her appearance as Principal McGee in the romantic musical comedy *Grease* and it's 1982 follow-up, *Grease 2* (her final film). Divorced from her first husband in 1947, the actress married actor and producer, Brooks West, with whom she remained until his death in 1984. After an extremely successful career in all major entertainment venues, Arden died in Los Angeles on November 12, 1990 from colorectal cancer and a heart attack.

E d w a r d   A r n o l d

Rotund gentlemen frequented movie screens in the form of character actors throughout the golden age of Hollywood. There was Hungarian funnyman S.Z. "Cuddles" Sakall, whose thick-as-goulash accent added humor and charm to his characters. There was also Sydney Greenstreet, a menacing villain in Warner Brothers' productions during the '40s. The portly club also included Charles Coburn, Eugene Pallette, Walter Connolly and one of the hardest working actors in the business: Edward Arnold. Arnold had a screen career that spanned forty years (from 1916 to 1956) and a film resume that listed some of Hollywood's biggest hits. He was one of the most popular character actors in the industry, occasionally being cast as leads, but best-known as a billowing, hot-headed tycoon, both in comedies and dramas of the period.

The actor came into the world as Gunther Edward Arnold Schneider on February 18, 1890, in a tenement flat on the Lower East Side of New York City, one of five children born to German immigrants. His father, Carl Schneider, was a fur cutter, who was placed in the Montefiore Home for Chronic Invalids, when young Gunther was only eight years-old. Unable to care for himself, Carl died there in the early years of the new century. Arnold's mother, Elizabeth (Ohse), took a job as a janitor to help keep food in the family's young mouths. She died in 1901. The Schneider children left behind faced extreme poverty and eleven-year-old Gunther, though not the eldest offspring, quit school to find work. At first a newsboy, he then found odd jobs and finally worked as a jeweler's apprentice. A May 1936 article in *Photoplay* magazine describes this job as consisting of "ten to twelve hours a day and paid him $3.00 a week as a sort of handy-boy to a manufacturing jeweler on John Street." More manual labor followed, including work as an oiler in the boiler of Columbia University, before the orphaned lad began to spend time at the East Side Settlement House, where he was involved in athletics and, eventually, drama.

The Settlement House hosted a production of William Shakespeare's *The Merchant of Venice* and young Gunther made his amateur dramatic debut as Lorenzo. It marked a turning point for the boy, who appeared in other Settlement House productions and eventually became known merely by his middle name, Edward Arnold. With the encouragement of the drama coach, he decided to devote all his time to the stage and made his professional debut in 1905 with the Ben Greet Shakespearean Players at the Trenton (New Jersey) Opera House, earning $25.00 a week. He then worked a season with actress and businesswoman Maxine Elliott, and later, three seasons touring in juvenile roles with Ethel Barrymore.

In 1915, Arnold made his way to Chicago, where he worked as an extra at the old Essany Film Studio on Argyle Street. He worked in dozens of short silent pictures until the company shuttered its doors in 1918, when he went back East and worked at World Studios in New Jersey. As the 1920s began, the actor returned to the stage, working on Broadway and touring in vaudeville. His career during this period culminated with a role as gangster Jake Dillon in the comedy-mystery *Whistling in the Dark*, which ran a resounding 265 performances beginning in early 1932. His turn in the play won him a movie contract with Universal and his first film project for the studio was *Okay, America!* (1932), in which he portrayed his most typical screen persona: a heavy on the wrong side of the law, the big boss, the bad guy. His youthful stage days behind him, Arnold recalled his early career as a promising and sought after supporting player in the movies. "The bigger I got, the better character roles I received."

Although middle-aged and perfectly cast in his character parts, the heavy-set actor also played occasional leads throughout the late 1930s and early 1940s. These were often played as less abrasive, usually sympathetic parts, such as the rich, fun-loving alcoholic who is in love with Joan Crawford in 1934's *Sadie McKee*. His leading role in *Diamond Jim* (1935), playing legendary financier James Buchanan Brady, solidified his place in Hollywood. Arnold had met the famed entrepreneur in his early theater days when the wealthy businessman would visit an actress in the company backstage. It is a role the actor reprised in 1940 for the film, *Lillian Russell*, with Alice Faye. His commanding presence helped him take leading parts in *Come and Get It* (1936) as well as *The Toast of New York* (1937), both with up-and-coming actress Frances Farmer.

His status in the industry as a true heavyweight (pardon the pun), was proven when he was named on the infamous 1938 Hollywood exhibitors list of "box-office poison" stars which also included Katherine Hepburn, Greta Garbo, Fred Astaire and Joan Crawford, among many others. The label was given by the Independent Theatre Owners of America in an article in the Independent Film Journal, listing certain well-known stars whose "box-office draw is nil." Despite the article, Arnold continued working very steadily, becoming a regular on the set of several Frank Capra films of the period, including *You Can't Take It with You* (1938), *Mr. Smith Goes to Washington* (1939, as exceptionally nasty political boss, Jim Taylor) and *Meet John Doe* (1941).

One of Arnold's best performances was as New England politician Daniel Webster in RKO's *The Devil and Daniel Webster* (aka *All That Money Can Buy*, 1941), opposite Walter Huston and James Craig. Although Thomas Mitchell was originally cast in the role, the actor was injured on the set and had to be replaced. Director William Dieterle hired Arnold and almost all of Mitchell's scenes, with the exception of a few long camera angles, had to be reshot. Huston, as Mr. Scratch (the Devil), is by far the more flamboyant character of the two in the movie's title, though Arnold more than holds his own in this retelling of the Faust legend. Among the many criticisms for the cast of the film, reviewer Bosley Crowther of the *New York Times* saved his kinder words for the two leads, calling Arnold "solid and sincere as Daniel Webster."

The 1940s saw an expansion in his interests, including having his memoirs published in 1940. Its title, *Lorenzo Goes to Hollywood*, was drawn from his very first stage role in *The Merchant of Venice*, back in his Settlement House days. His growing interest in politics led to a stint as the president of the Screen Actors Guild from 1940-1942. The decade also brought a contract with MGM, where the hard-working actor appeared in *Johnny Eager* (1941) with Robert Taylor and Lana Turner, the non-musical version of *Kismet* (1944) with Ronald Colman, the studio's all-star remake of *Grand Hotel*, this time called *Weekend at the Waldorf* (1945), and *Annie Get Your Gun* (1950) with Betty Hutton, among many others.

Arnold's personal life would yield three wives and just as many children. He married his first spouse, Harriet Marshall, while on tour in Richmond, Virginia in 1917. The union lasted ten years and produced three children: Elizabeth, Jane and William, the latter sporting an unimpressive acting career as Edward Arnold, Jr. in the '30s and early '40s. His second wife was former concert singer Olive Emerson, whom he married in January 1929 in Union City, New Jersey. Arnold and Emerson were married for nineteen years when the actor filed for divorce in the spring of 1948, citing extreme cruelty, though he did not elaborate. His final marriage was to Cleo McLain in 1951.

Besides continuing to make movies in the late '40s and early '50s, Edward worked on both radio and television, particularly in television theater and playhouse productions. His radio appearances were highlighted by a six-year run on the ABC program, *Mr. President*, where Arnold would play a different President of the United States in each of the half-hour episodes, which ran from 1947 to 1953. On April 26, 1956, in the early hours of the morning, Edward Arnold died at his home in Encino, California from a cerebral hemorrhage associated with atrial fibrillation. The actor was attended by his son-in-law, Dr. William Orlando. A prolific and popular star, Arnold left behind a screen legacy of high professionalism, a variety of screen credits and utter enjoyment.

Fay Bainter

Academy Award-winning actress Fay Bainter spent her youth and early adulthood honing her craft on the stage and it wasn't until she was past forty that she made her first Hollywood film. Unlike many who depended on age or unique personality traits to define their supporting role, a 1918 magazine article declared that Bainter, then in her twenties, proved that "the acting of character need not be confined to eccentric types or old persons." Known for her trademark husky, mahogany voice, she became a fixture of top-notch productions during the 1930s and '40s.

She was born on December 7, 1893, in Los Angeles, the daughter of Charles F. Bainter and Mary Okell. She began acting at the age of five in "pageants and other amateur entertainments" in her hometown.

According to Bainter, her father was a "dreamer of dreams that never came true, of inventions that never became practicable," and she eventually became the breadwinner for her family. Barely remembering a time when she wasn't trodding the boards, Bainter was discovered by theatrical producer Oliver Morosco who cast her in his production of Nance O'Neil's *The Jewess*. While appearing in Morosco's play, members of the theatrical troupe found her a lovable tyke and saw to it that she "never lacked such tangible evidences of their affection, such as fruit, cake and candy." Morosco kept her working throughout her youth in his stock company (until she "grew too tall for children's parts), appearing with the likes of Charles Ruggles and Richard Bennett (father of Constance and Joan). She then went on to play ingénue roles in various troupes in the Northwest, before traveling to New York to seek fame on the renowned stages of the Great White Way.

At seventeen, with meager savings and renting a "cheap room... in a neighborhood frequented by the lesser theatrical people," she made the rounds, trying to find acting jobs. She eventually made her Broadway debut in the 1912 musical, *The Rose of Panama* at Daly's Theater, following up with a role in *The Bridal Path* the following year. These, however, were not very successful attempts and she toured yet again in stock, appearing with famed actress Minnie Maddern Fiske in 1914 and taking her advice to "pretend that every performance you give is your opening performance on Broadway," where she returned, successfully this time, in 1916 in *Arms and the Girl*. The play's popularity led to a silent film version in 1917, with Billie Burke taking the role played by Bainter on stage. She attained true stage stardom, when she was featured as Asian girl, Ming Toy, in *East is West* in 1918, which ran 680 performances thru the summer of 1920.

After a long courtship in the early 1920s, Bainter married Lieutenant Commander Reginald Venable in June 1921. The couple had one child, Reginald Venable, Jr. in 1926. While engaged in 1920, Venable made the New York papers due to an unconventional naval maneuver used to see his beloved Bainter. At sea on his ship, the *U.S.S. Ingram*, he met the White Star liner *Olympic*, on which his fiancée was returning to New York from Europe. The ships met offshore of Sandy Hook, and the *Ingram* followed the corresponding ship to port, where Mr. Venable boarded the liner in quarantine. Passengers found intrigue in the incident, thinking the Navy Department had sent the destroyer out to meet and honor John W. Davis, the returning Ambassador to Great Britain. Although Navy officials regarded the event as unusual, they didn't consider it serious enough to cause Venable to be officially reprimanded.

Her career on stage was successful throughout the '20s and early '30s, reaching a zenith in 1934 when she played Fran opposite Walter Huston in *Dodsworth* to capacity crowds at the Shubert Theater. Although Huston went on to recreate his role in the successful 1936 film version, popular movie actress Ruth Chatterton took the role of Fran, the Midwestern wife of a self-made tycoon who finds herself in mid-life crisis. Just before opening on stage in *Dodsworth*, however, Bainter made her film debut at MGM in *This Side of Heaven*, costarring with Lionel Barrymore. It was the start of an onscreen career that lasted over three decades. She almost immediately began her tenure as Hollywood's favorite aunt, mother or spinster, sometimes nervous but always poised, completely opposite, it can be noted, from her self-serving, shallow Fran Dodsworth. Her characters weren't always nice, but they were dependable.

In 1938, Fay made movie history for being the first (and even into modern history one of the few) actress to be nominated for both a Best Actress and Best Supporting Actress Oscar in the same year. After only four years in the film industry, she had already made her mark. Her Best Actress nod came for her performance in Warner Brothers' *White Banners*, in which she played Hannah, the housekeeper with a past, and the Best Supporting Actress nomination for *Jezebel*, as fretting Aunt Belle in the Deep South. Ironically, she was up against her *Jezebel* costar, Bette Davis, for the top actress prize. When the big night came in early 1939, it was Davis who won the Best Actress category, but Bainter held her own, winning as Aunt Belle. Davis was complimentary toward her fellow actress, to say the least, in her 1962 autobiography *The Lonely Life*. On Bainter's role in *Jezebel*, she said: "Her contribution to the film and to my performance was immeasurable. It just wouldn't have been the same picture without her."

As the '40s approached, Bainter essayed a number of matriarchs which landed her third, fourth and fifth billed under top stars of MGM, RKO and other studios. She followed up her acclaimed performances in

White Banners and *Jezebel* with *Mother Carey's Chickens*, as, of course, Mother Carey. In *Young Tom Edison* (1940), she played Edison's mom, and in *Our Town* (also 1940), she portrayed William Holden's mother. At Twentieth Century-Fox she continued the trend, in *Maryland* (1940) for John Payne and *State Fair* (1945) for Jeanne Crain. She made numerous films throughout the '40s and early '50s, alternating her work load with television and the stage. In 1961, she returned to the big screen to earn her third Academy Award nomination as the wealthy and influential dowager Mrs. Amelia Tilford in *The Children's Hour*, a remake of the 1936 film *These Three*.

Bainter died of pneumonia on April 17, 1968, in Los Angeles at the age of seventy-four. After a funeral service at All Saints' Episcopal Church in Beverly Hills, she was buried next to her husband, who had died four years earlier, in Section 3 of Arlington National Cemetery in Virginia.

LYNN BARI ... 20th CENTURY-FOX PLAYER

Lynn Bari

Known by many film fans as "Queen of the B's" (a title also attributed on various occasions to Lucille Ball, Evelyn Ankers and Claire Trevor), beautiful and sultry Lynn Bari could more aptly be called "Queen of the Bad Girls," which she demonstrated in dozens of films, both big budget and small, at 20th Century-Fox during the late '30s and 1940s. At 5' 7," the statuesque actress was at her best as bitchy other-women and sexy man-traps, though she also excelled in occasional leading lady roles which showed her to be a striking female star with intriguing possibilities. Her come-hither looks and shapely figure were matched with a deep, velvety seductive voice that, on-screen, led male co-stars astray and planted doubt in the minds of their wives and girlfriends. She was a Hollywood gem but her career, as hard as she tried, never successfully made it off the second tier of stardom.

Bari was born Marjorie Schuyler Fisher in Roanoke, Virginia on December 18. The year of her birth has been listed by various sources as 1913, 1917 and 1919. Her father, John Fisher, died when Bari was a child and her mother, also named Marjorie, moved the family, which included young Marjorie and her older brother, John Owen Fisher, to Boston. While in Massachusetts, the young widow met and married Reverend Robert H. Bitzer, a Religious Science minister. The Reverend relocated his new family to southern California, where he accepted a position as head of the Institute of Religious Science in Los Angeles.

In 1933, the tall teen-ager went on a casting call for chorus girls to be featured in the MGM musical, *Dancing Lady*, which starred Joan Crawford and Clark Gable. Hired as a chorine, she decided it was time for a name change that would suit her budding career. Combining the first name of stage star Lynn Fontanne and the last name of author and playwright James M. Barrie, of whom she was a fan, she became Lynn Bari from then on (According to Bari biographer Jeff Gordon, Lynn's mother had an interest in numerology and adjusted the spelling of "Barrie" accordingly, shaving off some letters). Her early movies cast her in uncredited bit parts, where she played, among other things, showgirls, secretaries and one of many in large crowds.

The turning point for her came in 1937, when she landed her first credited role, as Miss Fenwick in *Lancer Spy*, an espionage thriller from 20th Century-Fox. The following year her screen presence expanded further with a featured part in an "A" picture called *Always, Goodbye*. Fifth-billed as Jessica Reid, it was the first of many nasty females that would become her trademark and she went head to head with movie stalwart Barbara Stanwyck, in a "mother-love" melodrama. She quickly gained career traction on the Fox lot getting leads in many of the studio's "B"-unit movies. An extremely active contract player, Bari appeared in twenty films in 1938 and 1939 alone. She said of her on-screen reputation, "I seem to be a woman always with a gun in her purse. I'm terrified of guns. I go from one set to the other shooting people and stealing husbands!"

During the war years of the 1940s, Bari became one of a host of studio glamour girls who found popularity as a G.I. pinup and was tagged "The Woo Woo Girl" and "The Girl with the Million Dollar Figure." These years also saw her at the height of her career, with interesting supporting roles or occasional leads in some of Fox's top pictures. In 1941, she played band singer Vivian Dawn in the Sonja Henie skating spectacular *Sun Valley Serenade*, which featured Glenn Miller and his Orchestra playing some of their most famous songs. Lynn was dubbed by singer Pat Friday for the romantic "I Know Why (and So Do You)" and the lively "It Happened in Sun Valley." The movie was so well received by the public that a follow-up picture was made the next year with Miller and his band called *Orchestra Wives*. Lynn was again cast in the secondary lead as band singer and scheming "other woman," Jaynie Stevens, and again dubbed while singing the Miller ballads "At Last" (as a duet with Ray Eberle) and "Serenade in Blue."

Bari's personal life didn't go as smoothly as her professional one during this time. She had married agent Walter Kane in 1939. Kane was a former vaudevillian who ran a talent agency with famed Marx brother Zeppo before becoming a confidante and assistant of billionaire, Howard Hughes. With more than a decade's difference in their ages, the Kanes divorced in 1943, and Bari married Sid Luft shortly after. Luft was a former amateur boxer and secretary, who became the assistant to dancing star Eleanor Powell. After several tempestuous years and two children (one child, a daughter, died shortly after birth), Bari and Luft also divorced and he would become the third husband of Judy Garland. The estranged couple would return to court on several occasions for custody and child support issues throughout the 1950s. Divorce was the end result of her third and final marriage to psychiatrist Nathan Rickles, whom she wed in 1955.

Throughout the '50s, her film work was sporadic and low-budget, including *Francis Joins the WACS* (1954), where she played support to the famed "talking" mule. She made several television appearances including a starring role in a summer replacement series on NBC called *Boss Lady* in 1952. In the comedy, which was part of the network's anthology series, *Fireside Theater*, she played Gwen Allen, the chief executive officer of her father's construction company. Her last film appearance was in *The Young Runaways* (1968), playing the mother of troubled teen, Patty McCormack. After working on the stage during the 1970s, she retired at the end of the decade. Bari died of a heart attack in Santa Barbara in 1989, survived by her son John Luft. Her body was cremated, and her ashes scattered at sea.

Florence Bates

"Wretched stuff! Give me a chocolate, quick!" Thus was the memorable response given by the silly, vain, wealthy dowager, Mrs. Van Hopper, upon taking some foul-tasting medicine in Alfred Hitchcock's *Rebecca* (1940). The self-absorbed widow was played by the delightful Florence Bates, and the Hitchcock classic was her first major film role, as well as the one with which she is most readily associated. In the thirteen years after *Rebecca*, she would appear in over sixty films, some in uncredited roles, some of which her scenes would be deleted. On the other end of the decade, she triumphed with a similar *grande dame* role in *A Letter to Three Wives* (1949). As Mrs. Manleigh, radio advertising mogul supreme, she is sheer perfection.

Born Florence Rabe on April 15, 1888 in San Antonio, Texas, she was the child of Jewish immigrant parents. Her biography includes a varied background, especially for the time in which she lived. After earning a math degree in 1906 from the University of Texas, she became a schoolteacher, met and married her first husband in 1909, had a daughter and got a divorce within a few years. Not the standard fare for females at the turn of the twentieth century. An attorney at one point (one of the first in the state of Texas), she was admitted to the bar in 1914. She also managed an antique shop, ran a bakery and was involved in oil drilling. A seemingly wise woman, she once said: "Never underestimate the intelligence of an opponent, an audience, or a child. Whenever you do, you get your come-uppance and you jolly well deserve it."

In 1929, she married again, and she and her husband moved to California. After settling in Los Angeles, she auditioned for and won the role of Miss Bates in a stage version of Jane Austin's *Emma* at the historic and prestigious Pasadena Playhouse. Due to the success of the production, the actress continued to work with the organization through the rest of the decade and she went as far as to adopt the last name of her character, Bates, as her own, becoming Florence Bates.

Except for a small uncredited role in a low-budget crime thriller from Universal, *The Man in Blue* (1937), Florence had no screen experience before she was personally cast by Alfred Hitchcock in his American debut film, *Rebecca*, in 1940. The director, along with the film's producer David O. Selznick, spotted the mature actress (she was fifty-two when she appeared in *Rebecca*) at the Pasadena Playhouse. Although produced in the United States at an American studio, *Rebecca* was a very English movie, based on a famed English novel, set in a very English manor and starring mostly native English actors. Bates' appearance as Edythe Van Hopper, the very American dowager, was quite memorable. Her character was nouveau-riche to the max, demanding, abrasive, obnoxious; everything that gave such Americans a bad name in Europe of the day. Her portrayal of an ultra-snob helped her land similar roles throughout the rest of her career.

Full-figured and matronly in appearance, and fiercely independent in character, Bates' roles included an assortment of wealthy socialites, high-level businesswomen and hard-fisted landladies. Some of her best films include *Love Crazy* (1941), *The Moon and Sixpence* (1942), *The Diary of a Chambermaid* (1946), *The Secret Life of Walter Mitty* (1948) and *Portrait of Jennie* (1948). She continued her film career into the next decade and also made several appearances in some of the most popular television shows of the 1950s including *My Little Margie, Our Miss Brooks, The Adventures of Ozzie and Harriet* and a very funny episode of *I Love Lucy* entitled "Pioneer Women," in which star Lucille Ball makes a bet that she can survive using nothing invented after the year 1900. Bates played her quintessential role of society matron yet again in this episode.

Her second husband, Will Jacoby, died in 1951. Her only daughter had died in childbirth a decade before and her only sister a few years prior. Florence Bates passed away in Burbank, California on January 31, 1954, from a heart attack. Her legacy as one of the great character stars during Hollywood's golden age is one which is appreciated into the 21st century.

Louise Beavers

African-American actress Hattie McDaniel famously said of her Hollywood career, which was filled with portrayals of domestics and servants: "I'd rather play a maid than be one." The quote summed up the limited opportunities for women of color in Hollywood during the 1930s, 1940s and 1950s, and along with McDaniel, Louise Beavers was one of the most active actresses of her race in this period. If credited for a film at all, Beavers was usually listed simply as "Maid" or "So-in-so's Maid," but even in her tiniest walk-on she provided warmth and humor and her contributions are well remembered by classic movie fans. Where Hattie McDaniel was characterized as "a big, black, bossy and beautiful maid who continually forgets her place," Beavers was rarely overbearing but always jolly; her spirits lifted and her demeanor ready to lift the spirits of others, usually the white stars of the films in which she appeared.

Cincinnati-born in 1902, Louise was the daughter of William and Ernestine Beavers. When Mrs. Beavers, a school teacher for Cincinnati public schools, became ill, the family moved to southern California, where young Louise graduated from Pasadena High School. From there she joined an all-female troupe called the Lady Minstrels and eventually the young woman became a real-life maid and assistant to Paramount silent star Leatrice Joy. She made her film debut as an uncredited slave in 1927's *Uncle Tom's Cabin* and continued with a relentless parade of "mammy" roles, which spanned over thirty years.

The "Mammy" archetype was present in entertainment venues and popular culture since the Civil War and was continued in motion pictures throughout the golden age. It represented an overweight, large breasted, middle-aged African-American woman, in a serving role to white households, whether to families or single people. Beavers' interpretation included a good-natured soul, usually Christian in belief and often of a slightly naïve personality. Her most famous part was opposite Claudette Colbert in the original version of Fannie Hurst's novel *Imitation of Life* (1934). As Delilah, she played a maid whose pancake recipe and Aunt Jemima marketing made a fortune for her white friend (Colbert), to whom she gave the recipe. Together the women (the Colbert character cuts Delilah in for a 20% share!) live together and raise their respective daughters in the same household. Delilah's daughter, Peola, is a light-skinned girl who passes for white, despite her mother's efforts to make her accept her true racial background.

Beavers had her critics, African-Americans who resented what they claimed was her perpetuation of racial stereotypes. To these Beavers responded: "While I might interpret the roles of ignorant people at times, I have heard it said that it takes intelligence to do such a part." Unfortunately, her breakthrough role didn't further her career other than afford her more of the same parts that she had played before. In her lighter moments, she played maids to both Mae West and Jean Harlow, a fun foil and confidante to these deco sex queens. Unlike uppity society matrons on screen who saw their maids as merely "the help," Harlow and West interacted with these women, if not equals, at least as an intimate, someone to whom they could discuss their men and their plans for those men. West was actually instrumental in hiring Beavers to play Pearl in her comedy *She Done Him Wrong* (1933).

In the 1940s, the actress appeared in dozens of roles, some in top level pictures with the screen's biggest stars, including *Holiday Inn* (1942), as Bing Crosby's loveable maid Mamie, who cares for the singer in the infamous inn while dishing out her own brand of homespun wisdom. In the hilarious classic *Mr. Blanding's Builds His Dream House* (1948), Beavers character, Gussie, spouts the movie's fun advertising catchphrase, "If you ain't eatin' Wham, you ain't eatin' ham," saving the day for boss Cary Grant.

In 1952, she took her turn with fellow film peers, McDaniel and Ethel Waters playing on television in the hit series *Beulah*, notable as the first TV show to carry an African-American woman in the starring role. A precursor to Shirley Booth's *Hazel*, Beulah was a maid who helped solve the problems of her white employers via her kitchen. Poor health, including diabetes, plagued Beavers later in life and in October 1962, the actress died of a heart attack (Her death was exactly ten years to the day of the death of Hattie McDaniel). She was posthumously inducted into the Black Filmmakers Hall of Fame in 1976.

Charles Bickford

"Actors," Charles Bickford once said, "seem to attach some kind of personal importance to heroism and youth, and insist on clinching in the sunset, first making sure that the touch of gray on top has been carefully shoe-polished out.   If they want to stay on the screen and make money, which is a point, too, they ought to be willing to grow old and act out villainy."

Charles Bickford was rough and tumble, the real deal. With his "crinkled hair, gruff voice and granite features" he portrayed strong men, both black-hearted and noble in dozens of Hollywood's most revered motion pictures. Although he held leading man status a handful of times early in his screen career, it was not a goal he sought out and his flexibility in Hollywood was a testament to his longevity there. The rugged-faced actor played ranchers as easily as he portrayed priests and his talent was recognized more than once with Academy Award nominations, though he never won the coveted prize.

In his autobiography, *Bulls Balls Bicycles & Actors*, Bickford claims he was born in the first minute of 1891. Bickford said of his birth, "It's appropriate that I should have come in on the wings of a blizzard. I've been blowing up a storm ever since." The New Year baby came to life in Cambridge, Massachusetts, the fifth of seven children. A tough guy from his earliest years, he was tried and acquitted at the age of nine of the attempted murder of a trolley motorman who had run over and killed his dog. His father, Lorettus, was a coffee importer, but his childhood influence was his maternal grandfather, who was a sea captain and told Charlie stories of adventure, which stirred in the youngster a sense of wanderlust.

His teen years found him drifting around the United States. He found a job as a lumberjack and for a time ran his own extermination business. He became a coal stoker in the U.S. Navy and took a job in burlesque on a dare before serving as a Lieutenant in the Army Corps of Engineers during the First World War. After the war ended, Bickford returned to show business, where he felt he'd found his niche. In April 1919, he opened with actor Thomas Mitchell in a play called *Dark Rosaleen* at the Belasco Theater on Broadway, after which he toured both in vaudeville and with stock companies. In 1925, he appeared back on the New York stage with an actor named James Cagney in a show called *Outside Looking In.* Both young red-headed newcomers garnered very good reviews which helped establish them in their field.

As talking films made a big splash with audiences, studios raided Broadway stages in an effort to find actors with good voices. In 1928, Bickford made his way to Hollywood, where he was offered a contract with Metro-Goldwyn-Mayer at the request of director Cecil B. DeMille, who was filming *Dynamite* (1929) at the studio. MGM then cast him opposite one of its biggest stars, Greta Garbo, in her talking movie debut, *Anna Christie.* Bickford played Matt, Garbo's tough Irish sailor boyfriend. It wasn't a bad way to begin a screen career and Mordaunt Hall of the *New York Times* proclaimed the actor "succeeds splendidly with his portrayal." Bickford could be arrogant and had a notorious temper, his difficulty to take direction from certain filmmakers and refusal of some scripts made his time at Metro short-lived.

When he sought a contract with other studios in town, he discovered that his difficult ways had gotten him blacklisted. He became an independent actor and worked steadily at RKO, Columbia and Paramount, though often in low-budget pictures. He played Irene Dunne's hot-headed husband in *No Other Woman* (1933) and grumpy gangster Big Steve Halloway in *Little Miss Marker* (1934), the film that boosted the stock of child-star Shirley Temple. Tragedy struck in 1935 on the set of the shipwreck adventure *East of Java*. During shooting at Universal, Bickford agreed to wrestle a lion with his bare hands, being assured it was tame and trained for films. The animal, however, viciously attacked the actor, his jaws closing on Bickford's throat, almost severing the jugular vein. The following week, Bickford was scheduled to sign a $2,500 a week contract with Twentieth Century-Fox and slated to appear again with Shirley Temple in *The Littlest Rebel*. Although he survived the attack, his neck was badly scarred. He insisted on reporting to Fox for his scheduled film role only to be sent back to the hospital by the director. Bickford spent the next ten months recuperating and lost out on the Fox deal. His days as a leading man were no more.

Once he was back on his feet, Cecil B. DeMille hired him once again for his glossy western, *The Plainsman* (1936), opposite Gary Cooper and Jean Arthur and cast a villainous Bickford selling arms to the Indians. The following year he reunited with Irene Dunne for *High, Wide and Handsome*, this time playing a corrupt bully. The late '30s and very early '40s were a low ebb in the actor's career, with appearances in films at Hollywood's lower budget studios, Monogram, Republic and Universal, although he was good support in a couple of A-list dramas, *Of Mice and Men* (1939) and DeMille's *Reap the Wild Wind* (1942). Bickford said of this glum period: "Gradually I noticed that I was slipping into those cruel, gravel-voiced roles of the chief jailer and the backwoods father and the escaped convict. I made lots of pictures - mostly 'Bs'- and then I began thinking of parts which would take me out of prison cell blocks and off quarterdeck of a hell ship and out of those seven-day epics into which I had gravitated."

Then in 1943, on the recommendation of the film's writer, George Seaton, he was cast as Father Peyramale, Bishop of Lourdes in Fox's *The*

Song of Bernadette, with Jennifer Jones. It was a top-notch production and Bickford was nominated for an Academy Award for Best Supporting Actor, saying of his efforts in the picture, "a great character actor was born." The quality of his movies improved immeasurably and continued to be of a high caliber throughout his career. The mid- '40s saw some of his best roles in films which included Fox's film noir, *Fallen Angel* (1945), the colorful western saga *Duel in the Sun* (1947), *The Farmer's Daughter* (1947) and *Johnny Belinda* (1948), with the latter two movies offering him Oscar nominations yet again. Ironically, for each of the films that he earned an Academy nomination, his female co-star won as Best Actress for the same movie: Jennifer Jones in *Bernadette*, Loretta Young in *The Farmer's Daughter* and Jane Wyman in *Johnny Belinda*.

He continued racking up quality films for his resume throughout the 1950s, including *A Star is Born, Not as a Stranger* and *The Court-Martial of Billy Mitchell*, all in 1955. He was part of a stellar cast in the sprawling drama *The Big Country*, alongside Gregory Peck, Jean Simmons and Charlton Heston. He also made numerous appearances on popular television shows including *Celebrity Playhouse* (playing another priest), *Wagon Train* and in 1962 became a regular on *The Virginian*.

In the summer of 1967, Bickford suffered from an attack of emphysema and was hospitalized at the University of California at Los Angeles Medical Center. His illness became complicated by pneumonia followed by a blood infection. On Thursday night, November 9, he passed away. He was survived by his widow, Beatrice Loring, whom he married in 1919 (and barely mentioned in his autobiography), and two adult children. His friend and frequent co-star, Jennifer Jones unsuccessfully attempted suicide less than an hour after hearing of Bickford's death.

Clara   Blandick

As the plain and careworn farm wife, Auntie Em, in *The Wizard* of *Oz*, one of the last words one would associate with character actress Clara Blandick would be "exotic," but her entrance into the world was rather exotic and romantic comparative to most in her generation. Her exit from the same world was just the opposite unfortunately, a sad ending to a life dedicated to her craft. Immediately recognizable as the dour but caring, pinch-faced Em, Blandick offered decades of characterizations, both on stage and screen.

Although 1880 is given most often as the year of her birth, Clara Blandick was actually born in 1876, which is clearly evident in the 1880 US Census, listing the toddler, age three and living with her family in Quincy, Massachusetts. June 4, to be precise, and having taken place on board a small American merchant ship, the *Willard Mudgett*, which was anchored in Hong Kong. Her birth name was Clara Blanchard Dickey and her father, Isaac Dickey, was the ship's captain. After living in Quincy, her family settled in Boston and it was there that she made her stage debut in *The Walking Delegate* at the Tremont Theatre, having taking portions of her middle and last name to create the professional name that she would hence be known as: Blandick. She then appeared in a production of *Richard Lovelace* with famed Shakespearean stage actor E.H. Sothern before moving to New York by the turn of the century. She made her Broadway debut in 1901, when she was cast as Jehanneton in *If I Were King*, which again starred E.H. Sothern in the lead, and ran for 56 performances at Garden Theatre.

In 1903 she originated the role of Gwendolyn in the Broadway premiere of E. W. Hornung's *Raffles, The Amateur Cracksman* opposite Kyrle Bellew. It was a part that would be played by Kay Francis and Olivia de Havilland in screen versions during the 1930s. Blandick continued working steadily on the stage throughout the first and second decades of the century including playing the lead in *Madame Butterfly: A Tragedy of Japan* for famed producer David Belasco, with whom she was under contract for a short period.

On December 7, 1905, Blandick married Harry Stanton Elliott in New York City. Prior to their marriage, Elliott had been an actor and a member of Harvard's class of 1900. By 1910 the couple appears to have been separated, with Elliott living and working in Nevada and they divorced in 1912, having had no children together. In the meantime, Clara made her film debut in the silent short, *The Maid's Double* in 1911 and continued to make a handful of pictures through 1917, though she preferred working on the stage. During World War I, she volunteered for the American Expeditionary Force in France.

In 1929, Blandick moved west to Hollywood and began a long career as one of that town's busiest character players. At fifty-three, she quickly made her name playing disapproving spinsters, dowdy aunts and nosy neighbors. Middle-age had taken the rose from her cheeks and she was cast as worried or meddling women. One stage co-star called her "Constipated Clara." She was Aunt Polly in both the 1930 version of *Tom Sawyer* as well as *Huckleberry Finn*, made the following year. In 1932, she appeared in Columbia's *Shopworn*, opposite Barbara Stanwyck. It was one of her meatier parts and somewhat more "glamorous" than the usual sullen Midwestern matrons she usually portrayed. As the snobbish and overbearing mother of Stanwyck's object of affection (Regis Toomey), she was able to sink her teeth into a real pre-Code potboiler.

After working steadily throughout the 1930s in roles varying from uncredited bits to more substantial supporting parts, Blandick was cast in the movie for which she would be most identified: *The Wizard of Oz*. Actress Sarah Padden was tested unsuccessfully, after veteran character actress May Robson turned down the part as too insignificant. MGM eventually hired Blandick, instead of using one of their own contract actresses, feeling no one in their stable of character players was right for the part. She received $750 for one week of shooting, the same as her on-screen spouse Charley Grapewin (Judy Garland, not yet a full-fledged star, was paid $500 per week). Like most of her Kansas contemporaries in the film, Blandick's Em had no colorful counterpart in Oz, a point to accentuate Dorothy's persistent longing to return to her black-and-white home.

During the 1940s, the actress continued working at every major studio (and some lesser ones) in town. She popped up in major A-list pictures including *The Wagons Roll at Night* (1940), *The Big Store* (1940), with the zany Marx Brothers, *Gentleman Jim* (1942), *Heaven Can Wait* (1943) and *Life with Father* (1947). She spent a short time under contract at Twentieth Century-Fox. After a couple of appearances on television, she retired from acting in the early 1950s.

Blandick lived in seclusion at the Hollywood Roosevelt Hotel in Los Angeles. Her health deteriorated during the 1950s and she suffered from extreme arthritis and began to go blind. On Sunday, April 15, 1962, she returned from Palm Sunday services at her church to the Shelton Hotel, where she then resided. She spent the afternoon laying out press clippings and memorabilia from her career. She perfectly styled her hair and adorned a royal blue dressing gown before taking a large overdose of sleeping pills. She then covered herself with a gold blanket and proceeded to pull a plastic clothes bag over her head. She had apparently planned the event earlier, having told her friend, James Busch, that she was disposing of her medications should anything happen to her. Her landlady, Helen Mason, found the body soon after and called the police, who declared the death a suicide. A heart wrenching note was found which read: "I am now about to make the great adventure. I cannot endure this agonizing pain any longer. It is all over my body. Neither can

I face the impending blindness. I pray the Lord my soul to take. Amen."
She was eighty-five.

Ward Bond

As a supporting player in well over 200 films, Ward Bond was one of Hollywood's busiest and most popular actors. Burly and broad-shouldered, he looked like a proverbial high school football coach and in fact, was playing football at the University of Southern California, alongside fellow teammate John Wayne when director John Ford cast them as extras in a film in 1929. The trio would make numerous films together over the next 30 years, including *The Long Voyage Home* (1940), *Three Godfathers* (1948) and *The Quiet Man* (1952). Like another great character actor, Thomas Mitchell, Bond was featured in two of Hollywood's most popular, most viewed films of all time, *Gone with the*

Wind (1939) and *It's a Wonderful Life* (1946), the latter as Burt, the gruff yet affable cop.

Born and raised in the middle West, Bond hailed from Benkelman, a tiny burg in the extreme southwest corner of Nebraska, where he and his family lived until 1919, when the sixteen-year-old moved to Denver, where he graduated from East High School. A born athlete, Ward made his way to the University of Southern California, where he was a starting lineman on the school's 1928 national championship team. He was hired, along with two dozen other USC Trojans, by director Ford as extras for his football flick, *Salute* (1929), which starred George O'Brien. Though Bond and "Duke" Wayne starting out on the same playing field (both figuratively and literally), as the years passed, Wayne became a film icon, one of the most popular and recognizable stars of the golden age and beyond, while his lifelong buddy remained in a supporting capacity. That said, Ward Bond was one of the hardest working, most dependable actors ever to grace both the large and small screen.

Specializing in masculine roles, the actor was usually cast as brusque cops, rugged cowboys and seasoned soldiers. When Ford first noticed the brash and outspoken Bond among the other football extras hired for *Salute*, he asked, "Who's that great big ugly guy?" The two, along with Wayne, forged a long running personal and professional friendship. Also, like Wayne, the actor was a staunch political conservative and was an ardent supporter of the anti-Communist activity movement in the 1940s and 1950s, holding membership in the Motion Picture Alliance for the Preservation of American Ideals.

Fearless onscreen and off, his hulking frame and deep, prominent voice added strength and presence to some of the most well-known movies throughout the entire golden age of American film. The actor appeared in no less than a dozen movies each year throughout the '30s, though in most of these early roles he was uncredited. Although never playing the lead himself, he supported most of Hollywood's biggest male stars. In 1939, Bond was cast in twenty-one pictures, including the Civil War epic *Gone with the Wind*, where he played Tom, the Yankee captain and poker buddy of Clark Gable's Rhett Butler. The '40s saw him as tough police detective Tom Polhaus in the classic crime drama *The Maltese Falcon* with Humphrey Bogart and later he played famous boxer John L. Sullivan opposite Errol Flynn in Warners' *Gentleman Jim*. In

Frank Capra's *It's a Wonderful Life,* Bond played small town cop Bert, whose scenes ranged from comedic to sentimental to dramatic, all of which Bond handled to perfection.

In the '50s, he continued to be a part of dozens of films, more and more often westerns (a genre which exploded in popularity during the 1950s and 1960s). Two of his most memorable movies of the decade were both John Wayne/John Ford collaborations, having become a part of Ford's stock company of actors. *The Quiet Man* (1952) and *The Searchers* (1956) both showed the actor to a very good advantage. Later in the decade, Bond had the opportunity to transition from movies to television, as so many other film actors had done, though he was wary about the change. Ford gave him a different perspective and told him, "Listen, you dumb Irishman. Don't you act for a living? Well, then you'd better act." He took on the lead role of Major Seth Adams on NBC's hit western *Wagon Train* from 1957 until his death in 1960. On November 5, the prolific actor had a massive fatal heart attack while in Dallas to attend a football game. He was only fifty-seven years old.

Beulah Bondi

Though she made a career out of playing wives, mothers and grandmothers, actress Beulah Bondi never married and never had children of her own. She lived to the ripe age of ninety-two and won her only major entertainment award a mere four years before her death, an Emmy for her portrayal of Martha Corinne Walton in a 1976 episode of *The Waltons* television series. It was the final screen performance of a varied career that had begun some 45 years before.

Bondi was one of the strongest character actresses of her day. Best known to movie audiences as James Stewart's Ma Bailey in *It's a Wonderful Life* (1946), she played Stewart's mother in four movies including his breakthrough picture, *Mr. Smith Goes to Washington* (1939). Although the actress perfected the kind and loving mother in

47

those films and many others, she was, however, extremely versatile, able to play everything from bewitched Puritan to hillbilly hen-pecker and often played characters older than she really was.

Chicago-born in 1888, Beulah Bondi made her first foray on the stage at the age of seven as the male lead of *Little Lord Fauntleroy*. Highly intelligent and well-educated, she graduated from the Frances Shimer Academy and gained Bachelor's and Master's degrees in oratory at Valparaiso University in 1916 and 1918. She then established herself as a stage actress, touring with theatrical stock companies throughout the country, making her Broadway debut in 1925. She appeared in the Pulitzer Prize winning *Street Scene* in 1929, as the gossipy neighbor Emma Jones and went to Hollywood to repeat her performance in the film version of the Elmer Rice drama which starred Sylvia Sidney. She was 43 years-old.

The following year she was fine as Walter Huston's prim, plain and prudish minister's wife in *Rain* ~ is it no wonder that Huston's Reverend Davidson was tempted by the smoldering Joan Crawford? In *The Trail of the Lonesome Pine* (1936) she was a soft-hearted hillbilly and in *The Shepherd of the Hills* (1941) she was a black hearted one, not surprisingly excelling at both. In 1936, she was one of the first five actresses nominated in the new Best Supporting Actress Oscar category for her role as Andrew Jackson's wife Rachel in MGM's *The Gorgeous Hussy*. She followed this with yet another nomination for *Of Human Hearts* (1938).

Bondi gave an interesting and powerful performance in *Maid of Salem* (1937), a Hollywood take on the witch-laden hysteria of Puritan New England. The film is bursting at the seams with extremely capable character actors (Gale Sondergaard, Edward Ellis, Donald Meek, Bonita Granville and others) and Bondi more than holds her own as the repressed and nervous wife of a harsh Puritan elder. In 1940 the actress tested for the role of Ma Joad in 20th Century-Fox's *The Grapes of Wrath*. She was so confident of being cast that she moved to an "Okie" camp near Bakersfield, California, to immerse herself in the character. While there, she got the news that Jane Darwell landed the part.

She was memorable as the kind adoption agent in *Penny Serenade* (1941) with Irene Dunne and Cary Grant, as she was for her markedly different role as crotchety and complaining Granny in Jean Renoir's *The Southerner* (1945). Then in 1946, she played the part for which she is most readily associated, Ma Bailey in Capra's classic, *It's a Wonderful Life*. Still playing the ultimate matron, she was given the opportunity to utilize her great range by playing the kind and understanding matriarch to James Stewart's George, while also playing the hard and bitter version of the same character in the scenes where George had never been born. The quality of her scripts declined in the 1950s and the number of films in which she appeared was scaled back dramatically, being replaced (like many other actors) with more work on television, culminating in her 1977 Emmy.

Beulah Bondi died at the Motion Picture Country House and Hospital in Woodland Hills, of injuries she sustained following an accident at her home. She was ninety-two years-old. She once summed up her feelings on her career which was sage advice for others in a similar state. "Give me a good supporting role, and that's all I ask. The life of a star with few exceptions is brief. It's like a merry-go-round only suddenly the music stops playing. Supporting players, unless typed, go on forever." Indeed, Miss Bondi's legacy of magnificent performances has sustained the test of time.

Walter Brennan

One of the finest and most successful character actors in Hollywood's golden age, Walter Brennan holds the distinction of being the only man to win three Best Supporting Actor Oscars during his career (Jack Nicholson and Daniel Day-Lewis have won three awards which include combinations of Best Actor and Supporting Actor). His success can also be attributed to the fact that he is one of the most recognizable actors in the American cinema. With his high-pitched, gravelly voice and careworn, weather-beaten face, Brennan ignited a scene when he appeared on the screen. Where most screen actors would fight nature and gravity to retain a youthful allure, Walter Brennan went with the grain at a younger age and embraced his physical shortcomings, including tooth loss, thinning hair and a slight frame, to play characters many years older than his actual age.

The second of three children born to Irish immigrants, Brennan came into the world on July 25, 1894 in Lynn, Massachusetts. His father, William John Brennan, was an engineer and initially, young Walter was to follow into his pop's footsteps, studying engineering at Rindge Technical High School in Cambridge, Massachusetts. His interest, however, shifted to acting while still in school, where he appeared in several plays and even worked in vaudeville while still in his teens. Upon graduation, Brennan worked at various jobs before enlisting in the U.S. Army during World War I, serving as a private stationed in France. While in service, his vocal chords were injured when exposed to poisonous mustard gas, leaving him with his trademark voice. After the war he raised pineapples for a time in Central America before moving to California, where he made, then subsequently lost, substantial money in real estate.

His need for funds led to his entry into films in the mid-1920s, when he began taking on jobs as a movie extra and stuntman. Brennan commented on these early Hollywood years in a 1972 interview with *Guidepost* magazine:

> "I got into pictures the hard way – as an extra. Year in, year out I hung around the studios, made the rounds of casting agencies, waited for the call backs that never came. I don't mean it wasn't painful while I was going through it – struggle generally is. A good many times during those years, Ruth [his wife since 1920] fed our family of three children on a dollar a day, plus what those chickens and our backyard garden contributed."

He had uncredited bit parts in dozens of pictures in the late '20s and early '30s, including stints in *The Invisible Man* (1933), *The Bride of Frankenstein* (1935) and a Three Stooges short, *Woman Haters* in 1934. When cast as a cab driver in *The Wedding Night* (1935), the actor impressed producer Samuel Goldwyn enough that he put him under contract. Goldwyn was preparing for his upcoming feature, *Barbary Coast*, starring Edward G. Robinson and Miriam Hopkins and directed by Howard Hawks. According to the Hawks biography, *The Grey Fox of Hollywood*, Brennan went to his audition for the role of a cackling codger called Old Atrocity and asked, "With or without," to which he was asked, with or without what? He was talking about his dentures and did the test without his falsies. Brennan not only gained the role, but the part was gradually expanded until he ended up with a much higher screen billing. Hawks called him "the greatest example of a personality that I've ever used," and *Barbary Coast* was his first of six roles working for the acclaimed director.

The following year he won his first Best Supporting Actor Academy Award, playing Swan Bostrom in the Goldwyn drama, *Come and Get It* (He is also distinguished for being the first actor to win the award, as it was the debut of the category that year). He repeated his victory in the category in 1938, again playing an aged curmudgeon in *Kentucky* at 20th Century-Fox. The same year he was a success for David Selznick as Muff Potter in the color film adaption of the Mark Twain classic *The Adventures of Tom Sawyer*. In 1940, he co-starred with Gary Cooper, an actor with whom he shared the screen often, in the classic *The Westerner*, for which he won his third and final Oscar as the corrupt Judge Roy Bean.

According to August C. Bolino in his book *Men of Massachusetts: Bay State Contributors to American Society*, Brennan's multiple wins in such a short period of time, though never considered undeserved, may have been somewhat circumstantial. Bolino explains that in the early years of the Academy Awards, extras were given the right to vote on the candidates. Brennan was extremely popular with the Union of Film Extras, of which he had been one for many years, and he won his category each and every time he was nominated. After winning his third Oscar, the Academy discontinued allowing extra players a vote. Brennan never won again, though he was nominated the following year for his work in *Sergeant York* (1941).

Whether playing comic imbeciles, warm-hearted fathers or sinister villains, Brennan always came through, mastering a wide range in acting ability. He did, however, stand out as rural oddballs and as strong support in many classic westerns over several decades. One of his occasional dramatic turns came in the 1946 western *My Darling Clementine*, where he played the uncharacteristically villainous role of Old Man Clanton. His career never wavered, and he worked steadily and consistently throughout the 1940s and 1950s, and in 1957, he gained even more popularity with audiences when he starred in the television situation comedy, *The Real McCoys*. As the irascible Grandpa Amos

McCoy, the sixty-three-year-old actor led the series through six years on the small screen, first on ABC then CBS. Brennan worked up until his death of emphysema on September 21, 1974 at the age of eighty. One of the most beloved, respected and successful actors of his generation, he left a treasure trove of fine performances to be enjoyed by movie lovers for decades to come.

N i g e l   B r u c e

With eyes popping from bewilderment or agitation and bushy moustache bearing more salt than pepper, English actor Nigel Bruce became one of the most recognizable supporting actors of the '30s and '40s. He was at his best as a flustered, sometimes blustery Englishman, usually with a bumbling, aristocratic air. His best-known characterization, however, is as the befuddled Dr. Watson, sidekick to Basil Rathbone's Sherlock Holmes in numerous movie mysteries during World War II.

His name rings of the British Isles and his genealogy and background followed suit. He was born William Nigel Ernle Bruce on February 4, 1895 in Ensenada, Mexico, while his parents were on an extended holiday (His brother Michael had been born there nearly a year earlier). He was the second son of Sir William Waller Bruce, 10th Baronet of Stenhouse and Airth, a descendant of Robert the Bruce, King of Scots. His mother was Angelica Mary Selby, daughter of General George Selby, Royal Artillery. To his family, and those who knew him best, young Nigel was known as "Willie," and he was educated at the Grange, Stevenage and at Abingdon School, Berkshire. Sir William died in 1912, with Michael succeeding his father as 11th baronet, less than a week shy of his eighteenth birthday.

During World War I, Willie joined the 10th Service Battalion of the Somerset Light Infantry, serving as a Lieutenant and later the Honourable Artillery Company in 1916. While fighting at Cambrai in 1917, he was badly wounded. Bruce's left leg was hit by no less than eleven bullets and he was confined to a wheelchair for over a year of convalescence before being able to walk again. His mother, Lady Bruce, died the same year.

After his discharge Bruce took a serious interest in acting and in May 1920, he made his debut stage appearance in *Why Marry?* at the Comedy Theatre in London's West End. The following year he married actress Violet Campbell (born Violet Pauline Shelton) and the two appeared together on Broadway in 1926. The actor continued on the stage throughout the 1920s and began appearing in British films in 1930. He then moved to the United States and became part of the illustrious British colony in Hollywood. He made numerous films throughout the 1930s, including *Stand Up and Cheer*! with Shirley Temple, *Treasure Island*, with Wallace Beery, and *The Scarlet Pimpernel*, with fellow Brits Leslie Howard and Merle Oberon (all 1934). The following year he appeared in *Becky Sharp*, which had the distinction of being the first motion picture to be shot in three strip Technicolor. He lent just the right amount of British appeal to two of director Alfred Hitchcock's classic suspensers of the early '40s, *Rebecca* (1940), as Maxim de Winter's easygoing brother-in-law, Major Lacy and *Suspicion* (1941), as the trusting and affable Beaky.

In 1938, Bruce was going through a difficult time with the failure of his current Broadway stage endeavor, *Knights of Song*, a very short-lived musical about the partnership of Gilbert and Sullivan. In his unpublished memoirs, *Games, Gossip and Greasepaint*, Bruce recalls how a message from a close actor friend made all the difference. "The telegram was from Basil Rathbone who said: 'Do come back to Hollywood,

Willie dear boy, and play Doctor Watson to my Sherlock Holmes. We'll have great fun together.' Basil can never realize how much that telegram cheered me up, as when I received it, I was in the mood to put my head in a gas oven." Rathbone states in his 1962 autobiography: "There is no question in my mind that Nigel Bruce was the ideal Dr. Watson... There was an endearing quality to his performance that to a very large extent, I believe, humanized the relationship between Dr. Watson and Mr. Holmes."

Originally meant to be a freestanding film in 1939, *The Hound of the Baskervilles*, based on the story by Sir Arthur Conan Doyle, was so popular that Twentieth Century-Fox developed a follow-up picture called *The Adventures of Sherlock Holmes*. The pair of films was true to form for turn-of-the-century period and story, but when Universal took over the franchise in 1942, the series setting was changed to World War II. Although many fans of the classic mystery series consider Bruce's Watson to be the quintessential characterization, Holmes purists find his incompetent, albeit loveable doctor lacking, as the original literary character created by Conan Doyle was less blundering and more of a mental helpmate for the sleuth. As far as good cinema goes, the comic relief provided by Bruce was a balanced contrast to Rathbone's solemn and serious Holmes. The duo made fourteen Holmes movies and over two hundred radio programs, the film series ending in 1946 with *Dressed to Kill*.

Although the Holmes run ended, Bruce continued making movies and being an active member of the British film colony in Los Angeles. In October 1953, Nigel "Willie" Bruce died from a heart attack in Santa Monica, California at the age of fifty-eight. He was cremated, and his ashes stored in the vault at the Chapel of the Pines Crematory in Los Angeles. He was survived by his wife and two daughters, Jennifer and Pauline. His last movie role, as Governor Coutts in *World for Ransom*, a nuclear espionage drama, was released posthumously the following year.

Billie Burke

       Billie Burke's fame crosses over classic movie fandom into the realm of "everyone else" even if the "everyone else" class doesn't know her by name. They do know, however, her role as Glinda, the Good Witch of the North in the quintessential film fantasy, *The Wizard of Oz* (1939). "Ah, yes," you say, "I DO know her! Wasn't she in a few other "old" movies, playing someone's fluttery mother?" Indeed.

       She was Hollywood's favorite female flibbertigibbet. Other actresses of the day may have dipped their toes into the water of wealthy, daffy, feather-brained matron roles but that was one characterization that Billie Burke had dibs on. As good as she was in carrying that particular persona, however, Burke had a full and luxurious career long before becoming Tinsel Town's number one bubble-headed society lady.

Show business was her family's bread and butter, as her father, William "Billy" Burke was a professional clown with the Barnum & Bailey Circus. "Billy Burke was a handsome clown," the actress wrote in her 1949 memoirs, *With a Feather on My Nose*. "I am tempted to say a "pretty" clown, because he had a round, open generous face with sparkling blue eyes, always shining, and beautiful bright red hair."

On August 7, 1884 (some sources cite 1885), in Washington, D.C., Billy and his wife, Blanche, welcomed their daughter to the world. Baby Burke explained in a 1917 *Photoplay* interview: "I'm afraid I was a dreadful disappointment to my father. He wanted a boy and not only was I not a boy, but I had no masculine proclivities from the start." The actress certainly must have made this statement tongue-in-check, as she later noted that her father, who was on tour when she was born, sent a telegram to her mother that read: "I DON'T CARE IF IT'S A BOY OR A GIRL, BUT DOES IT HAVE RED HAIR?" Regardless, she was called "Billie" after her beloved padre, though her given name was Mary William Ethelbert Appleton Burke.

The family toured with Burke the Elder throughout the United States and, with lean times before them, eventually settled in London, while Billie was still a child. According to the actress, the Burkes had "diggings on Kensington Road in one of those dreary London flats in which the landlady fetches your mutton on a tray and your bath in a bucket." At her mother's urging, she began acting on the stage and made her debut in 1903 in the two-act musical comedy, *The School Girl,* at the Prince of Wales Theatre. After other shows in England, the young actress returned to the United States and began appearing on Broadway, beginning with *My Wife* in 1907 with John Drew, uncle to Lionel, Ethel and John Barrymore. Burke gained quite a following and her salary mirrored her popularity. With strong financial gains, she was able to buy a home, in 1910, in the town of Hastings-on-Hudson, located in Westchester County. She called the three-story estate Burkeley Crest and lived there with her mother (her father had died in 1906).

While acting in New York, she met producer and impresario Florenz Ziegfeld. A famed showman and creator of the *Ziegfeld Follies*, he was also a notorious womanizer, newly divorced from his common-law wife, Anna Held. Ziegfeld and Burke were deeply attracted, and the actress wrote years later: "...even if I had known then precisely what tortures and frustrations were in store for me during the next eighteen years because of this man, I should have kept right on falling in love." The two married in 1914, and had a daughter, Patricia, two years later. In 1916, Burke made her movie debut in *Peggy*, a silent film comedy which was popular and led to a salary that was reportedly one of the highest paid to any actress of the day.

With her money and fame and the popularity of her husband's productions on Broadway, Billie became a trendsetter of fashion and popular culture. She continued to make silent movies until 1921, when she returned to her first love: the stage. The Roaring Twenties were for the Ziegfelds, as the decade was for many families; a time of prosperity and affluence, but as the Stock Market Crash of 1929 hit the nation hard, it did the same for the show business couple. Their investments were greatly diminished to the point that Billie had to make her way back to motion pictures.

She made her movie "comeback" in 1932, when director George Cukor asked her to play the mother of newcomer Katharine Hepburn in his new project, *A Bill of Divorcement*, which co-starred John Barrymore. In the summer of 1932, while Burke was filming *Divorcement*, Florenz Ziegfeld died, having been ill for some time. The producer's death left his wife with debt and she continued working full-time in films to strengthen her financial status. Her second film, after *A Bill of Divorcement*, was again with Hepburn (in what was also her second picture). *Christopher Strong* (1933) cast Burke as yet another middle-aged aristocratic matron, the characterization – with fluttery humor added – which would become the cornerstone of the rest of her career.

That characterization was no more evident than in her next film. *Dinner at Eight* (1933) was an all-star extravaganza made at MGM and showcasing many of the studio's biggest stars, including Wallace Beery, Jean Harlow, Lionel and John Barrymore and Marie Dressler. As a self-centered society birdbrain, Billie was perfection. The movie and her role (as well as her trademark 'disturbed-chandelier tinkle of a voice and sparrow like flutter of hands') established her as one of Hollywood's brightest comediennes and held her in good stead for the rest of the decade and beyond.

A filmization of the life of her late husband was planned at Universal in 1933 with William Powell slated to play Ziegfeld and Burke to play herself. The production proved too costly, however, and the rights were sold to MGM, who staged it on a grand scale, retaining Powell as the late producer, but casting Myrna Loy, Powell's frequent co-star, as Billie Burke. The studio felt the real Mrs. Ziegfeld was too old to play a younger version of herself, as well as the fact that Powell and Loy had enjoyed enormous success as husband and wife sleuths Nick and Nora Charles in MGM's *The Thin Man*, two years earlier. *The Great Ziegfeld*, released in 1936, was a greatly sanitized version of events, downplaying the impresario's dalliances and paramours at Burke's request. According to the actress, the film netted her "very little" in the way of film rights because it was tied up in various "splits and shares and commissions." A big hit, the movie won an Oscar as the Best Picture of 1936 and Burke gained a contract with Metro.

The remainder of the decade held more of the same, with Burke appearing in the classic ghost-comedy *Topper* (1937) and its two sequels, as well as *Merrily We Live* (1938), with her *Topper* co-star Constance Bennett, the latter film reaping her an Oscar nomination as Best Supporting Actress. In 1938, she was chosen to play Glinda in *The Wizard of Oz*, a role she admitted was her favorite, as it reminded her of the ones she dominated on the stage. Her MGM contract ended in 1941, but she continued to work steadily throughout the decade and into the next, with a featured part as the mother of the groom in the original version of *Father of the Bride* (1950), with Spencer Tracy.

Along with her continuing film work, she was heard on the radio, most notably in her own program, *The Billie Burke Show* from 1943 to 1946, a situation comedy in which she played her usually daffy character. She also hit the stage, though less frequently, and was seen regularly on television. In the 1960s, she decided on retirement, saying: "Television directors had no patience with little old ladies. It just wasn't fun anymore, and that's why I quit after 60 years in show business." She lived out her last years quietly, and in May 1970, the actress died of natural causes at the age of eighty-five. She never remarried after Ziegfeld's death and both are interred at the Kensico Cemetery in Westchester County, New York.

John Carradine

When actor John Carradine said, "I've made some of the greatest films ever made - and a lot of crap, too," he was absolutely right on both counts. The character great had a career that spanned six decades and included Shakespeare, Dracula and most things in between. Tall and lanky of frame, gaunt and thin of face, he was a character, both on screen and off, a self-proclaimed "ham," who begat a dynasty of thespians that carried his name forward on stage and screen.

On February 6, 1906, Richmond Reed Carradine was born in the Greenwich Village section of New York City. His father, William Issac Shelby Duff Green Reed was a correspondent for the *New York Herald* and part-time graphic designer, who died from tuberculosis when young Carradine was only two. In his autobiography, *Endless Highway*, John

Carradine's son, David, writes that his grandmother, born Genevieve Richmond, went back to school after her husband's death and became a surgeon. Her second husband was a Philadelphia paper manufacturer named Peck, who according to David Carradine, "thought the way to bring up someone else's boy was to beat him every day just on principle."

Naturally artistic, John studied sculpture and spent some time at the Graphic Art School in Philadelphia, before hitchhiking around the South for a period, sketching local businessmen and their daughters. "If the sitter was satisfied, the price was $2.50," he later recalled. "It cost him nothing if he thought it was a turkey. I made as high as $10 to $15 a day." His travels through Dixie included a stint in jail for vagrancy (which resulted in a beating and a broken nose that led to his specific facial "look" during his long acting career) and time with a traveling acting troupe as caricaturist. This period with a group of players enhanced the interest in acting which began when he was eleven and saw Shakespeare for the first time. In 1925, at the age of nineteen, Carradine made his stage debut in New Orleans, in a version of *Camille*. He continued with the troupe, playing a variety of roles and made his way across the country to California, Los Angeles specifically. Always the extrovert, he would cavort up and down the streets of Hollywood in a long cloak, reciting his beloved Shakespeare in his booming baritone voice.

After making his film debut in 1930's *Tol'able David*, as a villainous hillbilly named Buzzard, Carradine appeared in numerous movies under the name Peter Richmond, the vast majority of which he earned no screen credit. Many of these early film appearances were at Universal studio in some of their signature horror films, including *The Invisible Man*, *The Black Cat* and *The Bride of Frankenstein*, foreshadowing of the many chillers in which the actor would lend his charismatic persona. He eventually settled in at Twentieth Century-Fox, where he signed a long-term contract in 1935 and changed his name to John Carradine. The same year he married his first of four wives, Ardanelle McCool. John adopted McCool's son, Bruce, from a previous marriage and the couple had a son of their own, future actor David Carradine in 1936.

After several years in small, unsubstantial parts, Carradine had a breakout role as a sadistic guard in the historical drama *The Prisoner of Shark Island* (1936). It was directed by John Ford and began the actor's long tenure as one of Ford's unofficial stock players, appearing in numerous classics with Ford at the helm, including the classic western, *Stagecoach* (1939), which featured him as a Southern gambler. Carradine clashed with the director on the set of 1940's *The Grapes of Wrath*. According to Ford biographer Ronald Davis, the director "loathed" Carradine but used him in several of his movies because he was such a gifted actor. Screenwriter Nunnally Johnson observed that "Carradine had an ego which was about three times John Ford's and Ford could not put him down in any way," which angered the director even further.

When his Fox contract ended in 1942, the prolific actor began freelancing and started an acting troupe of his own, focusing on Shakespearean drama, financed by money made from his film work. His roles of choice were *Hamlet* and *Macbeth*, but he also made occasional appearances on Broadway as non-Shakespearean characters, including a long run as the Ragpicker in *The Madwoman of Chaillot* beginning in 1948. To continue to support his company of Shakespeare players, Carradine took whatever acting jobs he could get for a quick buck, including *Voodoo Man* in 1944 at low-budget Monogram Pictures, co-starring his fellow horror icon Bela Lugosi.

This string of films ruined his reputation in Hollywood as a serious film actor but along the way, he played one of his best roles and one in which he found personal gratification. *Bluebeard* (1944) was a minor horror film made by one of the kings of low-budget pictures of the day, Edgar G. Ulmer. As Gaston Morrell, a French puppeteer who murders women in 19th century Paris, Carradine portrayed the villain using an understated elegance rather than the ham-handed dramatics he usually employed in other roles. *Photoplay* magazine put it quite plainly: "John Carradine gives one swell performance."

Carradine and his wife Ardanelle had separated within three years of their 1935 marriage but didn't file for divorce until 1944. Custody and alimony disputes ensued and Carradine left California to avoid jail time. He married actress Sonia Sorel, with whom he worked in *Bluebeard* and moved back to Hollywood to be cast in *House of Dracula* (1945), taking on the role of the vampire Count.

The actor worked as regularly on television in the '50s as he had on the big screen during the '30s and '40s. He portrayed Dracula in numerous productions throughout the last decades of his career, including *Billy the Kid vs. Dracula* in 1966. One of the hardest working actors of his generation, Carradine appeared in hundreds of movies and television shows. His legacy as a fine actor and particularly one who excelled in the horror genre has carried on. Some of the titles in which he appeared even in the last years of his life included *The Tomb, Buried Alive* and *Evil Spawn*. His marriage to Sonia Sorel produced sons Christopher, Keith and Robert, and ended in a bitter 1957 divorce. He was married twice more, first to Doris Rich, who died in a 1971 fire, then to Emily Cisneros, who survived him. At eighty-two, Carradine died in Milan, Italy on November 27, 1988 of multiple organ failure. His last words were reportedly, "Milan: what a beautiful place to die."

Jack Carson

About his esteemed profession, Jack Carson said: "Being a comedian is almost like being a doctor – the more troubles you discover and understand, the more gladness you can bring to an audience." A popular and hardworking actor in Hollywood during the golden age, Carson occasionally made leading man status, but his greatest roles were strong supporting guys. He excelled at being the fun and funny best friend to the male star or the goofy smart aleck who bumbled his way into trouble and sometimes into the arms of the female second lead. He was one of the greatest second bananas of the 1940s and made an indelible impression on audiences of the day and modern fans of classic film.

A 6' 2," 220 lb. beefy, burly buffoon Jack Carson was handsome in a cocky, every-Joe kind of way. His elastic face could do a fast draw

65

double-take to match the screen's best comedians and the affable actor could be the second-string brother of Bob Hope. His best years were spent at Warner Brothers, where he was a comic staple in some of the studios best lightweight offerings. His usual partner in comedy crime was Dennis Morgan, with whom he co-starred in more than a half-dozen Warners' productions. He did, however, make the grade when the occasional dramatic role came his way.

John "Jack" Elmer Carson was born in the rural farming community of Carman, Manitoba, Canada on October 27, 1910. His parents, Elmer and Elsa moved to Milwaukee, Wisconsin, where Elmer, as a successful insurance executive, would open his company's first office outside of Canada. In Milwaukee, Carson would attend Hartford School, and St. John's Military Academy, in the suburb of Delafield. While in school, he and chum Dave Willock, who would later become a supporting actor in Hollywood as well, began performing together. Carson recalled their antics in a 1941 article for the *New York World-Telegram*:

> "In high school Dave and I were a team in sports and drama, we followed this by creating a comedy routine when we were at the military academy. I recall at our final graduation ceremonies the academy principal, who I had always considered a pompous old ass, became my hero when he invited us to do our Willock and Carson comedy act in front of the packed auditorium, a routine that had, though I say it myself, the audience roaring with laughter."

After attending Carleton College in Minnesota, the two formed a vaudeville act and hit the road on the small theater circuit. By the mid-1930s, they hit Hollywood, gaining bit roles at RKO. In 1937, Carson made fourteen film appearances, some credited, some not, from features to shorts. During this period the comedian began periodically working in radio, specifically on the *Bing Crosby Kraft Music Hall* in 1938. Throughout the late '30s and early '40s, he wisecracked his way to his own program, *Everybody Loves Jack*, in 1943.

He made the most of small roles in forgettable movies until he made the move to Warner Brothers and by 1941 his bit parts and walk-ons were replaced with fun supporting and second leads beginning with *The*

Strawberry Blonde, a remake of the 1933 Gary Cooper vehicle called *One Sunday Afternoon.* The film starred James Cagney and Olivia de Havilland, with Rita Hayworth as the title character, a turn-of-the-century hotsy-totsy being fought over by Cagney and Carson. A big hit at the box-office, the picture also garnered Carson good reviews, with *Variety* raving, "Jack Carson is excellent as the politically ambitious antagonist of the dentist."

In 1943, he gave arguably his finest dramatic display as the good-hearted but ill-treated Albert Runkel in Warners' *The Hard Way*, starring Ida Lupino. He and Dennis Morgan would co-star in several other features for the studio, but none so artistically successful as this. Not to say the movie was high art. It was basically what was known at the time as a "woman's picture" with hints of film noir, very similar in many ways to *Mildred Pierce* (1945), another personal success for the actor. In *Pierce*, he played Wally Fay, a sleazy business associate of Joan Crawford's Mildred, always on the make, whether it be for a buck or a skirt.

As his career was reaching its peak in the late 1940s, he played a rare lead in the colorful musical *Romance on the High Seas* (1948), which featured the film debut of a cute blond Big Band singer named Doris Day. In between wives, Carson began dating his perky co-star, who also was just getting out of a marriage. Day recalled their relationship in her 1976 autobiography, *Doris Day: Her Own Story.* "Jack was a very sweet, considerate man, whom I liked very much but I wasn't in love with him. I spent a lot of time at his place and often stayed there with him, but Jack was a closed man who couldn't communicate.... He was basically a lonely man who drank too much." The singer broke it off and married her third husband Marty Melcher in 1951.

In 1954, Carson had another dramatic success as a backstabbing publicist in the first remake of *A Star is Born*, with Judy Garland and James Mason. A more mature and less buoyant Jack appeared in the film adaption of Tennessee Williams *Cat on a Hot Tin Roof* in 1958, playing Gooper Pollitt, patriarch to the "no-neck monsters." He appeared in a host of television programs throughout the 1950s. In 1962, Carson was diagnosed with stomach cancer and died the following year in Encino, California. The actor left behind a great body of work in all aspects of the entertainment industry.

Charles Coburn

Character actor Charles Coburn was born in the South, just as the Reconstruction era was ending. Acting was something he was drawn to from a very early age. "I can't remember wanting to be anything but an actor," Coburn recalled in his later years. "My mother and father were devotees of the theatre, although they were never on the stage. I suppose my desire to be an actor originated when my mother read me stories about theatre people. The glamour and excitement of their lives intrigued me, and I wanted to be like them." Even though his film career didn't get substantially started until he was past sixty, it was indeed an exciting one, with the performer sharing the screen with the biggest names in Hollywood during the 1940s and '50s. His was one of the most recognizable faces on the big screen.

Charles Douville Coburn was born in Macon, Georgia on June 19, 1877, the son of Emma Louise Sprigman and Moses Douville Coburn. His family moved to his father's birthplace of Savannah before Charles' first birthday and in that city, he began his show business career at age fourteen handing out programs at the Savannah Theater. He advanced to usher and eventually the theater's manager at eighteen. He was given a bit part by a visiting company in *The Mikado*, his stage debut. Failing to find other parts in his hometown, he left at nineteen to head for New York. He unsuccessfully made the rounds of Broadway producers and supported himself by working in the package delivery department of a store, as well as his old gig as an usher.

Frustrated with his lack of success, Coburn was on the verge of returning home to Savannah when he accepted a job as advance man for a theatrical company. While working in this job in 1898, he appeared in a Chicago stock company's production of *Quo Vadis*, making his professional stage debut at $12 a week, plus room and board. After touring with various repertory troupes, he made his first Broadway appearance at the Fourteenth Street Theatre in 1901 in *Up York State*, then taking his first leading role in a road tour of *The Christian* in 1904.

Coburn's theatrical path started out differently that it would end up. "I thought I wanted to be a comic opera comedian," he recalled. "I could sing and dance a bit. That ambition died when I played Shakespeare." In 1905 he began his own company, The Coburn Shakespearean Players. It was then that he met Ivah Wills, playing Orlando to her Rosalind in *As You Like It*. The young acting couple fell in love and married the following year. They ran the company together for twelve years, even performing for two days at the White House at the special request of President and Mrs. William Howard Taft in 1910.

Coburn made his film debut in the title role of the short film, *Boss Tweed* (1933), the first installment of a series of thirteen *March of the Years* pictures, dramatizing the true incidents involving the notorious New York political boss. The series was inspired by the *March of Time* radio shows and included other historical news events of the past, including the Lizzie Borden murder case. It was produced at Columbia Pictures, where Coburn would make many of his best movies in the '40s. The actor then went on to appear in a small role in the low-budget crime drama, *The People's Enemy* in 1935 but it wasn't until his beloved wife's death in 1937 that he went all out for a career in motion pictures. The actor admitted a low point in his life when Ivah died. "I was lost," he said. "There seemed to be nothing left, nothing to live for. Then I received an offer to do a picture [*Of Human Hearts* (1938)]. I accepted." Soon the "portly old gent with an ever-present cigar and monocle" was showing up in numerous Hollywood hits throughout the late '30s and 1940s.

Coburn played any number of comfortable fathers or uncles, sage judges, numerous doctors and salty old men. In *Idiot's Delight* (1939), he costarred with Clark Gable, Norma Shearer and a menagerie of supporting characters. *The Lady Eve* (1941), had him as the gambling father of con-artist Barbara Stanwyck, and in *The Devil and Miss Jones* (also 1941), he played a department store tycoon who goes undercover to find the instigators of a union in his business. For the latter he was honored with an Oscar nomination as Best Supporting Actor. He also scored dramatic kudos as Bette Davis' incestuously creepy uncle in *In This Our Life* (1942) at Warner Brothers.

In 1943 Coburn was cast as Benjamin Dingle in *The More the Merrier*, alongside Jean Arthur and Joel McCrea. Taking place during the World War II housing shortage in Washington, DC, the film features Coburn's Dingle as an elderly gentleman who plays cupid to a young man and woman with whom he is sharing a cramped apartment. The role won Coburn an Academy Award as Best Supporting Actor and further cemented his status in the Hollywood character hierarchy, as well as filling his bank account with upwards of $7,500 a week, according to one report.

He continued to appear in high quality pictures, including *Heaven Can Wait* (1943), *Knickerbocker Holiday* (1944) and *The Green Years* (1946), for which he snapped up another Academy Award nomination. Politically, Coburn served as a vice-president of the Motion Picture Alliance for the Preservation of American Ideals, founded in 1944 by a group of Hollywood luminaries who were opposed to leftist influence in the motion picture industry. Its membership included such prominent members of the entertainment community as Irene Dunne, Clark Gable, Walt Disney, Gary Cooper, John Wayne, Ginger Rogers and Barbara Stanwyck among others. His '50s film work consisted of fun parts in

Monkey Business (1952), with Cary Grant, *Gentleman Prefer Blondes* (1953), with Marilyn Monroe and *How to Be Very, Very Popular* (1955), with Betty Grable.

On the personal front, Coburn surprised those closest to him by remarrying at the age of eighty-two. On June 30, 1959, he wed Winifred Jean Clements Natzka, widow of former New Zealand bass opera singer Oscar Natzka. At forty-one years old, Winifred was exactly half Coburn's age. The couple had one child, a daughter named Stephanie, born in November 1960. After completing a record-setting run of a production of *You Can't Take It With You* in Indianapolis, the actor complained of throat soreness. He entered the Lenox Hill Hospital in New York on Monday, August 28 for a check-up and underwent a "minor throat surgery" before dying of a heart attack in that facility on Wednesday, the 30th, with his wife by his side. He bequeathed his collection of theatrical papers and photographs to the University of Georgia's Hargrett Rare Book and Manuscript Library. According to Coburn's wishes his body was not to lie in repose in a public room and he was cremated with his ashes scattered in Georgia, Massachusetts, and New York. A well-liked and respected figure in the Hollywood community, Charles Coburn left behind a fine acting legacy.

Joyce Compton

      With her blonde good looks and a honey-sweet Southern accent, Joyce Compton, more often than not, played a ditzy blonde, cute as a button but dumb as a rock, in numerous screen classics (and a few forgotten duds). She was cast along with Hollywood's biggest stars including Cary Grant, Barbara Stanwyck and Joan Crawford, and on occasion, stole the scene in which she shared with these big-name bigwigs. There were movies for which she received no screen credit but whether her contribution was a bit or a beefed-up featured part, Compton was usually recognizable and always fun.

She was born Olivia Joyce Compton on January 27, 1907 in Lexington, Kentucky. Some biographical sketches erroneously list her birth name as Eleanor Hunt, a mistake made in an early press release for the film *Good Sport*, in which she appeared with an actress of that name. A true daughter of the South, both her parents, Henry and Golden Compton, were of southern stock, hailing from Mississippi and Kentucky respectively. She moved with her family to Oklahoma while still a girl and after graduating from high school, attended Tulsa University, where she studied dramatics and art. She loved creative endeavors and in the late 1920s, when her career started taking off, she told an interviewer: "Art and music are my two big loves. I would rather play the piano or paint than almost anything else. I studied practically nothing but dancing and art during the two years I attended Tulsa University in Oklahoma."

The Comptons left Tulsa in 1924 and made the trek for California, when Joyce won a beauty contest, which led to her appearance as an extra in Cecil B. DeMille's *The Golden Bed* in early 1925. She signed a contract with First National Pictures and in 1926 was named a WAMPAS Baby Star, which was a big career boost in 1920s Hollywood. WAMPAS stood for Western Association of Motion Picture Advertisers, which was formed in 1921, and its Baby Stars were a group of starlets chosen each year whose potential for motion picture fame was noteworthy. Joyce's "class" of 1926 held names that would go on to big success including Mary Brian, Joan Crawford, Dolores Del Rio, Janet Gaynor, Mary Astor, Fay Wray, and Dolores Costello. Although her Baby Star exposure didn't spark immediate stardom, Compton did continue to work steadily. She left First National in 1927 and did some freelance work before signing with Fox Film Corporation. She gave memorable support to her buddy Clara Bow in *Dangerous Curves* and *The Wild Party* in 1929.

It was during this period that she began seeing a young actor named Joel McCrea. The two were briefly engaged but broke it off after McCrea's mentor, Will Rogers voiced his dislike for Compton. According to Jamie Brotherton and Ted Okuda, in their biography of female star Dorothy Lee, the actress claimed McCrea and Compton were quite an item. Lee recalled: "A couple of times, RKO paired me up with Joel McCrea and tried to make it look like we were dating, which was ridiculous... he was crazy about Joyce Compton, a pretty blonde actress. Joel idolized Will Rogers, and for some reason Will took a dislike to

Joyce... (and) told Joel, 'She's not the kind of girl you ought to marry,' so Joel dumped Joyce."

Her time at Fox saw her cast in undemanding ingénue roles and in 1933, after presenting a comedic flair in many of her films, she signed with the Mack Sennett Studio, where she made a series of two-reel shorts, and also worked for comedy giant Hal Roach. Not surprisingly, she played the dumb blonde, and cemented her screen persona for the rest of her career. The pace and long hours were exhausting, and she eventually went back to freelance work.

As a free agent, Compton made several dozen movies during the mid and late '30s, many of them hits, working with the cream of the Hollywood crop. The best and most popular of this period was her appearance in Columbia's *The Awful Truth* (1937). She played nightclub singer Dixie Belle Lee, Cary Grant's ditzy rebound girlfriend during his separation from wife, Irene Dunne. Compton's rendition of "My Dreams Are Gone with the Wind," while a floor air jet blows her skirt hither and yon is hilarious and one of the most memorable scenes in the entire film. Other pictures during this prosperous phase were *Artists and Models Abroad, Trade Winds* (both 1938) and *Rose of Washington Square* (1939). In 1940, she made a fun and kooky would-be-detective named Christine Cross in the B-movie mystery *Sky Murder*, with Walter Pidgeon at MGM.

During the 1940s, the actress was seen in small bit parts such as her fun yet quick scene as a "dumb blonde" witness at a murder trial in *They Drive By Night* (1940), as well as larger supporting roles, like Beulah in *Bedtime Story* (1941), with Fredric March and Loretta Young. She was still living with her parents, or rather, they were living with her. The family lived in an English style farmhouse on Davana Road in Sherman Oaks. It was built in 1936, with the money Joyce earned from her movie work. The Compton's lived at the Davana Road house when Joyce's mother, Golden, died in 1953.

The mid '40s offered several fine movie performances for the hardworking actress. In 1945, she played a pivotal role in the holiday classic *Christmas in Connecticut*. As Nurse Mary Lee, she, with her honey-drawl accent, persuaded magazine tycoon Sydney Greenstreet to arrange a homespun Yuletide weekend for her sailor boyfriend (Dennis Morgan). The same year she was seen (if you look really quickly) as a waitress in the Warner Brothers' melodrama, *Mildred Pierce*, and three years later had a lighthearted role as (what else) a Southern Belle in *A Southern Yankee*, with Red Skelton.

The 1950s saw a drastic decrease in the number of roles available. Joyce worked sporadically in television and made only a handful of movie appearances. She turned to nursing as a new career and married for the first time at the age of forty-eight to William Francis Kaliher, a Long Beach businessman. The wedding took place at the Hollywood Presbyterian Church in November 1955, but by the next year the couple would be divorced. She made her last acting gig in 1961, on the forgotten TV show, *Pete and Gladys*.

Compton died at the Motion Picture and Television Hospital in Woodland Hills, California, on October 13, 1997. She was ninety. Her final resting place is at Forest Lawn Memorial Park. A woman of deep religious faith, Joyce Compton's headstone sums up her essence: *Christian Actress, Beloved Daughter, Devoted Friend.*

Gladys Cooper

Gladys Cooper was the definitive aristocratic snob on-screen throughout the 1940s. Stone faced, with a sneer when called for, her characters names alone painted the picture of haughty, upper-class females who feared little and disapproved much. Mrs. Strafford, Lady Frances Nelson, Mrs. Henry Vale, Lady Jean Ashwood and Clarissa Scott were appellations that carried solid social status and knew their way around a tea cart.

In 1913, Gladys Cooper made her first film, a silent short called *The Eleventh Commandment* and in 1969 she appeared in her final feature, *A Nice Girl Like Me*, a British comedy about unwed motherhood. The fifty-six years in between were filled with a multitude of roles performed on both stage and screen, a rich career for a woman who started out in front of a camera at the age of six, as a photographer's model. Born in Lewisham, London in December 1888, Cooper was discovered by actor/producer Seymour Hicks and in 1905 began touring with his company in the musical, *Bluebell in Fairyland*. A noted beauty of Edwardian England, she continued appearing in musicals and operettas throughout the early 20th century and became a pin-up of sorts during and after the First World War.

Although she made occasional forays in silent films made in Britain, she didn't embark on a serious career in the cinema until relatively late in life, sharing her American screen debut with master director Alfred Hitchcock in his classic, *Rebecca* in 1940. She played Maxim de Winter's tweedy, outdoorsy sister, Beatrice, no-nonsense in both dress and manner, telling Maxim's new, plain and very shy bride (Joan Fontaine), "I can see by the way you dress you don't care a hoot about how you look." She quickly made a name for herself playing stodgy upper-crust bluebloods.

Her first of three Academy Award nominations was for what would arguably be her best-known role, that of Bette Davis' domineering and extremely overbearing mother in the Warner Brothers classic, *Now, Voyager* (1942). A wealthy widowed Boston matriarch, Cooper's Mrs. Henry Vale controls and dictates her spinster daughter's life to the point of the pitiful creature's nervous breakdown. Stifling and humorless, her parental tyranny is one of the great examples of movie motherhood born in hell. When her reign of terror over her emotionally victimized offspring begins to lose its power, she takes the no-holds-barred approach of tossing herself, cane and all, down the stairs, risking broken brittle bones for the chance to regain her daughter's attention and power over her decisions. Cooper was superb and based on the strength of this performance alone, Mother's Day could be recalled as a national holiday.

Her second Oscar nod came the following year in *The Song of Bernadette*, again in an unsympathetic part, that of a bitter, disbelieving nun. The same viperous venom she dispensed on Bette Davis' character in *Now, Voyager* was cast upon Bernadette of Lourdes (Jennifer Jones), of whom she was jealous and spiteful. The look on Cooper's face when she discovers the hideous tumor on the young woman's knee, the result of tuberculosis of the bone, makes her second nomination from the Academy easy to understand. Although she portrayed a penniless prioress, the contemptuous piety of her socially ambitious roles shined through and added the right amount of superiority needed to convey her great acerbity toward the future saint.

Her elitist villainess credentials came to a hoity-toity head as the snobbish control freak, Mrs. Hamilton in the holiday fantasy, *The Bishop's Wife* (1947). She did disdainful dowager like nobody else. It is great fun to watch her hard-as-nails, cold-as-ice exterior completely melted by the suave charms of handsome angel Dudley (Cary Grant). In a movie which featured a cavalcade of wonderful character actor talent (Monty Woolley, Elsa Lanchester, James Gleason and so many more), Gladys truly shined.

Though she focused her career on film roles during the 1940s, she shifted back to the theater during the 1950s and 1960s with limited appearances in pictures. She also worked in television during these years with a very notable part in a 1964 episode of *The Twilight Zone* titled "Night Call," in which she played an elderly woman who gets weird phone calls from the beyond. She received her third and final Oscar nomination for Best Supporting Actress in the 1964 musical hit, *My Fair Lady*, playing Henry Higgins' mother. In 1967, at the age of 79, she was honored with the title of Dame Commander of the Order of the British Empire for her contributions to acting. Gladys Cooper died from pneumonia, in 1971 at the age of 82 in Henley-on-Thames, England.

Laird Cregar

"I realized that I would have to find my own parts. I am, after all, a grotesque. That is, an actor who doesn't fit readily into parts. I needed special parts. I am too big, too tall, too heavy. I don't look like an actor. If I wanted to act, I would have to find plays I could act."

Very few today, other than hardcore classic movie fans, have heard of Laird Cregar. His movie roles were powerful, albeit few in number. His brief career included only sixteen film appearances between 1940 and 1945, with most being colorful character parts in pictures ranging from comedy to horror. The majority of the parts he played were dark-souled "heavies." Heavy is ironically one of the first words associated with the tragic star, as his 6' 3" frame carried what most sources claim to be 300 lbs. On film, his oversized characters were an oxymoron, a menacing hulk, with a booming voice, yet effeminate and cultured. Sadly, it was his girth that brought him to prominence and eventually caused his demise.

Many older sources claim Cregar's year of birth is 1916, and it has been said that the actor liked to shave a few years off as well, but searches in both the 1920 and 1930 US Census reveal that Samuel Laird Cregar was indeed born on July 28, 1913 in the Mt. Airy section of Philadelphia. Sammy, as he was called by his family and close friends, was the youngest of six sons of Edward Matthews Cregar, a former professional cricket player, who died when Samuel was only two years-old, and Elizabeth Cregar, nee Smith. As a lad, Cregar went to England to attend Winchester Academy and while there worked as a page boy for the Stratford-Upon-Avon Players, where he developed a desire to become an actor. "From that time on," he later recalled, "all I've ever wanted to do is go on stage."

He returned to the United States to continue his education, graduating from the Episcopal Academy in Philadelphia. He then began acting in local stock companies before winning a scholarship to the famed Pasadena Playhouse in 1936, where he trained for the next two years. Then it was back and forth between the east and west coast in various stage productions before he embarked on a personal endeavor to play Oscar Wilde after seeing Robert Morley in the Broadway version of the infamous writer's life. Cregar felt sure the part was perfect for him and after finding backers for the production, had a successful run with the play in both Los Angeles and San Francisco in the spring of 1940. His performance was a popular one and he even received a fan letter from his idol, John Barrymore, who called him "one of the most gifted young stage actors in the past ten years."

With the success of *Oscar Wilde*, Hollywood came calling, with several studios showing interest in the actor. After making screen tests with some of the biggest studios in town, Darryl Zanuck persuaded him to sign with Twentieth Century-Fox. Cregar had tiny roles in two unforgettable pictures early in 1940 before making his feature debut at Fox as a burly fur trapper in the historical drama *Hudson's Bay*. He followed this up with a role in the studio's big Technicolor version of *Blood and Sand*, starring Tyrone Power and Rita Hayworth. As the pompous and flamboyant bullfighting critic Curro, he more than held his own with a swath of Fox stars and veteran stock players.

The actor proved himself capable of comedy in *Charley's Aunt* (1941) with Jack Benny, but when he played corrupt and obsessive police inspector Cornell in the film noir classic *I Wake Up Screaming* (1941), he cemented his typecasting as a film heavy, with *Variety* claiming, "... Laird Cregar is the picture." He made another nefarious noir nod in *This Gun for Hire*, on loan-out to Paramount in 1942, and more comedy back home at Fox in *Heaven Can Wait* (1943), playing the Devil, full of charm and charisma. Cregar's homosexuality found its way into many of his screen roles, sometimes nuanced, often not, as seen in *Blood and Sand*, when he screams almost orgasmically upon Tyrone Power's triumph in the bull ring: "I tell you he is the greatest of the great! The first man of the world!"

His sexual preference was common knowledge around the Fox lot and actor Henry Brandon, best known for his role as villainous Barnaby in *March of the Wooden Soldiers*, recalled how Cregar's actions were received by the top brass.

> "Sammy had a little boyfriend who was a dancer in a musical in Hollywood. One night, the boyfriend was sick, so Sammy went on for him, and was in the chorus – and he was a star at the time! I happened to be in the theatre that night, and I couldn't believe my eyes! And he was incredibly graceful, floating like a balloon; still, it was incongruous to see this great fat man among those little chorus boys. Well, Zanuck found out about it, and put his foot down with a *bang*!"

Another incident in 1943 required studio intervention to protect Cregar's image. He had become romantically involved with a twenty-nine-year-old minor actor named David Bacon, known best for appearing in *The Masked Marvel*, a low-budget 1943 serial. Bacon, the son of the former lieutenant governor of Massachusetts, was erratically driving his sedan in the Venice Beach area before running over the curb, climbing out of the car and collapsing as witnesses made their way to him. He asked them for help but was dead before he could say more. He was wearing only a swimsuit and a small knife wound was discovered in his back. A wallet and camera were found in his car, and when the film from the camera was developed, the only image was of Bacon, nude and smiling on the beach. Although the case was never solved, it was suggested that his attack took place at a gay bathhouse in Venice Beach and photos circulated in the media connecting him with Cregar, who mournfully claimed the dead actor was "such a good friend."

While the David Bacon incident was unfolding, Cregar was finishing up filming on his latest project, *The Lodger*, which cast him as Jack the Ripper. Yet again, Fox's favorite heavy was as dark and creepy as ever, screen traits that Laird was trying desperately to shed. It was, however, an opportunity that showered him with accolades and offered him a starring role alongside Merle Oberon. With the success of *The Lodger*, Cregar informed the press that "my fan mail has jumped 150%, mostly from women, and a surprising number of young girls." The attention only accelerated his desire to lose weight and create the appearance of a leading man, something he had always yearned for.

He had dieted down for his role in *The Lodger*, losing seventy pounds, but with another picture slated for him with a starring role, he doubled down on his reducing efforts. *Hangover Square* was a project developed specifically with Cregar in mind. His character, a demented pianist, was almost identical to the homicidal maniac he portrayed in *The Lodger*. Wanting desperately to get away from the hulking bad-guys that had made him famous, the actor refused to accept the role in *Hangover Square* and Zanuck put him on suspension. With his contract option coming up, Cregar felt pressured to take the role and eventually did so, albeit grudgingly. George Sanders, Cregar's co-star in both *The Lodger* and *Hangover Square*, later wrote that "...a tragic resolve was born in Laird's mind to make himself over into a beautiful man who would never again be cast as a fiend."

The determined actor began a drastic crash diet during filming, eating no more than 500 calories a day. Reflecting on his minimal intake, Cregar admitted, "Two slices of crisp bacon, two pieces of dry toast and a cup of coffee with cream isn't much for a guy like me." At the end of November 1944, after filming completed on *Hangover Square*, Cregar checked into the Good Samaritan Hospital in Los Angeles for abdominal surgery to aid in his weight loss. The procedure was performed a few days later but the extreme dieting had put a great strain on his heart which failed him. After a second heart attack, his body couldn't rally and on December 9, Laird Cregar died. He was only thirty-one years old.

Twentieth Century-Fox security stood guard at Forest Lawn Memorial Park in Glendale, while family and friends attended the private funeral for the fallen actor on December 13. *Hangover Square* was released the following February, with much praise going to its late star, including *Time* magazine, who summed up what many in the film colony wondered as well: "The late Laird Cregar, brilliant and touching... will have cinemaddicts pondering sadly on the major roles he might have played."

Jane Darwell

Many character actors and actresses played roles that supported the stars and the movies in which they appeared and that was the extent of their contribution, brilliant as it may have been, but sometimes the actor was lucky enough to make a role so much their own that it became iconic and they would forevermore be known for creating that specific part. One such player was Jane Darwell and the role was Ma Joad in *The Grapes of Wrath*. She not only represented the Depression-era dust bowl via Hollywood, but also won an Academy Award in the process. She appeared in four movies that were nominated for the Best Picture Oscar: *Gone with the Wind* (1939), *The Grapes of Wrath* (1940), *The Ox-Bow Incident* (1943) and *Mary Poppins* (1964). Her signature character was a pleasantly plump, homespun mother, who wore a no-nonsense disposition as easily as she did a mid-western calico dress.

Jane Darwell was the name she took professionally, in an attempt to keep her original family name from the disgrace of being associated with an "actress." Born Patti Woodard in Palmyra, Missouri, on October 15, 1879, she was the daughter of William Robert Woodard, president of the Louisville Southern Railroad, and Ellen Booth, the daughter of a Presbyterian minister from Seymour, Indiana. Her family moved to Chicago when she was four, and she graduated from the exclusive Dana Hall in Boston where she studied voice and piano.

Early on she had thoughts of becoming a circus rider, then changed her mind to singing opera, but at her father's objections, she compromised by becoming an actress and "Jane Darwell" emerged. She began her career by joining a stock company in Chicago in 1906, then later various troupes around the country, making her Broadway debut in a single matinee performance of *The Wedding Day* in December 1909. She made her film debut in 1913 and appeared in no less than eight short silents in that year alone. The actress worked steadily in silent features for the next two years (showing up in a couple of early Cecil B. DeMille productions) before returning to the stage, including two more stints on the Great White Way.

Other than a small, uncredited role in 1923, Darwell had a fifteen-year hiatus from movies, which ended in 1930, when she was cast as the Widow Douglas in Paramount's *Tom Sawyer* and reprised the role the next year for the follow-up *Huckleberry Finn*. It was the kind of role she excelled in and became known for: Stout, folksy matrons with a steely disposition. The actress signed with Twentieth Century-Fox in the mid-1930s and appeared in numerous Shirley Temple features including *Bright Eyes*, *Curly Top* and *Poor Little Rich Girl*, all in 1936. By the end of the decade she was given a memorable part in David O. Selznick's Civil War epic *Gone with the Wind* (1939) as Atlanta busybody Dolly Merriweather.

The following year produced her most famous role as Ma Joad in the Fox classic, *The Grapes of Wrath*. The film was directed by John Ford, who wanted solid character actress Beulah Bondi to play the role of the Joad matriarch, who held her family together. Fox boss Darryl F. Zanuck wanted Darwell, who ended up with the role and the Academy Award to go with it. Jane must have won Ford over, however, as *Grapes* was the first of six pictures she made for the acclaimed director. She also made several films with the movie's star, Henry Fonda, declaring in one magazine interview, "I've played Henry Fonda's mother so often that, whenever we run into each other, I call him "Son" and he calls me "Ma" just to save time."

By the time the Oscars were awarded in early 1941, however, the actress had experienced a career slow down with *Variety* reporting that "Jane Darwell, who received the award last night for supporting actress for her work in '*The Grapes of Wrath*' has worked only five weeks since appearing in this picture and has been unemployed for the past seven months." With her top honor under her dramatic belt, however, she was back on the screen later that year in several features including the high profile *The Devil and Daniel Webster* with Walter Huston. Her next big film was *The Ox-Bow Incident* (1943) for director William A. Wellman, in which she played "Ma" Grier, member of a lynch mob, an uncharacteristically unsympathetic role in contrast to the usual earth mothers she portrayed. She was cast in the film after character actresses Sara Allgood and Florence Bates were unable to take the part.

Darwell was back on Broadway in early 1944 in a comedy called *Suds in Your Eye*, in which she played an Irishwoman who owns a junkyard. It ran for thirty-seven performances and had some positive press, although a certain reviewer for *The New Yorker* deemed in "too damn folksy." As the 1950s approached, the actress split her time between the stage, the big screen and the increasingly popular medium of television. Film work during the period included a role as the isolation matron in the gripping women's prison drama, *Caged* (1950), with Eleanor Parker and the lighthearted Bob Hope romp, *The Lemon Drop Kid* (1951). On television, she appeared on *The Loretta Young Show* in 1954, the same year she starred with Andy Clyde in an episode of *The Pepsi-Cola Playhouse* called "Santa's Old Suit," which aired during the Christmas season. In 1961, Darwell played the mother of Walter Brennan's character, Amos McCoy, on the popular TV show, *The Real McCoys*, though she was only fifteen years older than the actor.

By the mid-1960s, Jane had retired from acting, making her last feature film in 1959 and only a handful of television appearances during the '60s. With severe heart problems, she was living at the Motion Picture

Country Home, a retirement community for members of the movie and television industry, when she was approached personally by producer Walt Disney about appearing in his upcoming feature, *Mary Poppins*. Disney wanted Darwell to play the poignant figure of the Bird Woman, during the vignette for the song, "Feed the Birds." At eighty-four and in poor health, Darwell wasn't sure, but Walt assured her that filming of the scene would be swift, and concessions would be made for her comfort. The actress agreed and "Feed the Birds" was reportedly Disney's favorite song. It would be her last role. Jane Darwell died on August 13, 1967, at the Motion Picture & Television Country House and Hospital in Woodland Hills, from a heart attack at the age of eighty-seven.

Harry Davenport

"Without a doubt, he was the greatest character actor of all time." That is high praise from anyone, but particularly from screen queen Bette Davis, who made the statement about fellow actor Harry Davenport upon his death. His cinematic stamina was amazing, with Davenport appearing in over one hundred and fifty motion pictures, usually playing wizened old doctors (from both the 19th and 20th centuries) judges, uncles, grandfathers, and the occasional minister and elected representative, all of which he portrayed as sage, endearing and usually with a whimsical sense of humor. Not only did he produce quantity in Hollywood but the quality of many of his movies was some of the best of the golden age. He appeared in some of the film colony's most prestigious and financially successful pictures, including *Marie Antoinette* (1938), *You Can't Take It With You* (also 1938), *Meet Me in St. Louis* (1944) and the grand-daddy of all blockbusters from the golden age, *Gone with the Wind* (1939).

Harry George Bryant Davenport was born in New York City, on January 19, 1866, the offspring of well-known actors Edward Loomis Davenport (1815-1877; considered by many as one of the best Shakespearean thespians of his day) and Fanny (Elizabeth) Vining (1829-1891), who graced the stage on both sides of the Atlantic during the 19th century. Harry was the youngest of nine children, two of which wouldn't survive childhood. The seven who did survive would follow in their parent's footsteps and take to the stage. He was raised in Philadelphia, but the family spent their summers in the town of Canton in north central Pennsylvania. In 1871, at the age of five, young Davenport made his stage debut in *Damon and Pythias* in his father's company. As a youth, he was in the juvenile company of *H.M.S. Pinafore*, appearing at the Broad Street Theater in Philadelphia. He eventually made his way to Broadway, making his debut in 1894, at the age of twenty-eight, in a musical called *The Voyage of Suzette*. In fact, much of his stage career was spent performing musicals and musical-comedy.

In 1913, while still appearing on the stage, Davenport co-founded the Actor's Equity Association (then known as "The White Rats") with famed vaudevillian, Eddie Foy, Sr. The labor union was formed in response to the exploitation of actors by theater owners, including the Shubert family and impresario David Belasco, among others. Before long, "The White Rats" had an enthusiastic membership, which would unite by refusing to appear on the stage in protest of their appalling treatment and cause a close-out of theaters in question. With no stage work for income, Harry sought out employment in movies and signed on with Vitagraph Studios in 1914, making his film debut in *Too Many Husbands*, at the age of forty-eight. Despite his late entry into films, he was very active in the industry, particularly starring in and directing silent short films, in which he appeared in over two dozen through 1921. Stage work began to be more readily available and Harry returned to his first love, the theater. He continued in that venue for most of the 1920s.

Davenport had married his first wife, Alice Shepard, in 1893. She would keep her married surname and become a silent film comedienne, making almost as many films as her husband. The couple divorced after three years but the union did produce a daughter, Doris, who would also become an actress and eventually marry silent matinee idol Wallace Reid. After his divorce from Alice, Harry married another actress, Phyllis

Rankin, with whom he shared the stage often. The two were married until Phyllis's death in 1934 at the age of sixty. In addition to this devastation, Davenport's last few plays on Broadway had been flops and his handful of film roles in the early '30s had been small and few and far between.

At the age of sixty-nine, when most would be finishing their working lives, Harry packed his belongings and moved to the west coast, where his adult children had already settled, to give the movies another try. He began making frequent appearances in numerous movies (nineteen in 1937 alone!), though not yet making his mark as one of the preeminent character actors of the golden age. Among the average pictures he took part in, he appeared in some of the top tier of the year, including *They Won't Forget* and *The Life of Emile Zola*, both for Warner Brothers.

1939 was also a banner year for the prolific actor. Besides playing an affable King Louis XI of France in RKO's *The Hunchback of Notre Dame* with Charles Laughton, Davenport portrayed the character with which he is arguably most associated and remembered, Doctor Meade in the Civil War epic, *Gone with the Wind*. As the aged Confederate physician, Davenport's Meade was sometimes grumpy, sometimes funny, and always compassionate. The actor was celebrated by his fellow cast members on the *GWTW* set for his sixty-ninth year in show business.

The following year saw the actor grace the screen in even more prestige pictures, including *All This and Heaven Too* with Bette Davis and Charles Boyer, *Dr. Ehrlich's Magic Bullet* with Edward G. Robinson, and *Foreign Correspondent*, directed by Alfred Hitchcock. His reputation was top-notch, and the offers continued. In 1944 he played another of the roles for which he is well-remembered, the spry and kindly Grandpa in MGM's colorful musical, *Meet Me in St. Louis*. He worked without pause for the rest of the decade. Then, on Tuesday, August 9, 1949, Davenport died of a sudden heart attack at the age of eighty-three. His remains were interred back east in Westchester County, New York. When asked how a man of his age could work as hard as he did, the actor would retort: "A man should stand on his feet at any age."

Brian Donlevy

Character star (and occasional lead) Brian Donlevy once gave a self-assessment of his own acting abilities. Of his talents he said bluntly: "I think I stink." The actor had the looks of a dashing leading man but chose instead to focus on playing heavies and tough guys of the first order, particularly in high profile film noirs of the 1940s. His reputation as a movie baddie grew to the point that Donlevy recalled getting letters from people asking, "if I kick my dog." He has been described as a durable character player and it is a very fitting summarization of his work in Hollywood during its golden years.

Like many of Tinsel Town's actors and actresses of the era, both the year and place of Donlevy's birth is disputed by various sources. Some list him as being born in Portadown, County Armagh, Ireland (now in Northern Ireland), on February 9, 1901, while others have his origins in or around Cleveland, Ohio as early as 1899. According to the obituaries of both Donlevy's parents (his father died in 1931, before the actor found stardom, his mother in 1939, when Brian had already established his Hollywood career), the couple married in Massachusetts in February 1902, then moved to Cleveland, where they welcomed their only child into the world.

Regardless, Waldo Bruce Donlevy made his entry around the turn of the 20th century. He was the son of Thomas and Rebecca, who raised him in Sheboygan Falls, Wisconsin, where Thomas worked as a superintendent at the Brickner Woolen Mills. Young Waldo led a colorful life during his early years. As a youth, he attended St. Johns Military Academy in Delafield and around the age of fourteen, ran away from home to join up with General John J. Pershing's campaign against Pancho Villa in 1916. Lying about his age, he became a teenaged bugler during the raid in New Mexico. Donlevy later served as a pilot with the Lafayette Escadrille in France during World War I.

He returned home and spent two years at the US Naval Academy at Annapolis, Maryland before deciding on a career change that took him to New York and the bright lights of Broadway. The Great White Way offered no immediate success. A longtime amateur poet, the would-be actor tried his hand at writing, and supplemented his income, thanks to his striking profile, as an Arrow collar model for famed illustrator J.C. Leyendecker. He finally broke through in September 1924, landing the small part of Corporal Gowdy in *What Price Glory*? The same year he appeared in a handful of silent films, beginning a career that would serve him well for years, but wouldn't take off for another decade. He did, however, continue to make a name for himself on the stage.

In 1935, Donlevy finally found his niche when he was cast in Samuel Goldwyn's *Barbary Coast* starring Edward G. Robinson and Miriam Hopkins. The actor played Robinson's henchman, a villainous brute named Knuckles Jacoby, who meets his maker at the end of a rope being hoisted by a group of vigilantes. It was just the kind of role he needed, and a new slick villain was born in Hollywood. He signed with 20th Century-Fox the following year and continued in black-hearted snake-in-the-grass roles like a corrupt political boss in *In Old Chicago* (1938), a nasty railroad rep in *Jesse James* (1939) and a sadistic sergeant in the French Foreign Legion in *Beau Geste* (also 1939), the latter garnering the up-and-coming Donlevy an Oscar nomination in the Best Supporting Actor category (he lost to Thomas Mitchell).

Although he appreciated the success his nefarious characters gained him, Brian was ready for a change. "I got a kick out of playing villains. But after four years or more, it began to get under my skin," the actor said. "Everywhere I went, kids looked sidewise at me. My wife stopped going to my pictures because she couldn't take the razzing I got." Based on the strength of his performance in *Beau Geste*, he signed a non-exclusive contract with Paramount in 1940 and was used by Preston Sturges in his directorial debut, the political satire *The Great McGinty*. It was one of Donlevy's most memorable of his rare leading roles, with *Time* magazine giving him high praise, saying: "*The Great McGinty* is shrewd, salty, adroit. It is also an actor's dream. Brian Donlevy makes the dream come true."

The war years at Paramount were fruitful ones for the actor with three of his best films produced in 1942: *The Great Man's Lady*, *Wake Island* and *The Glass Key*. His personal life didn't go as smoothly during the latter half of the decade with his second marriage to singer Marjorie Lane (whose singing voice was used to dub dancer Eleanor Powell's musical numbers) ending in a nasty divorce in 1947, with Donlevy reportedly paying out over $160,000. The couple shared custody of their only child, a daughter named Judy. With the quality of his film roles slipping, Donlevy made the transition to radio in 1949 as lead character Steve Mitchell in the adventure series *Dangerous Assignment*. The show made its way to television in 1952 for nearly 40 episodes with Donlevy in tow.

Television work continued throughout the 1950s and 1960s with occasional feature film appearances. A third marriage (his first was to Yvonne Grey from 1928-1936) to Lillian Arch Lugosi (ex-wife to vampire-player Bela) took place in 1966. Donlevy spent his later years writing poetry and short stories and continuing to appear in low-grade westerns. Bouts with acute alcoholism had taken their toll and on April 5, 1972, he died of throat cancer at the Motion Picture County Hospital in Woodland Hills, California. He would be remembered as a strong actor, whose contributions to film were solid and significant.

Dan Duryea

Slimy, sleazy, slick and smarmy. No, these aren't demented dwarfs in an off-beat version of Snow White, they describe the kind of roles actor Dan Duryea was most famous for in his almost three-decade career in Hollywood. He was great as an instigating weasel, either stirring up trouble or landing smack dab in the middle of it or both. In William Wyler's *The Little Foxes* (1941), he recreated his stage role of smart aleck buffoon Leo Hubbard, pawn to his uncle's financial shenanigans. Two film noir classics, *The Woman in the Window* (1944) and *Scarlet Street* (1945) showed Duryea in some of his best roles, as blackmailer and low-life pimp respectively. His lanky frame, slicked back blond hair and devious grin made him the definitive creep of the film noir period, with other standouts including *Ministry of Fear* (1944) and *Black Angel* (1946). The 1950s saw a shift in parts for the actor, primarily in the crime drama and western genres.

Dan Duryea was born on January 23, 1907, in the New York City suburb of White Plains, the second son of Richard and Mabel Duryea. In contrast to the nimble-minded, lazy characters he portrayed on-screen, the actor graduated White Plains High School, then went on to study English at Cornell University, where he became president of the school's drama society. It was a post previously held by future MGM star Franchot Tone. Also proving his scholastic mettle, Duryea was elected into Cornell's Sphinx Head, the university's oldest honor society for seniors. Pressed by his parents to pursue a more traditional and stable career path, he went into advertising and worked in that field for six years before suffering a stress-related heart attack. From that point on he followed his initial interest of acting.

Starting out in summer stock, Duryea made his way to Broadway where he debuted in a small part as a "G-man" in the Sidney Kingsley play *Dead End* in 1935 and three years later landed a plum supporting role in Lillian Hellman's Southern drama *The Little Foxes*, starring *grande dame* Tallulah Bankhead. After working on the film version of *Foxes* in 1941, the actor spent the rest of the decade playing every negative character attribute from whining to menacing, making a particular impact in the rising genre of film noir. With European film director Fritz Lang he made three noir hits in a row beginning with *Ministry of Fear* and continuing with *The Woman in the Window* (both 1944), then *Scarlet Street* (1945), which was a follow-up of sorts to *Woman in the Window*, reuniting the wiry weasel with Edward G. Robinson and Joan Bennett. As Johnny, the brutish thug who pimps his girlfriend Kitty (Bennett) out and uses her to bilk a meek bank clerk (Robinson), Duryea is one of the best sleazeballs of the era.

After the war he continued playing hoodlums and hoods who liked to slap women around and signed a lucrative contract with Universal Pictures. His films, however, weren't as high quality as those made earlier in the decade, though he did contribute to some fine and interesting dramas, including *Another Part of the Forest* (1948), a prequel to *The Little Foxes*, and *Criss Cross* (1948), another gritty noir offering co-starring Burt Lancaster. The 1950s saw an increase in television work for

Duryea with guest appearances in the western hit *Wagon Train* and his own series, *China Smith*.

Unlike the shady and repugnant characters he had created on the screen, Duryea was a devoted spouse of thirty-five years to his wife Helen (until her death in 1967), a self-proclaimed "ordinary, peace-loving husband and father." He knew what his fans expected out his characters. Such an unglamorous and upstanding off-screen life proved a testament to the actor's ability to create an array of degenerates and boors throughout his career. Dan Duryea died of cancer in 1968 (a year after his beloved wife) at the age of sixty-one.

Barry Fitzgerald

Irish actor Arthur Shields wrote of his brother, beloved screen character Barry Fitzgerald, upon his death, "Barry was a very shy little man and he was uncomfortable in crowds and really dreaded meeting new people, but he was not a recluse and did enjoy certain company, especially when the 'old chat' was good." The description, though an apt one, was quite the opposite of the screen persona of the impish and eccentric character actor who hailed from Ireland and became a favorite on U.S. cinema screens. The diminutive and irascible performer was much loved and became one of the best-known faces in Hollywood pictures during the 1940s and 1950s.

Fitzgerald was born William Joseph Shields on March 10, 1888, in Walworth Road, Portobello, Dublin, Ireland. He had six siblings (some sources say seven) including fellow actor Arthur Shields, with whom he co-starred in several films. According to Arthur's wife Laurie regarding the Shields family, "Every child was encouraged to develop his natural talents, especially those dealing the arts or service to others." A loveable pint-sized actor (5' 4") with a playful, expressive face and a thick brogue, Fitzgerald graduated from Skerry's College Dublin in preparation for a career in civil service. He worked as a junior executive in the Department of Industry and Commerce. Bored with his day job, he began an interest in the theater and took up acting as a hobby making his debut with The Abbey Theatre in the play *Hyacinth Halvey* (1914). He subsequently began acting full-time at the age of forty-one and starred in the Abbey's production of Sean O'Casey's *Juno And the Paycock*, a role that he recreated in his film debut for director Alfred Hitchcock in 1930.

Director John Ford brought Fitzgerald to the United States, along with other members of the Abbey, including brother Arthur, to appear in the film version of another Sean O'Casey play, *The Plough and the Stars* at RKO. He decided to stay in Hollywood and was cast in lackluster supporting roles with an exception in *Bringing Up Baby* (1938), a screwball comedy with Cary Grant and Katharine Hepburn. He gained career traction giving fine performances, again in films for John Ford, first *The Long Voyage Home* (1940) and *How Green Was My Valley* (1941). Then, in 1944, he appeared in Leo McCarey's *Going My Way* and was fully established as one of the industry's best and most sought-after character actors. As Father Fitzgibbon, the feisty Roman Catholic priest, he was the personification of the Emerald Isle, Hollywood style (Ironically, the actor was a Protestant off screen). The movie was nominated for ten Academy Awards and won seven, including Best Picture and in an unprecedented move, Fitzgerald was nominated for both the Best Actor prize as well as Best Supporting Actor for the same role. He won the Supporting category and his co-star, Bing Crosby, copped Best Actor for the year.

The middle-aged star had wide-spread appeal and was offered many roles after his Oscar win. The *New York Times* stated it very specifically in a 1945 article. "Today Barry Fitzgerald is in greater demand by the studios than any character has ever been in the history of the film city. One conservative estimate, by people who figure such things out, has it that if the 56-year-old Irish actor accepted all of the parts that have been offered to him in the past four months he would be working in front of the cameras, night and day, for the next two years."

His popularity soared as the screen's resident Irish representative, scrappy attitude, heavy brogue and leprechaun demeanor in tow. He was top billed in René Clair's *And Then There Were None* based on Agatha Christie's famed whodunit, a film that was comprised almost entirely of top notch supporting actors and actresses. Fitzgerald was again cast as the lead in the significant film noir *The Naked City* (1948) at Universal. In 1952, John Ford hired the actor to play the role for which he is arguably best remembered, matchmaking Michaleen Oge Flynn in *The Quiet Man*. It was the last time Ford and Fitzgerald worked together in a film.

As the actor's fame grew, so did his need for privacy. Fred Stanley at the *New York Times* expressed Fitzgerald's feeling on his newfound notoriety. "He finds it all rather bewildering. He resents the disruption of his previously inconspicuous private life. He can't even browse in Los Angeles book shops or join in a discussion with strangers at some out-of-the-way barroom or drug store without being tagged as Father Fitzgibbon. His old clothes and cloth cap, which once kept him inconspicuous, now make him a marked man."

Walt Disney had hoped to cast Fitzgerald in his work in progress *Darby O'Gill and the Little People*, which was being considered as a potential project for the Disney studios as early as 1946 when the actor was at his peak. The film didn't make it to theaters until 1958, though it was without Fitzgerald, who turned down the role due to health concerns which had developed by the time filming actually began. He did make a few television appearances in the 1950s, including a 1955 episode of *Alfred Hitchcock Presents* called "Santa Claus and the Tenth Avenue Kid," in which he played a cynical paroled convict given a job as a department store Santa who matches wits with a bad-tempered brat. "I would rather be a villain on the screen and bop someone on the head occasionally than play the most noble of characters," he said. "A villain doesn't have to be repressed - and audiences have a sneaking affection for him, especially if he is picturesque. And besides, it's easier to portray villainy."

In failing health, Barry Fitzgerald moved back to his native Dublin in 1959 where he would star in his final film, an Irish comedy called *Broth of a Boy*. He plays fictional Patrick Farrell, who at 110 claims to be the world's oldest living gent. The *New York Times* said of the actor's swan song: "Mr. Fitzgerald behaves as benignly as befits a man three score and ten, who is playing the oldest man on earth. Nevertheless, the scowl, the sudden, elfin smile, the occasional rages, the beauty of a brogue and a dented derby and ragamuffin clothes make his caricature an endearing one." A year and a half later, on January 4, 1961, Fitzgerald died in a nursing home in Dublin after undergoing exploratory brain surgery.

Gladys George

During Hollywood's golden age, Gladys George played world-weary women and she played them well. For one reason, she had a certain been-around-the-block look about her face and carriage that lent itself to the characters she portrayed. Don't get me wrong, she was attractive, but she wore the look of a woman who knew how the world worked and had worked much of it herself. She played a long line of dames, broads and gangster's molls and worked at most of the major studios of the day, with her best-known roles in Warner Brothers melodramas.

On stage practically from the cradle, she was born Gladys Clare Evans in Patten, Maine on September 13, 1902, the year stated on her Maine birth certificate, though other years have been given. Her parents were touring Shakespearian actors Sir Arthur Clare, from England and Boston-born Abbie Hazen, whom she joined when she was three years-old to form a vaudeville act called "The Three Clares." As the toddler became the focal point of the act, the name was changed to "Little Gladys George and Company" and found success with a sketch called *The Doll's Dream*, written by Sir Arthur. The family of vaudevillians toured the United States throughout Gladys' youth and she eventually yearned to try her hand at the legitimate theater. The teenager made her way to New York and debuted on Broadway in the autumn of 1918 in a play called *The Betrothal* for director Winthrop Ames.

The following year she made her film debut for producer Thomas Ince in a silent picture called *Red Hot Dollars*, which was the first of seven movies she appeared in before 1921. She then returned to the stage where she worked steadily until 1934, when she screen-tested for Paramount in Hollywood. Although that test didn't pan out, it led to a contract with MGM and she made her first talking picture, *Straight is the Way*. Although an unforgettable movie, it allowed George to use her husky voice to good display as a "bad girl."

The actress was back on Broadway shortly afterward with a successful show as well as a scandal in her lap. Married and divorced (to actor Ben Erway) in the 1920s, George had married for the second time in 1933 to millionaire paper manufacturer Edward Fowler. She was cast in the stage comedy *Personal Appearance* in October 1934, which was a hit and ran for over a year at the Henry Miller Theatre. During the show's run, she and her handsome costar, minor actor Leonard Penn, were caught in a clinch by her suspicious husband, Fowler. The incident hit the headlines and the cuckolded Fowler sued for divorce. Ironically, her role in *Personal Appearance* was that of a nymphomaniac movie star. Despite George countersuing Fowler for infidelity, the husband won the divorce, which prohibited George from remarrying in New York for a period of three years. Not to be deterred, Gladys and Leonard Penn (who was half a decade younger) were married in September 1935, not in New York, but in neighboring Connecticut.

After her successful run on Broadway, the actress was back in Hollywood, on loan-out to Paramount for a leading role in a melodramatic soap opera, *Valiant is the Word for Carrie* (1936). A prime example of the mother love and sacrifice films that were extremely popular with audiences in the '30s and '40s, Gladys received good notices with Frank Nugent of the *New York Times* proclaiming, "Miss George's return to the screen after an unkind absence is occasion for rejoicing..." Even better still, the actress was recognized by the Academy with an Oscar nomination for Best Actress. Next up was as leading lady to Spencer Tracy in MGM's *They Gave Him a Gun* and later that year, what would be her best-known leading role in *Madame X*. Another mother's sacrifice story, it was the second, and many claim, best version, of the oft-told tale. With that, however, her starring career virtually dried up and was replaced by a string of films that cast George in rich and interesting character roles, that used her raspy voice and hard-boiled visage to their best advantage.

Her time at Metro wound down in 1938 with the juicy role of Madame du Barry, the infamous courtesan who challenged Norma Shearer as head honcho in the French court in the luxurious *Marie Antoinette* (which also featured her then-husband, Leonard Penn in a small role). Next, she moved over to Warner Brothers, where she gave rousing support to James Cagney in *The Roaring Twenties* ("He used to be a big shot") in 1939. One of her most recognizable roles came in 1941, when she played Iva Archer in John Huston's classic, *The Maltese Falcon*. Although she had little screen time, she was very effective as the adulterous widow of Miles Archer. In 1943, she played an aging alcoholic star who is usurped by newcomer Joan Leslie in *The Hard Way*. It was a small supporting part, but one which displayed the nuanced pathos that her roles became known for.

The remainder of the decade found her parts getting smaller and smaller, though still strong characters, made more so by her noticeable acting skill. She was used to good advantage in the all-star post-war classic, *The Best Years of Our Lives* (1946). In 1949, she was sassy as hard-boiled broad, Lute Mae Sanders in the Warner Brothers' hard-boiled melodrama, *Flamingo Road*, starring hard-boiled Joan Crawford. She then began the early '50s with several roles, though most were inconsequential, with the exception of *He Ran All the Way* and *Detective Story*, both in 1951.

Gladys and Leonard Penn divorced in 1944 and two years later she married Kenneth Bradley, a hotel bellhop who was twenty years her junior. This marriage also ended in divorce in 1950. She suffered with various health issues in her later years, including throat cancer and cirrhosis of the liver and she died on December 8, 1954. Although an overdose of barbiturates was initially suspected, an autopsy revealed that George died of a brain hemorrhage. She was only fifty-two.

Bonita Granville

Child stars have been a large part of Hollywood history ever since the days of silent films, with Jackie Coogan leading the way alongside Charlie Chaplin in *The Kid* (1921). Often these wide-eyed moppets would drain the tear ducts of adoring audiences or make them chuckle with a cute quip directed at an unsuspecting adult co-star. During the Depression years of the 1930s, Shirley Temple was the leader of the juvenile pack, becoming the number one box-office star for four consecutive years: 1935, 1936, 1937 and 1938. She wasn't, however, the only Tinsel Town tyke to grace movie screens during the decade. Deanna Durbin and Judy Garland were singing and dancing at Universal and MGM respectively. Jackie Cooper was breaking hearts in *The Champ* (1931) and finding mischief in *Our Gang* shorts while Jane Withers was being a scamp in B-level flicks. Yet with all this cherubic precociousness swirling 'round her, Bonita Granville made a mark for herself as one of the most dependable young actresses of the day. Though many film fans know her best as the star of a series of four Nancy Drew mysteries made at Warner Brothers in the late 1930s, it is her performances as malicious pre-teens and reprehensible brats for which she gained prominence in the film community.

Some film encyclopedia entries for Granville state that she was the "daughter of show people." More specifically, she was the daughter of Bernard 'Bunny' Granville, a veteran vaudevillian who worked often with Will Rogers and was a longtime headliner in the famed Ziegfeld Follies. Her mother was Rosa Timponti, an actress whose own mother was a ballerina with the distinguished Ballet Russes in Monaco. Born in New York, New York on February 2, 1923, Bonita made her stage debut at age three and her movie debut at nine in the drama *Westward Passage* (1932), after her family made the move from New York to California. The following year she had a small part in the Oscar-winning, *Cavalcade*, then appearing in several films in uncredited roles.

In 1936, she gave what was arguably her best performance as the vicious schoolgirl Mary Tilford in Samuel Goldwyn's *These Three*. Based on Lillian Hellman's play *The Children's Hour*, the film centers on the devastating effects of a lie, in this case concerning a trio of friends, two female and one male, who are accused of hanky panky in a girl's school. As the source of the lie, Mary leverages her manipulation of her less obnoxious peers to perpetuate the lie for her own gain. Granville's performance was powerful and gained her a nomination as Oscar's Best Supporting Actress, up against adults in the Academy's first year to offer the award. In addition to the flattering nomination, the youngster ranked a rave review from esteemed author and then film critic Graham Greene. In the May 1, 1936 edition of Britain's, *The Spectator*, Greene wrote: "The more than human evil of the lying sadistic child is suggested with quite shocking mastery by Bonita Granville. It has enough truth and intensity to stand for the whole of the dark side of childhood."

She followed up with several more brash brat roles including the teen-aged leader of a group of "bewitched" lasses accusing Claudette Colbert of sorcery in a precursor to *The Crucible* called *Maid of Salem* (1937) at Paramount. After her turn as girl-detective Nancy Drew, Granville began taking on ingénue roles, not exactly leading lady fare but maturing in age and nature from her juvenile parts. She gave engaging performances in *The Mortal Storm* (1940), *Now, Voyager* (1942) and *Hitler's Children* (1943), a topical melodrama about the Hitler Youth movement of Nazi Germany.

In 1947, the actress married oil millionaire Jack Wrather. The Texas-born petroleum tycoon had tried his hand at film production in 1946 and his debut project was a film noir called *The Guilty* for low-budget Monogram Pictures and starred Granville. The actress appeared in only a handful of pictures after her marriage, opting instead to become an executive at her husband's company, the Wrather Corporation. An extremely wealthy man, Wrather's business concerns included the dry-docked Queen Mary in Long Beach and the Disneyland Hotel in Anaheim, which he constructed in 1955, when Walt Disney's funds were insufficient to build the resort himself. During the 1950s Granville acted sporadically in television, focusing more behind the camera as a producer of the Lassie TV series, which was owned by the Wrather company. Upon her husband's death in 1984, Granville, an astute businesswoman, became the chairman of the board, a post she retained until her own death of cancer in 1988.

Sydney
Greenstreet

Like Lucile Watson, Sydney Greenstreet got a late start in a movie career. The corpulent actor was sixty-one when he made his film debut, but what a motion picture to start out in: *The Maltese Falcon.* He not only was well-received by audiences but was nominated for an Academy Award for his role in the classic noir drama. The actor didn't make a movie outside the decade of the 1940s, as the *Falcon* was released in 1941 and his last appearance was in 1949, and within those eight years, Greenstreet made less than twenty-five films, yet he became one of the most popular and recognizable character stars of the entire golden age of Hollywood. Although he usually played a menacing villain, his occasional forays into comedy were just as fun and memorable.

Sydney Hughes Greenstreet was born on December 27, 1879, in Sandwich, Kent, England, one of eight children born to a tanner, John Jack Greenstreet and his wife, Anne Baker. From age seven to seventeen, he attended the Dane Hill Preparatory School in Margate, where he appeared in amateur stage productions and excelled in school athletics. As a young man, in 1899, he tried his hand as a supervisor on a tea plantation in Ceylon, but severe drought drove him back to England two years later. Upon his return, he took a position as manager for an agency in Harrow for Watneys, Coombes and Reed's Brewery for a year, then, turned his attention toward the stage.

As he had hoped to do with his time in Ceylon, Greenstreet, hoped to make his fortune. He began an apprenticeship with the Ben Greet School of Acting in London, making his stage debut in 1902 as a villain (foreshadowing of his future?) named Craigen in a production of *Sherlock Holmes* at the Marina Theatre in Ramsgate, Kent, after which he toured England with Greet's Shakespearean company. In 1905, he traveled with the group to America and made his Broadway debut. He then toured the globe playing various roles, from musical comedy to Shakespeare, settling in the United States in 1909. His reputation as a versatile actor was well-established and Hollywood came calling for his entre into films. He consistently refused, citing other commitments.

In the spring of 1941, Greenstreet was touring with the well-known husband and wife acting team, Alfred Lunt and Lynn Fontanne (with whom he worked often on stage) in a production of Robert Sherwood's *There Shall Be No Night*. The last stop on the tour before closing for a summer vacation was Los Angeles, where Warner Brothers producer Hal Wallis caught a performance. In his autobiography, *Starmaker*, Wallis recounts his thoughts on Greenstreet for an upcoming project he was casting called *The Maltese Falcon*.

"Enormously fat, almost 350 pounds, he seemed to rejoice in his size. He had a deep chuckling laugh, a fruity voice, and a manner that was alternatively genial and menacing. I felt he would be perfect for the part of the fat man (appropriately named Gutman), who was the villain of the piece. His test was marvelous. We only had to tone down a slight effeminacy in the playing to make it perfect."

With no excuse before him, the actor agreed to make the picture. Preview audiences for *The Maltese Falcon* responded to the question on the opinion poll, "Who gives the best performance," with "the fat man." Indeed, after the film's release, fan mail arriving at the studio was addressed simply to "Fat Man." With his diminutive (in comparison) on-screen cohort, Peter Lorre, he formed a film partnership that was a reliable and popular union. The rotund Greenstreet and the wiry, pop-eyed Lorre appeared together in a total of nine pictures and became known as the "Laurel and Hardy of crime." As a tribute to an unusually high-profile movie debut, Greenstreet was nominated for the Best Supporting Actor Oscar, though ultimately, the coveted prize went to Donald Crisp for *How Green Was My Valley*.

With a Warner Brothers contract under his substantial belt, he was placed in some of the studio's top-drawer movies and, as with Peter Lorre, was often cast with Warners' rising star, Humphrey Bogart. In *Across the Pacific* (1942), he played yet another menacing heavy, with the *New York Times'* Bosley Crowther perfectly summarizing the new film actor's on-screen persona, saying he was "entirely an enigma – malefic yet dignified, urbane and full of enviable refinement, yet hard and unpredictable beneath." For his appearance in the iconic classic, *Casablanca* (1942), Warners' enticed him with exceptional pay for what was essentially a small role. The part of Signor Ferrari, the sinister owner of the Blue Parrot, was enlarged specifically for him and Greenstreet was paid $3,750 a week, with featured billing. Although the actor's part was originally supposed to take only five days to shoot, set delays put filming way behind schedule and Greenstreet spent most of July waiting on-set for his scenes to be shot, ultimately being paid over $13,000.

He occasionally branched out from his evil roles to take part in one of the studio's dramatic pictures, such as *Devotion* (filmed in 1943 but released in 1946), playing novelist William Makepeace Thackeray in the story of the famed Bronte sisters, or lighthearted fare like the Yuletide classic, *Christmas in Connecticut* (1945). As magazine mogul Alexander Yardley, Greenstreet showed a fun side of his characterizations rarely seen by audiences, yet still playing a power-hungry control freak. He continued into the latter part of the decade with a loan-out to MGM for the star-powered drama *The Hucksters* (1947), then back to Warners for the film version of Wilkie Collins' mystery, *The Woman in White* (1948), as the perverse Count Fosco. In 1949, the last year of his film career, he continued what he had done so well, portraying totally corrupt Southern sheriff Titus Semple in *Flamingo Road* with Joan Crawford.

In his personal life, Greenstreet had married Dorothy Marie Ogden in 1918 and the couple had one son named John Ogden Greenstreet, who was born in 1920. As he aged, diabetes and kidney disease, among other ailments, contributed to his declining health. On January 18, 1954, in Los Angeles, Greenstreet died at the age of seventy-four. Although his movie career was short, it was successful, and his films are some of the most remembered and revered to modern classic movie fans.

Virginia Grey

MGM head honcho, Louis B. Mayer, once told beautiful Virginia Grey, "You have everything but luck." The actress appeared in many dozen films over the course of forty-plus years, yet never hit the "big time," breaking through to full-fledged stardom, like many of her contemporaries. She did, however, make a very welcome addition to the many movies in which her comely face and lovely frame showed up. A gorgeous honey-blonde with blue eyes, Grey supported Hollywood's biggest stars, and unlike most well-known character actors, who had very distinctive features and mannerisms, her beauty and outgoing nature were among her screen virtues.

Virginia was born on March 22, 1917 in what was then known as Edendale, a historic district of Los Angeles, near the old Mack Sennett studios. She came from a show-business family, her father, Raymond Standish Grey, or as he was known more simply, Ray Grey, was an original Keystone Kop with Sennett, who later worked his way up to become a director of two-reel silent comedies for his boss. Virginia recalled being babysat by one of her father's fellow players, pre-stardom Sennett starlet, Gloria Swanson. When Ray died in April 1925, at the age of thirty-five, Virginia's mother, Florence, went to work at Universal Studio as a film cutter, to support her three daughters. While visiting her mother at work, Virginia was spotted by producer Paul Kohner, who gave her a screen test. The following year, at the age of ten, she made her film debut in the big-budget silent screen adaptation of *Uncle Tom's Cabin* (1927), playing Little Eva. She made a handful of other movies as a child-actor, including *The Michigan Kid* and *Jazz Mad* (both 1928), and joined the famous Meglin Kiddie dancing troupe (which also featured Judy Garland and Shirley Temple early in their careers) before eventually leaving the movie business to finish her education.

Grey briefly trained to be a nurse before returning to more lucrative work on the screen in the early '30s. With stunning looks and statuesque figure, she joined the ranks of chorus girl in several productions and played many uncredited bit roles before signing a contract with MGM in the middle of the decade. Like many contract beauties of the day, Virginia was given lead roles in the studio's B-pictures, like the standard programmer, *Bad Guy* (1937) with Bruce Cabot, and supporting parts in their larger more prestigious productions. When Jean Harlow died suddenly in 1937, Grey was one of the young hopefuls who tested for the part of her fill-in (filmed only from the back) to finish up production of the blonde star's last movie, *Saratoga*. She met the picture's male star, Clark Gable, who was married to his second wife, Ria Langham at the time, and the two began a romantic relationship, with Gable securing small parts for Virginia in two of his upcoming films: *Test Pilot* (1938) and *Idiot's Delight* (1939).

Grey and Gable had an on-again/off-again romance for years. Howard Strickling, head of publicity for Metro said of the pair: "Clark and Virginia had a great relationship. If he was lonesome, you know – I mean Virginia was always there." Gable had entered into a serious romantic relationship with blonde star Carole Lombard as early as 1936. In his biography of the comedienne, *Fireball: Carole Lombard and the Mystery of Flight 3*, author Robert Matzen relates Lombard's knowledge of Gable's strong attraction to Grey, whom Lombard liked. During filming of *Idiot's Delight*, Carole had gotten wind of a rumored dalliance between Clark and one of the leggy chorines (not Virginia, who was also in the film) who backed up his character in the "Puttin' on the Ritz" musical number. The enraged blonde star, who had become a regular visitor to the sound stage, demanded of the film's director, Clarence Brown, to "Get that whore out of here," continuing, "...either she goes, or Gable does!" The next day, the offending young lady had been dismissed. Lombard did not, however, say anything about Grey's presence on the set and according to Matzen, "never made a fuss when Gable strayed in Virginia's direction," choosing instead to "pick her battles."

In 1939, Virginia gave one of her most memorable, though small in content, roles as Joan Crawford's lovely and sarcastically humorous co-worker in MGM's classic comedy, *The Women*. As Pat, the pretty perfume peddler, Virginia shines and practically steals her scene with Crawford. Despite her bright spot in *The Women*, however, she never seemed to get traction with audiences, and stardom seemed to elude her. Grey reflected, quite candidly, about her lack of good roles in a 1941 issue of *Silver Screen* magazine, telling interviewer Dick Mook:

> "In the first place," she said, "the studio has never put on a publicity campaign for me and I have never gone out for any freak or sensational publicity - like sweaters, or mannish attire or romances or night-clubbing with a different fellow every evening or creating scenes in the places I do patronize. So, without the studio telling everybody they are going to "do things" with me, on the strength of the bits I play there isn't much for gossip writers and columnists to say about me."

After more secondary roles in such films as *Another Thin Man* (1939) with William Powell and *The Big Store* (1941) with the Marx Brothers, Virginia left MGM in 1942 and worked at various studios around town, including Fox, Republic and Universal. After Carole Lombard was killed in a plane crash in 1942, Grey was Gable's most consistent of many girlfriends, and it was assumed by friends and gossip columnists that she would be the next Mrs. Gable. To everyone's surprise, including Virginia's, Clark married Lady Sylvia Ashley in 1949. A heartbroken Grey never married, many say due to the huge torch she carried for "the King."

113

The 1950s were a busy time for the actress professionally. She made regular appearances on television, including three episodes of *The Ford Television Theatre*, three of *Fireside Theater* and numerous other showings of the episodic anthology programs that were so popular during the decade. On the big screen, she was hired by longtime friend Ross Hunter in some of his biggest films, including 1955's *All That Heaven Allows* with Jane Wyman and Rock Hudson, *The Restless Years* in 1958 and *Portrait in Black* with old MGM friend Lana Turner in 1960.

Still attractive but settling into middle-aged roles, Virginia appeared in the steamy and seemy *Love Has Many Faces*, again with Turner, in 1965 and made her last feature film in a small role in the 1970 disaster epic *Airport*. On July 31, 2004, at the age of eighty-seven, Grey died of a heart attack at the Motion Picture and Television Fund's home and hospital facility in suburban Woodland Hills, California. Upon her passing, fellow MGM stock player, Ann Rutherford, called the actress a "nifty lady." Many classic film fans would heartily agree.

E d m u n d G w e n n

Film star Maureen O'Hara called him "a sweetheart," and continued on to say that "by the end of the movie, I think he really believed he was Santa Claus and so did we!" Of course, she was talking about her 1947 Christmas classic, *Miracle on 34th Street* and the "sweetheart" was her beloved co-star, Edmund Gwenn. Okay, okay, he was the perfect choice to play Kris Kringle. He looked like Santa, he had the soft-spoken gentleness, yet protective strength of the old gent and he even won an Academy Award for his portrayal to prove it. It was, however, not the only role this talented and versatile actor created. His range was wide and his parts eclectic, so to pigeonhole him into this one picture would be a disservice not only to him, but to those who aren't aware of the all the other wonderful characterizations he fashioned, both on stage and screen.

The actor was born in the Wandsworth district of London, as Edmund John Kellaway on September 26, 1877. He was the eldest child and his father, John Kellaway, a customs clerk, wanted him to follow in his footsteps. Theodore Strauss of the *New York Times* explained, "As the oldest son, and therefore the only one that mattered, in the household of a government civil servant, Edmund was carefully groomed for a position of consequence in the Empire." First a student at St. Olav's College, then attending King's College, London, the stage-struck young man informed his father of his desire to be an actor. The elder Kellaway, a stern Victorian, was livid and tossed his son out of the house, with the promise that if he failed, he could not return home and further prophesied that his offspring "would die in the gutter, a rogue and a vagabond."

In 1895, at the age of eighteen, he joined English actor Willie Edouin's company, playing parts "that required him to be vulgar, rough, and often noisy." He then travelled to Australia, where he remained for three years, before returning to England in 1904. While appearing in a small part in London, the actor (now calling himself Gwenn) was spotted by playwright George Bernard Shaw, who offered him the leading role of the Cockney chauffeur in his play *Man and Superman*. Gwenn happily accepted. He later spoke of his mentor to Helen Ormsbee of the *New York Herald Tribune*: "I was grateful to Shaw. Mind you though, you're just as good an actor on the day before you make a hit as on the day after. But nobody knows it."

He appeared in several of Shaw's plays and spent three years in his company. Throughout the next decade, Gwenn played in productions by well-known English playwrights, including John Galsworthy and J.M. Barrie (author of *Peter Pan*). Military service as an officer in the British Army during World War I disrupted his career temporarily, though he made his film debut in a silent short while on leave in 1916. He continued working on stage after the war and occasionally in movies, including the silent version of *The Skin Game*, based on Galsworthy's play, in 1921 and the sound version of the same title in 1932. The latter would be directed by young filmmaker Alfred Hitchcock. It would not be the last time the actor and director worked together on a picture.

In 1935, Gwenn was working on Broadway in *Laburnum Grove*, when he answered the call of Hollywood and made his first American film appearance as Katharine Hepburn's father in RKO's *Sylvia Scarlett*, also starring Cary Grant. He then made several films on both sides of the Atlantic, including the movie version of *Laburnum Grove* in England, before settling in Hollywood in 1940. That same year he was part of a large supporting cast in MGM's sumptuous and very British literary spectacle, *Pride and Prejudice*, playing the wise and perpetually patient Mr. Bennett. Then, moving completely across the spectrum, the actor was equally engaging as a cherubic assassin, working again with Hitchcock in a small but powerful role in *Foreign Correspondent* (how else would a hit man be described in a Hitchcock picture?).

He worked steadily throughout the 1940s, playing a wide range of characters from bad guys to, eventually, the most loveable man there is. In 1941, he joined a band of some of Hollywood's very best character actors in *The Devil and Miss Jones*. The movie starred the ever-entertaining Jean Arthur but the supporting cast is a veritable Who's Who of classic second bananas, including Charles Coburn, Spring Byington, "Cuddles" Sakall, Florence Bates, William Demarest and Regis Toomey. In the film, Gwenn played Mr. Hooper, a haughty and supercilious department store head who makes everyone's life very unpleasant. He countered this meanie role with a part in *Between Two Worlds* (1944), made at Warner Brothers, in which he portrayed Scrubby, a supernatural steward on a depressing ghost ship. It was a different kind of role in a different kind of film that was a remake of *Outward Bound* (1930). Gwenn gave a fine performance as a wise psychiatrist in *Bewitched* (1945) at MGM, a unique B-picture and an early attempt to delve into the topic of multiple personalities.

Although he was regularly in demand as an actor, Gwenn wasn't a household name in the mid-1940s. His role as Kris Kringle in 20th Century-Fox's *Miracle on 34th Stree*t would change that, as well as his stature in Hollywood. The part was originally offered to Gwenn's cousin, fellow character actor Cecil Kellaway but South African-born Kellaway refused it, claiming "Americans don't like whimsy." Apparently, he was wrong, as *Miracle* was a hit and made a star of his cousin, who happily took the role. Along with the mainstream popularity of the movie and his part in it, Gwenn gained a personal victory by winning the Best Supporting Actor Oscar in 1948 at the age of seventy-one. Over at the *New York Times*, reviewer Bosley Crowther (a tough nut to crack as critics go) said of Edmund Gwenn:

> "...if ever the real Santa wants to step down, Mr. Gwenn is the man
> for the job. His candor with Mr. Macy, an awesome tycoon; his

charm with little Sue and his genuine attitude of generosity toward everybody are cherishable in this dark day."

Fox wasted no time in ushering its new senior citizen star into another picture. *Apartment for Peggy* (1948), starred Jeanne Crain, then one of the studio's top stars, and William Holden (not yet the star he would become in the next decade), as young marrieds on a college campus. Gwenn played an elderly professor who contemplates suicide before meeting the sweet and sprightly Crain. The charm that the actor exuded in *Miracle on 34th Street* is recaptured in the lighthearted, yet heartwarming film, a charm that he continued to display in many of the remaining movies of his career. The 1950s brought more work for the hardworking Gwenn, both in movies and television, with his most memorable film of the decade, also one of his last, the black comedy, *The Trouble with Harry* (1955), again directed by Alfred Hitchcock (reportedly one of the filmmaker's personal favorites of his pictures).

Like many of his generation in Hollywood, Gwenn lived out his last days at the Motion Picture Home in Woodland Hills, California. He died there after suffering a stroke and finally contracting pneumonia on September 6, 1959, just three weeks shy of his eighty-second birthday. Gwenn had married only once in his lifetime, in 1901, to actress Minnie Terry. Some sources say the marriage lasted only a matter of hours, but articles and newspaper clippings from 1902 and beyond show that the two were wed for at least a matter of years, though at some point, in the early part of the 20th century, the marriage was dissolved. Upon his death, his estate was divided, according to his will, with a third going to his former wife, a third going to his sister, Elsie Kellaway, and a third for his longtime live-in valet/butler, Ernest Bach. There was a dispute over Bach's portion between the valet and former Olympic athlete Rodney Soher, who shared Gwenn's Beverly Hills home in his later life.

Alan Hale, Sr.

A tall, brawny American actor with a mass of fair, crimped, wavy hair, Alan Hale is often mistaken for his son, Alan Hale, Jr., who became famous as The Skipper on the 1960s television sitcom, *Gilligan's Island*. Alan the Elder, however, had a long and illustrious career, appearing in over two hundred Hollywood films of both the silent and classic era and became one of the most recognizable character actors of the golden age.

Hale was born Rufus Edward Mackahan in Washington, D.C. on February 10, 1892. His early attempts as an opera singer failed, and at one point young Hale contemplated a career as an osteopath, attending the Philadelphia College of Osteopathy before beginning a career on the stage, first in vaudeville and as part of theater stock companies. In 1911, he joined the Lubin Film Studios in Philadelphia, Siegmund Lubin being a pioneer in the burgeoning silent film industry. He then made films for legendary director D.W. Griffith at Biograph studio and throughout the 1910s appeared in dozens of silents, both shorts and full-length movies. His early film resume included a role as a villain in the classic *The Four Horsemen of the Apocalypse* (1921), starring romantic icon Rudolph Valentino.

In 1914, Hale married Gretchen Hartman, a Chicago-born actress who began appearing on the stage in her teens, then moving to silent films, where she became a popular figure. Besides Alan, Jr., she and Hale, Sr. had two daughters, Jeanne and Karen. The couple remained married for the rest of Alan's life. As the actor's family expanded, so did his career, with more work on stage in New York, on screen in Hollywood and even behind the camera as director on more than a handful of films for the Cecil B. DeMille Company during the 1920s.

His real claim to character actor stardom came in the 1930s as one of the busiest members of the Warner Brothers stock company. Warners employed a legion of character actors and actresses who filled cast rosters for the studios many productions. Besides Hale the extensive group included Frank McHugh, Guy Kibbee, Aline MacMahon, Una Merkel, Allen Jenkins, Ruth Donnelly and many others. In 1937, he made his first appearance of many with Errol Flynn in the studio's costume spectacle, *The Prince and the Pauper*. It was a warm-up of sorts to his most famous role during the period.

The following year, Hale was cast as Little John in the colorful masterpiece, *The Adventures of Robin Hood*, which starred Flynn as the dashing Robin of Locksley. It was a role that he had portrayed on film sixteen years earlier in the 1922 silent classic, *Robin Hood*, with Douglas Fairbanks, Sr. playing Robin. His association with the role didn't end there, as he played Little John, albeit an older, less vigorous version, yet again in *Rogues of Sherwood Forest,* at Columbia in 1950, this time with John Derek playing Robin, Earl of Huntingdon, the son of Robin Hood. The Technicolor extravaganza of the late '30s is the version which cemented the burly actor's fame at Warners, however, and he would continue to support Flynn and other leading men at the studio throughout his career.

His roles during the 1940s were more of the same that he had created during the Depression years; loveable buffoons, boisterous sidekicks and gentle giants. In *The Private Lives of Elizabeth and Essex* (1939), Hale played Flynn's enemy, the Earl of Tyrone, Irish revolutionary in Tudor times. In *They Drive by Night* (1940), he was cast as the fun-loving boob with money, married to the wicked Ida Lupino. He's the ever-loyal sidekick to James Cagney in the Warner Brothers' war flick, *Captains of the Clouds* (1942) and a sailor opposite Humphrey Bogart in *Action in the North Atlantic* (1943). His list of movie appearances was varied if his characterizations were not.

In addition to his work as an entertainer, Hale held patents for several inventions. Not just random, useless concoctions, but sliding theater seats, a hand-held fire extinguisher and "greaseless potato chips." After a full life, both personally and professionally, the actor died on January 22, 1950 at the age of fifty-seven of a liver infection. Ironically, if not appropriately, his last role was Little John in *Rogues of Sherwood Forest*, released after his death.

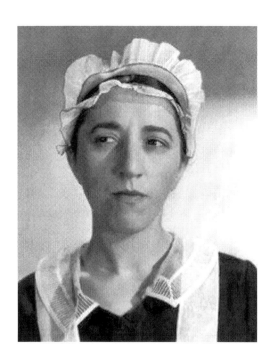

Margaret
Hamilton

"I was in a need of money at the time, I had done about six pictures for MGM at the time and my agent called. I said, 'Yes?' and he said 'Maggie, they want you to play a part on the Wizard.' I said to myself, 'Oh Boy, *The Wizard of Oz*! That has been my favorite book since I was four.' And I asked him what part, and he said, 'The Witch' and I said, 'The Witch?!' and he said, 'What else?'" That is how actress Margaret Hamilton described being cast in the classic fantasy *The Wizard of Oz* (1939). The hatchet-faced actress made the role iconic and created a character that would be ranked No. 4 in the American Film Institute's list of the 50 Best Movie Villains of All Time, just behind Hannibal Lecter, Norman Bates and Darth Vader, making her the highest-ranking female baddie. But as memorable as she was in *Oz*, she also added bristling, disapproving presence to dozens of films and television appearances from the 1930s through the 1980s.

The youngest of four children, Hamilton was born in Cleveland, Ohio, and had an early interest in acting and working in local theater. Upon her parent's wishes, she attended Wheelock College, or as it was founded in 1888, Miss Wheelock's Kindergarten Training School. While there she served as president of the senior class, as well as playing Jo in a school stage production of *Little Women*. Upon graduation, Margaret did indeed become a kindergarten teacher. Her true passion, however, remained in the theater and in April 1932, at the age of 29, she made her Broadway debut in *Another Language*, later traveling to Hollywood for the film version at Metro Goldwyn Mayer. She reprised yet another of her stage roles for the screen in *The Farmer Takes a Wife* (1935), which also marked the movie debut of Henry Fonda. After steady film work in a string of supporting parts, with an exceptional turn in Samuel Goldwyn's *These Three* (1936), she was cast in the role of her lifetime. She was, however, not the first choice for the sinister and infamous Wicked Witch of the West.

Oz producer Mervyn LeRoy envisioned a slinky, glamorous witch of the West, cavorting around the haunted castle in green eye shadow and black sequins. His conception was influenced by the wicked queen in Disney's outrageously popular *Snow White and the Seven Dwarfs*, which premiered in late 1937. LeRoy wanted attractive actress Gale Sondergaard, whom he had directed in the 1936 hit, *Anthony Adverse* (for which Sondergaard won the very first Best Supporting Actress Academy Award), but when it was decided that the witch would be ugly and scarier than originally anticipated, Sondergaard was out and thirty-six-year-old Hamilton was hired at $1,000 a week. Seeking steady employment over the potential ups and downs of show business, Maggie Hamilton, as she was called by those who knew her best, followed a common-sense approach as her personal career philosophy. "At 1,200 or $1,500 a week, I knew I wouldn't work much," she stated. "And I had my young son and I wanted to work all I could [Hamilton Meserve was born in 1936 and Margaret had just been divorced from his father before being hired for *Oz*]. So I never let them pay me more. And I never went under contract."

An incident on the *Oz* set in December 1938 put her out of commission for weeks and made her wary about scenes which included fire. During the filming of the segment in which Hamilton's character exits Munchkinland in a burst of flame and smoke, the actress received burns on her face and hand when the fire used for the special effect rose prematurely from the trap door from which she was to disappear. Making matters worse, the green makeup used on her skin contained potentially toxic copper-oxide and had to be removed before her burns could be treated, which was an extremely painful process. When she returned to the set after a hospital stay, she claimed, "I won't sue, because I know how this business works, and I would never work again. I will return to work on one condition - no more fire work!"

Although best-known as the scariest gal in Oz, outside that realm the actress played characters more in line with her Wicked Witch alter ego, Miss Almira Gulch; sour-faced spinsters and gossipy snoops who lived in the neighborhood. She was at her crabby, disapproving best in *The Adventures of Tom Sawyer* (1938), *My Little Chickadee* (1940) and *The Beautiful Blonde of Bashful Bend* (1949) among others. Ironically, as abrasive as her screen image was, she always carried an interest in nurturing children, even serving on the Beverly Hills Board of Education in the late forties.

Having graced the stage in New York and the large screen in Hollywood, the industrious Hamilton also found work on the radio with a regular role in the *Ethel and Albert* series, playing Aunt Eva. Among her many television appearances, she garnered a steady gig on the 1960s soap opera, *The Secret Storm*. In the '70s, she became the popular spokesperson for Maxwell House coffee, starring in numerous television commercials as Cora, the wise New England storekeeper who recommended the name-brand brew. She also appeared on children's shows, including *Sesame Street* and *Mr. Roger's Neighborhood*. Hamilton died of a heart attack in 1985, at a nursing home in Salisbury, Connecticut.

Edward Everett Horton

He had the bewildered and befuddled charm which played out perfectly in comedies of the 1930s and 1940s. His classic double take (sometimes even a triple take!) was famous among the character actor fold. Edward Everett Horton was the perfect fluttery fussbudget, nervous sidekick to the film's star and he excelled as the straitlaced but very funny manservant. He sometimes appeared as an effete busybody, not abrasive or malicious, as Clifton Webb could play a similar role, but loveable and warm.

Brooklyn-born on March 18, 1886, his parents were Isabella S. (née Diack) and Edward Everett Horton, a foreman in the composing room for the *New York Times*. He attended Boys' High School in Brooklyn and Baltimore City College, then, spent time at Oberlin College in Ohio and finally Columbia University, where he studied history and German, though he didn't graduate from either institution.

When he was twenty-one years-old, he became a member of the chorus at the Dempsey Opera Company, which was then presenting Gilbert & Sullivan comic operas on Staten Island. He then joined the Louis Mann theater troupe in 1908 as a bit player in New York City, making his debut with a walk-on part in *The Man Who Stood Still*. A well-known stage actor, Mann once told his protégé, "My boy, I cannot understand why you continue on these blessed boards, when right in this town, there's a demand for good street cleaners." But Mann's words were either good-natured ribbing or an attempt at tough love, as he kept Horton in his company for three years, increasing the importance of his roles, as well as his salary from twenty-five to seventy-five dollars per week. The young actor eventually moved on to the Orpheum Players Stock Company at Philadelphia's Chestnut Street Theater, as a juvenile lead, until the theater was closed for fire regulation infractions. He stayed in Philadelphia and joined the Beulah Jay's Little Theater, which had opened in March of 1913, and prided itself on being semi-professional. After honing his craft in several other companies, Horton moved to California in 1919 to join Thomas Wilkes, who ran the Majestic Theater in Los Angeles. It was during this period, after six years with the Wilkes company, that he began making movies.

He made his film debut in 1922 as Edward Horton, adding the Everett after his first couple of years in the industry. He leaned toward comedy and was cast in the lead role of the 1923 version of *Ruggles of Red Gap*. He made several two-reel short films and with the advent of sound pictures, he thrived. He appeared in Warner Brothers' *The Terror* (1928), the second "all talking" film and the first "all talking" horror movie. The 1930s ushered in a fertile period of moviemaking for Horton, with appearances in some of the best-known films of the decade, including *The Front Page* (1931), with Pat O'Brien and the sophisticated comedies directed by Ernst Lubitsch, *Trouble in Paradise* (1932) and *Design for Living* (1933), both starring Miriam Hopkins.

In Paramount's *Alice in Wonderland* (1933), he played the Mad Hatter, looking very similar to the Tenniel drawing of the character, and one of the few actors in the oft-filmed fantasy whose countenance wasn't obliterated by costume or disguising makeup. The following year Horton was cast in the Fred Astaire-Ginger Rogers fluffy foot-fest, *The Gay Divorcee*, in which he danced the delightful "Let's K-nock K-nees" number with a young, pre-stardom Betty Grable. His success in this film led to appearances in two more Astaire-Rogers musicals, *Top Hat* (1935) and *Shall We Dance* (1937). Frank Capra cast the actor in his superb fantasy, *Lost Horizon* (1937), where he played jumpy paleontologist Alexander P. Lovett, who falls in love with the enchanted valley of Shangri-La. In 1938, the actor played Professor Nick Potter in *Holiday* with Cary Grant and Katharine Hepburn, a role he also played in the earlier 1930 version. Although she didn't have much nice to say of the majority of her *Holiday* co-stars, actress Doris Nolan, who played Hepburn's sister, called Horton "a wonderful actor... a very amiable chap."

The actor was blessed both with fun and popular roles, as well as financially. By 1936, the actor was earning a salary comparable to most leading stars. Regarding his financial status he said: "I have my own little kingdom. I do the scavenger parts no one else wants, and I get well paid for it." Horton added, "It's not that I really need the money, it's simply that I like money - lots of it. I must admit I'm sometimes over-frugal." Indeed, Mr. Horton was well-known off-stage as a frugal gentleman, who spent his money wisely and on those he loved. He invested in a 22 acres estate in California's San Fernando Valley, which he named "Belleigh Acres" and included homes for his siblings and their mother. A "confirmed bachelor," Horton never married, though he maintained a very private, decades-long relationship with actor Gavin Gordon, fifteen years his junior. Mississippi-born Gordon played smaller roles in some bigger films (with the exception of *Romance* (1930), in which he was cast as Greta Garbo's romantic interest), though he may be recognized by horror film fans as Lord Byron in the fun prelude to *Bride of Frankenstein* in 1935.

Throughout the late '30s and 1940s, Horton continued to make colorful appearances in numerous pictures but also continued to work in the theater. He first played the role of Henry Dewlip in the stage comedy,

Springtime for Henry in 1932 and took the show on the road in the summer of 1939 in a revival that was so popular, that the actor took it from coast to coast, then on to Canada and Cuba for ninety-six weeks! A 1940 issue of *Time* magazine commented on Horton's success in the part, saying he had "plenty of opportunity for the jittery mugging that averages him eighty to one hundred thousand dollars a year in Hollywood." He continued to play the role in revival tours for more than twenty-five years, including the show's 1951 Broadway revival.

In the mid '40s, Horton hosted a radio show (Kraft Music Hall) and later in the decade he began to make appearances on television, which was becoming more popular every year. In the 1960s, he played an ancient medicine man called Roaring Chicken on the comedy series *F-Troop* and a similar character, Chief Screaming Chicken on the campy *Batman* TV show. Yet, for most viewers of the late '50s and early '60s, Horton was best-known for a role in which he didn't show his face. His voice was recognized far and wide as the narrator of the Fractured Fairy Tales segment of the *Rocky and Bullwinkle* animated series from 1959 to 1964.

In his later years, the actor grew feeble and in the late summer of 1970, he was hospitalized at Glen Falls, New York, while vacationing at his summer home on Lake George's Kattskill Bay. Diagnosed with cancer, his condition improved enough for him to go back to his home in California. Horton died in Encino on September 29, 1970 and his remains were interred at Forest Lawn Memorial Park Cemetery. In the 1950s, the State of California forced the actor to sell a portion of his estate for construction of the Ventura Freeway. Shortly after his death, that section of road was renamed "Edward Everett Horton Lane."

Walter Huston

Motion Picture Classic, a movie fan magazine from the Depression years, summed up one very talented and popular actor from that era when it printed: "Roles fit others, but Walter Huston fits the roles." Although he started out playing leads in the early 1930s, Huston really came into his own in the late '30s and 1940s, when he created some of the most interesting and well-rounded characters in movies of the day. Even as a leading man during his early years in pictures, his parts had a depth of character and were much more interesting to watch (as a character study) than many of the shiny male stars who headed marquees.

Hailing from Scotch-Irish ancestry, Huston was the son of Elizabeth (née McGibbon) and Robert Houghston, a farmer who founded his own construction company. He was born in Toronto, Canada on April 5, 1884 (some sources give 1883), one of four children. While attending the Lansdowne Street School, the youth began working in a local hardware store and later in construction, and eventually studying at the Shaw School of Acting in Toronto, where he made his stage debut in 1902. Huston once told a reporter that acting was something he had wanted to pursue early on, stating, "to be an actor, in our family, was about an outlandish a notion as to be a gnome or a five-footed cow." Crossing over into the United States, he joined a road company and made his first appearance on the New York stage in a melodrama called *In Convict Stripes*, which was written by Hal Reid, the father of future film actor Wallace Reid.

In 1904, while on tour in St. Louis, Walter met a young newspaper journalist named Rhea Gore. Three years older than Huston, Gore had gone to the theater where the actor was appearing in *The Sign of the Cross* to cover the play for her paper. After a whirlwind courtship, the couple married, and Huston left the theater to become an engineer, working at electric power stations in Missouri. Rhea bore a son, John in 1906, the couple's only child. He would grow up to be the skilled director who was behind the camera on a multitude of classic films, beginning with *The Maltese Falcon* in 1941. Walter and Rhea divorced in 1912 but even as the marriage began to crumble earlier in the decade, the actor had ventured back to the stage as a vaudevillian. He met a woman almost two decades his senior named Bayonne Whipple and they created an act called Whipple and Huston. Together they performed a skit developed by Walter called "Spooks" in which he sang a comic ditty called "If You Haven't Got the Do-Re-Mi." The skit was the cornerstone of their act for the next several years. They joined together personally as well, marrying in 1915 and parting ways nine years later.

In January 1924, Huston made his way back to the legitimate theater, being cast by producer Brock Pemberton in the title role of the play *Mr. Pitt*. His Broadway debut brought praise from one reviewer who wrote that the actor "made one of the conspicuous hits of this season and given one of its most beautiful performances." Later the same year, Huston garnered a lead role in Eugene O'Neill's *Desire Under the Elms*. The play was a hit, winning the New York Drama Critics' Circle Award and Walter Huston became a stage star. He worked steadily on Broadway for the rest of the decade, appearing in several successful plays, including

Kongo, which he would bring to the movie screen in 1932. He gained a reputation of dependability when it came to playing a part well.

Like many stage actors being wooed by Hollywood to help make the transition to talking pictures smooth with their clear and dramatic voices, Walter signed on with Paramount studio. He made his feature film debut in *Gentlemen of the Press* (1929), an early talkie co-starring Kay Francis, another newcomer to moving pictures, with whom he had appeared on Broadway. As his movie career started taking off, Huston excelled in both leading roles and character parts, like the villain who always wears black in Paramount's *The Virginian* in 1929. The following year he starred in *Abraham Lincoln*, as honest Abe himself. Directed by silent movie legend D.W. Griffith, *Lincoln* is a creaky antique when watched today, with Huston, however, proving his depth of character acting even more. *The New York Times'* Mordaunt Hall praised the actor's "genuinely fine and inspiring performance." He finished up his Paramount commitment the same year with the romantic melodrama *The Virtuous Sin*, again with Francis.

He then went under contract with MGM, making several quality pictures there and extending his reputation as a fine and solid actor of fine and solid films. At Metro he scored several hits including *The Beast of the City*, *The Wet Parade* and *American Madness*, all in 1932. Huston had the unique capacity to play in unconventional, even unusual films, which only strengthened his association with the strong characters he was portraying. He was the fire-and-brimstone missionary who was determined to save the soul of prostitute Sadie Thompson in the South Seas in *Rain* (1932), with Joan Crawford. It was a flop, but Huston withstood the bad reviews. In *Kongo*, also 1932, he went out even further on the dramatic limb by playing a cruel and vengeful paraplegic who lived among the natives in the jungle along the Kongo.

In the winter of 1934, Huston went back to the stage to create his definitive role in *Dodsworth*. Based on the 1929 novel by Sinclair Lewis, the play was an enormous success, with much of the credit going to Walter. As the title character, the actor reaped his share of good notices including one from Brooks Atkinson at *The New York Times*, who wrote: "He has returned to remind us that he is one of the best actors our theater has developed." Huston reprised the role for the screen in 1936 and Atkinson continued his praise for that performance as well. "Among the virtues of *Dodsworth*, place Walter Huston foremost." He was widely recognized for his efforts in the film and won the New York Critic's Circle Award for Best Actor as well as being nominated for the Academy Award in the same category.

During the 1940s, Huston settled into even more character driven roles and was part of talented ensemble casts. His parts were rich and varying and he added greatly to any film in which he appeared. In 1941, he portrayed Satan, aka Mr. Scratch in *The Devil and Daniel Webster* (also called *All That Money Can Buy*). Like *Dodsworth*, it was a film which showcased his special skill at creating a character all his own and making the most of it. He was honored with another Oscar nomination as the Dark Prince, not dark in Huston's interpretation at all. In fact, the actor portrayed Mr. Scratch with homespun humor and a likable rustic quality.

The same year that *The Devil and Daniel Webster* was released, the actor made a cameo appearance in Warner Brothers' classic mystery, *The Maltese Falcon*. The film marked the directorial debut of Walter's son, John, and he took the bit role as a favor. He did, however, have to promise studio boss Jack Warner, infamous for his frugality, that he wouldn't charge him for his services, however small. At Warners' the next year he played the father of songwriter and Broadway star George M. Cohan (James Cagney) in the hit musical, *Yankee Doodle Dandy*.

Huston continued to offer strong support in top drawer films including *Dragon Seed* (1944) at MGM, *And Then There Were None* (1945) at Fox and *Duel in the Sun* (1947) for producer David O. Selznick. In 1948, John had persuaded Warner Brothers to buy the movie rights to *The Treasure of the Sierra Madre*, a 1927 novel by B. Traven about a trio of gold diggers in 1920s Mexico. As one leg of the acting triangle, John wanted his father to play the decrepit old miner, Howard. In correspondence regarding the production, author B. Traven had reservations about Walter, stating "he is too robust, too healthy and looks too young for the part." A fan of the elder Huston, Traven added, "If you can make him look over seventy, and make him act as if he were to give up his ghost any minute... this part will add tremendously to his fame." Add to his fame it did. Walter not only got the part (persuaded by his son to do it without his false teeth), but he would go on to win an Oscar for Best Supporting Actor of 1948. When he accepted his Academy Award the following year, the elder Huston said, "Many years ago.... Many, MANY years ago, I brought up a boy, and I said to him, 'Son, if you ever become a writer, try to write a good part for your old man sometime.' Well, by cracky, that's what he did!"

On Thursday, April 5, 1950, just a year after his only Oscar win, Huston celebrated his sixty-sixth birthday in fine spirits, enjoying a luncheon with several friends, including his agent. Later that evening, he complained of severe pain in his back and was unable to attend a birthday dinner in his honor. On April 7, he died of a heart attack in his suite at the Beverly Hills Hotel. His third wife, actress Nan Sunderland (whom he had married in 1931), was in New York at the time and called immediately. A non-denominational funeral service was held, and he was cremated, with his ashes buried at Belmont Memorial Park in Fresno, California. Besides a fine resume of film and stage work, Huston left an acting legacy in the form of his family, award-winning director, actor and screenwriter John, and Oscar-winning granddaughter Angelica.

Percy Kilbride

Few actors are associated with a character they created more than Percy Kilbride, with his characterization of good-natured slacker, Pa Kettle. His slow, twangy voice was unmistakable, even on the radio, and his hawk-nose, gaunt features and thin, wiry body made for Hollywood's most recognizable country bumpkin. His easy-going hicks graced many films during the 1940s and '50s. According to a UP columnist in 1945, he was a favorite of casting directors who thought he "looks and sounds more like an old rusty gate in the summertime than any other actor they know."

Percy William Kilbride was born on July 16, 1888, in the South of Market District of San Francisco. His father, Owen Kilbride was a machinist who hailed from Canada. His theatrical career began at the age of twelve as a call boy and bit player at the Central Theater in his home town. He later played his first part in *A Tale of Two Cities*, before touring with various road companies. He took a hiatus during World War I, when he served in France as a Private in the 80th division infantry. After the war ended, he continued working in regional stock companies for the next decade.

In 1928, after years in repertory troupes, Kilbride made his debut on Broadway in the short-lived *The Buzzard*. A film debut came in 1933 with the pre-Code drama *White Woman*, starring Carole Lombard, then another small movie role in 1936. He continued to work throughout the '30s on Broadway and in the autumn of 1940 appeared in the hit *George Washington Slept Here*, as the wry handyman, Mr. Kimber. Warner Brothers studio planned a film version of the play for 1942 starring comedian Jack Benny. When Benny saw the Broadway show, he insisted that Kilbride be brought out to Hollywood to reprise his role as the deadpan Kimber. Although studio head Jack Warner didn't see the appeal in Kilbride that Benny did, he relented and hired the actor, who practically stole the film.

He then went on to appear in the Spencer Tracy-Katharine Hepburn drama *Keeper of the Flame* in 1942 and the high-profile bio-pic *The Adventures of Mark Twain*, again at Warner Brothers in 1944. The following year was a banner one for Kilbride, who appeared in three A-list pictures, all completely different in genre. He was in the independent drama, *The Southerner* with Zachary Scott, then over to Twentieth Century-Fox for the film noir, *Fallen Angel*, with Dana Andrews and Linda Darnell and *State Fair*, Rodgers and Hammerstein's bright, colorful musical hit.

At the age of fifty-nine, the actor found long-term fame. Along with Marjorie Main, he was cast in *The Egg and I*, a comedy based on Betty MacDonald's bestselling novel about city folks who attempt to build their own farm. Fred MacMurray and Claudette Colbert were the stars, but Kilbride and Main completely stole the picture as Ma and Pa Kettle. Ma was the loud, brash, domineering country mama to a large brood of young'uns and Pa was her lazy, but good-hearted bumpkin husband. The parts were made for Main and Kilbride and they were so popular that Universal created a film especially for their characters, titled simply, *Ma and Pa Kettle* (1949). The popularity of the characters and their first solo venture sparked a series of *Kettle* films featuring Main and Kilbride, who eventually tired of his "Pa" role. After seven installments of the series, the actor bowed out.   Two more films were made with Marjorie Main reprising her "Ma" but without Kilbride, the magic was gone. He turned down an offer to play the Kettle role on television saying, "There's no kick to doing him over and over again."

In 1964, Kilbride and his friend, actor Ralf Belmont, were walking at the intersection of Yucca and Cherokee in Hollywood when they were struck by a speeding car. Belmont was killed instantly and Kilbride was taken to the Good Samaritan hospital, where he underwent brain surgery. He died three months later from atherosclerosis and terminal pneumonia which were caused by his head injuries. He was seventy-six years old. A lifelong bachelor, Kilbride lived alone in a modest Los Angeles apartment.

Patric Knowles

One of the most successful movies of the late 1930s was the Technicolor smash hit from Warner Brothers, *The Adventures of Robin Hood*, starring dashing Errol Flynn as the title character and an array of the studio's stock players as Robin's merry men. Flynn's closest sidekick in Sherwood Forest was Will Scarlett and the actor creating Master Scarlett was British-born Patric Knowles, who, off-screen, was once described as "Flynn's boon companion in debauchery." Although he never made it to leading man status, he was a popular second lead and handsome member of several ensemble casts in many of Hollywood's most memorable pictures.

Reginald Lawrence Knowles was born in Hosforth, Yorkshire, England on November 11, 1911, of Irish heritage. Although expected by his family to join his father's bookbindery business, he ran away to become an actor at the age of fourteen. He was forced to return but on the second try the acting bug bit, and he debuted in local and regional theaters including the Abbey and Oxford repertory companies, playing Shakespeare. In 1932, he began going by Patric, instead of Reginald, and made his first film appearance in *Men of Tomorrow* (which also happened to be the screen debut of Robert Donat). He continued making features in England for the next few years including *Crown v. Stevens*, made at Warner Brothers' British studios in 1936.

After being recommended for the studio's main branch in California, Knowles traveled to America later that year and made his Hollywood debut in a Kay Francis romance called *Give Me Your Heart*. Warners wanted to use the tall, handsome and very British actor as a threat to their rapidly rising star Errol Flynn. The two were acquaintances at Teddington Studios, Warners' film foothold in Britain, and instead of becoming rivals, Flynn and Knowles became great pals, costarring in several features in the next two years, including *The Charge of the Light Brigade*, *Four's a Crowd*, *The Sisters* and, of course, *Robin Hood*. They became so close, in fact, that Flynn was named godfather to one of Knowles' children. After appearing with George Brent, who was a licensed pilot, in the movie *Give Me Your Heart*, Knowles became interested in flying. Later, during filming of *The Adventures of Robin Hood*, the actor introduced his buddy Flynn to flying at the local airport, and their "joyriding in planes" got them in hot water with the studio. Knowles enlisted in the Royal Canadian Air Force, during World War II. Because of an eye ailment, he became a flying instructor.

When it became apparent that his standing at Warner Brothers was becoming stagnant as a supporting second lead, Knowles began freelancing in 1939. At RKO he appeared in *Beauty for the Asking* and *Five Came Back*, both with young RKO contract player Lucille Ball. He then moved over to Fox and played one of his best roles of the decade in John Ford's Oscar-winning film, *How Green Was My Valley* (1941), as one of the sons in a Welsh coal mining family. Later that year he signed on with Universal and was featured in several of their high-profile movies of the period, playing good guys in the horror classics *The Wolf Man*

(1941) and *Frankenstein Meets the Wolf Man* (1943). He also played straight man to Universal's top comedy duo Abbott and Costello in *Who Done It?* (1942) and *Hit the Ice* (1943).

After finishing out his time at Universal, Knowles set up shop at Paramount, where he was regal and refined while being passed over by Paulette Goddard in favor of Ray Milland in the top costumer, *Kitty* (1945). He also appeared in *Masquerade in Mexico* (also 1945), *The Bride Wore Boots* (1946) and supported Bob Hope, who played a bumbling barber in the French court, in *Monsieur Beaucaire* (1947). The rest of the decade saw more film roles, but major movie fame eluded him.

In the 1950s, the actor switched his attention to television. Like so many others in his profession, TV offered many opportunities and regular work. Knowles played in several live television playhouse productions, westerns, including *Wagon Train*, *Maverick*, *Have Gun – Will Travel*, and *Gunsmoke*, as well as private eye shows. He occasionally made big screen appearances like his fun part as Rosalind Russell's handsome suitor in *Auntie Mame*, the number one moneymaking film of 1959 (having been released late in 1958). He continued acting until the early '70s and published a novel called *Even Steven* in 1960. Knowles died in Woodland Hills, California on December 23, 1995. He was survived by his wife, Enid, whom he had married in 1935, and two children. A handsome and well-liked Brit, Knowles never hit the big time, but made his mark as a quality supporting player nonetheless.

Elsa Lanchester

With her unruly, auburn hair, upturned nose, dimpled chin and large dark eyes, Elsa Lanchester cut a striking and energetic figure in the films in which she appeared. Most wouldn't call her beautiful in her youth, but one couldn't take their eyes from this distinctive, elfin creature with a unique, lilting twitter of a voice. Her graceful movement betrayed her dancing roots and her confidence on stage and screen was unwavering. Often known better for being Mrs. Charles Laughton off-screen, this extremely engaging actress brought color and vitality to her roles and was one of Hollywood's longest-running character icons.

Elsa Sullivan Lanchester was born in Lewisham, London, England on October 28, 1902. Her parents, James "Shamus" Sullivan and Edith "Biddy" Lanchester were militant socialists, described by their daughter as pacifists, vegetarians and atheists, both very active members of the Social Democratic Federation (SDF), Britain's first organized Marxist party. The couple did not believe in the institution of marriage and were considered quite Bohemian. Edith was the daughter of prosperous English architect Henry Jones Lanchester and in 1895, at the age of twenty-four, the outspoken feminist announced that she intended to live with Sullivan, an Irish factory worker of common birth, without the benefit of legalized marriage. The young woman's parents were so outraged that her father had her committed to an asylum with the help of a hired "mental specialist," who claimed Edith was threatening "social suicide." Upon this diagnosis, Henry Lanchester signed emergency commitment papers, under the Lunacy Act of 1890 and, assisted by Edith's brothers, forcibly delivered his daughter to the Priory, an institution at Roehampton. The affair became known as the Lanchester Kidnapping Case and made headlines in newspapers far and wide in the autumn of 1895. After being interviewed by Lunacy Commissioners, who deemed her sane, Edith was released and left the asylum with her lover, never speaking to her father again. The couple bore their first child, Waldo Sullivan Lanchester in 1897 and their second, Elsa, five years later.

The eccentric family led a very unconventional lifestyle for Victorian and Edwardian times and James and Edith encouraged nonconformity. Although the household was supported by meager means, enough funds were managed to send Waldo to Mr. Kettle's, a private progressive school for boys. Young Elsa was homeschooled by her mother, until local authorities required formal tutelage whereupon the girl was sent to the all-boys school of her sibling. In 1912, when she was ten, she attended free dancing courses at the creative school of Raymond Duncan, the eccentric brother of famed dancer Isadora Duncan and was then enrolled, by means of a scholarship, in the latter's Bellevue School of Dance in Paris.

During her time under Isadora's instruction, Lanchester grew to immensely dislike the infamous dancer, calling her an "untalented bag of beans" in a 1970 television interview with host Dick Cavett. With the onset of the First World War, Elsa, not yet in her teens, returned to England and began teaching the form of free movement dance she had learned from Duncan. By the age of sixteen she organized the Children's Theatre in London, recruiting and training local youth for performances, but by 1921, the group was shut down by the London County Council for violation of child labor laws. Her reputation as "outrageous" grew with stints as an artist's model for English sculptor Jacob Epstein, among others (sometimes nude), and an occasional turn as a hired co-respondent in divorce cases. In addition, she continued her stage work, making her music hall debut in 1920 and her first legitimate stage appearance as a shop girl in the one act West End play *Thirty Minutes in a Street* in 1922.

In 1924, Lanchester and her partner, Harold Scott, opened a nightclub on Charlotte Street called the Cave of Harmony, a haven for London Bohemia. Although the main focus was midnight performances of one-act plays and cabaret songs, Lanchester also included revivals of aged Victorian ballads and bawdy Cockney songs, including odd ditties such as "Rat Catcher's Daughter." The Cave of Harmony became a popular haunt for toney artists and intellectuals, including writers H. G. Wells, Aldous Huxley, Evelyn Waugh, and future film director James Whale, who would play an important part in Elsa's life during the next decade. Her work at the Cave of Harmony was a labor of love, reaping little in financial gain and she participated in stage work elsewhere while continuing her tenure at her own establishment.

In 1927, the colorful actress made her professional film debut in a supporting role in *One of the Best*, a silent costume drama produced by prestigious Gainsborough Pictures (Her first actual film appearance was in an amateur motion picture by her friend and author Evelyn Waugh called *The Scarlet Woman: An Ecclesiastical Melodrama* in 1925). Yet, even more memorable for her personally, if not professionally, was her participation, that same year, in a play by Arnold Bennett called *Mr. Prohack*, in which she was cast opposite a young character actor named Charles Laughton. The two actors reportedly were paid the same salaries, though Laughton played the title role and Elsa was cast in the smaller part of his secretary. They acted together in a set of short films the following year and in February 1929 were married. They continued to act together on occasion including in *Payment Deferred* on the London stage in May 1931, then traveling to the United States to debut the show on Broadway in September, where it ran for 70 performances in the autumn of '31. Laughton was cast in the movie version, released in 1932, though Lanchester was not.

It was during this period that Laughton confessed to his wife of his homosexual tendencies. In her 1983 autobiography, *Elsa Lanchester, Herself*, she recounted the night he disclosed his secret. The actor arrived home late one evening in 1931 with Jeffrey Dell, who was adapting *Payment Deferred* for the stage, a policeman and a boy who apparently wanted money from Laughton, all in tow. According to Lanchester:

> "I was in bed when Charles came upstairs. 'Something awful has happened,' he said to me. 'I have something to confess.' He said that he had picked up the boy, and it wasn't the first time he had done it; that he was homosexual partly, and he cried. I said, 'It's perfectly all right, it doesn't matter. I understand it. Don't worry about it.' That's why he cried. When I told him it didn't matter. [...]

> Later on, I would ask Charles what really happened, and once he told me that he had had a fellow on our sofa. The only thing I said was, "Fine, okay, but get rid of the sofa." We did. We sold it."

When Laughton appeared in court concerning the incident, the judge called the money given to the boy "misguided generosity," and a tiny paragraph at the bottom of a local newspaper read: "Actor warned about misguided generosity." Only the boy's name was listed.

When he began his film career in Hollywood in 1932, Laughton appeared in no less than six movies, while Elsa found herself with no work. While back in London, Lanchester was contacted by famed English producer Alexander Korda who approached her with the idea of a filmed version of the married life of King Henry VIII and his many wives, with Charles as the king and Elsa as Anne of Cleves. The end result was *The Private Life of Henry VIII* (1933), which garnered Laughton an Academy Award as Best Actor and introduced Lanchester to American audiences. As Henry's forth and least attractive wife, she played her role with humor and confidence and offered what some consider the best scene of the film (A humorous take on the royal honeymoon with Henry and the homely Anne playing cards in their wedding bed). With her husband's career taking off, Lanchester signed a contract with MGM, making small character appearances in *David Copperfield* and *Naughty Marietta* (both in 1935).

A lackluster entre into Hollywood films sent the actress back to London, where she was contacted by her old friend, director James Whale, who offered her a dual role in his latest project: *Bride of*

Frankenstein. Whale had conceived of the idea early in production that the actress who was hired to play authoress Mary Wollstonecraft Shelley in the film's prelude, would also portray the monster's bride. Lanchester gladly accepted the opportunity and made her way back to Los Angeles. Between Whale's conception of the Bride's look and makeup artist Jack Pierce's execution of it, Lanchester's character became one of Hollywood's most recognizable icons, much copied by party-goers and parodied by comedians for decades. The actress viewed the part to be both a blessing and a curse, offering her widespread fame, while at the same time stereotyping her mercilessly. Still, the film was both a commercial as well as critical success for Universal Studio. After her appearance in *Bride*, she and Laughton crossed the Atlantic again to work together in a stage revival of *Peter Pan* at the London Palladium, with Lanchester as the eternal youth and her husband as Captain Hook. The couple also appeared together in two British pictures, *Rembrandt* (1936) and *The Beachcomber*, aka *Vessel of Wrath* (1938), before returning yet again to the United States for Charles to star as Quasimodo in *The Hunchback of Notre Dame* for RKO in 1939.

It would be 1941 before the actress would make another movie (*Ladies in Retirement* with Ida Lupino), but from then on, she would establish herself firmly as one of Hollywood's most solid supporting players, working steadily throughout the decade. Lanchester played any number of airy, twittery maids and servants of various character, most notably in *The Spiral Staircase* (1946), *The Bishop's Wife* (1947) and *The Secret Garden* (1949). In *Passport to Destiny* (1944) she played a London charwoman who makes her way to Germany in an attempt to assassinate Hitler. It is a strange cinema curio of the B-level variety, which was Lanchester's only top-billed role.   Her energetic and versatile performances did not go unnoticed critically with Oscar nominations as Best Supporting Actress in 1949's *Come to the Stable* and 1957's *Witness for the Prosecution* (in which she appeared yet again with husband Laughton), the latter actually garnering her a Golden Globe.

In the late '40s and 1950s, along with supporting film roles, Elsa spent much time on the stage. In 1948, she gave her 2,000th performance at Los Angeles' Turnabout Theater, an event celebrated with a full house and a party thrown by the establishment's management. The Turnabout was a very well-received Hollywood revue which consisted of a combination of adult marionette comic-drama, live music and comedy. Considering her early days at the Cave of Harmony, it fit the actress like a glove. The Laughtons became American citizens on April 28, 1950, and both continued to work steadily. Lanchester also made numerous television appearances during this period, most notably as Edna Grundy, traveling companion to Lucy and Ethel in the "Off to Florida" episode of *I Love Lucy* in 1956. She continued to work with Laughton and the two remained married until his death in December 1962.

The 1960s and 1970s held a mixture of very lighthearted work on both the large and small screen as well as a few examples of the macabre. She worked for Disney, appearing in several of that company's live-action films, including *Mary Poppins* (as Katie Nanna; 1964), *That Darn Cat* (1965) and *Blackbeard's Ghost* (1968), and in 1969 played in a two-part episode of *Walt Disney's Wonderful World of Color*. Her darker roles included supporting parts in *Terror in the Wax Museum* (1973) and in the original rat-thriller *Willard* (1971).

In 1983, the actress penned her second autobiography, *Elsa Lanchester, Herself*. She had written an earlier memoir in 1938 called *Charles Laughton and I*, recounting her early years with her actor-husband. After suffering a stroke in 1984, she battled heart problems for several years. The independent actress died of bronchopneumonia at the Motion Picture and Television Country House and Hospital in Woodland Hills, California on the day after Christmas, 1986. She was eighty-four years old. Lanchester once said: "There is no such thing as a person that nothing has happened to, and each person's story is as different as his fingertips," and indeed, her story was as different as they come.

Carole   Landis

When Jacqueline Susann wrote her runaway blockbuster novel, *Valley of the Dolls* in the 1960s, her characters were (sometimes) thinly veiled recreations of celebrities she had encountered throughout her long, and often uneventful, show business career. Although many who read *Valley of the Dolls*, thought beautiful blonde showgirl Jennifer North was based on Marilyn Monroe, the character was, in fact, a composite of three women. The first was Susann herself who, like Jennifer, fought breast cancer and underwent a mastectomy. The second was showgirl Joyce Mathews, who was twice married to famed comedian Milton Berle (when Uncle Miltie was asked why he remarried the blonde Mathews, he wittily replied: "She reminded me of my first wife") and the third was the beautiful and tragic Twentieth Century-Fox player Carole Landis. Susann had met the shapely Hollywood siren when the two appeared on Broadway in *The Lady Said Yes* in 1945, and a sexual affair ensued becoming what Susann biographer Barbara Seaman called "one of the most intense relationships of her life." Although best known for her 1948 suicide, reportedly over her broken affair with married British actor Rex Harrison, Carole Landis had a decade long career playing second leads and supporting parts, usually as a catty or ambitious female.

Early life was not kind to the blue-eyed beauty. She was born Frances Lillian Mary Ridste on New Year's Day in 1919 in Fairchild, Wisconsin. Her father, Alfred, a railroad mechanic of Norwegian descent abandoned his family shortly before Frances' birth (there were two older siblings, a brother and a sister) and her mother, Clara, remarried a man named Charles Fenner, though this was a short-lived union. It has been suggested by biographer E.J. Fleming that Fenner was actually the child's biological father by way of an adulterous affair, though this has never been confirmed. While Frances was still a toddler, Clara moved her family to San Bernardino, California, where she worked as a waitress and took on a variety of menial jobs "that would bring food for [her] children."

Young Frances matured quickly, and she began competing in and winning beauty contests at twelve! In January 1934, at the tender age of fifteen, she eloped with nineteen-year-old Irving Wheeler. When her mother discovered the marriage, she had it annulled within weeks, but Frances was determined to reinstate the union and asked her father, Alfred Ridste, who had remarried and also lived in San Bernardino, to sign the form allowing her to marry underage. He finally relented, much to her mother's chagrin, and she and Wheeler remarried in August of the same year. Their marital bliss was fleeting and within a month, Frances moved out, though they didn't conduct an official divorce.

She dropped out of San Bernardino High School, saved up some money and headed for San Francisco to pursue a career in show business. She landed a job singing and dancing at the Royal Hawaiian nightclub in a skimpy hula outfit. Building on her experience she got a job as a singer with the Carl Ravazza band, at the Rio Del Mar country club. She then changed her name to "Carole Landis," taking the first part from Carole Lombard, who was her favorite actress, and moved to Hollywood.

Landis began her film career in 1936, as a chorus girl and extra in several Warner Brothers and MGM extravaganzas, including *Gold Diggers of 1937* (1936), *The King and the Chorus Girl* (1937), *A Day at the Races* (1937) and *Varsity Show* (also 1937). While working at Warners, she met famed choreographer Busby Berkeley, who helped her get a contract with the studio for $50 a week. They began a personal relationship which brought estranged husband Irving Wheeler to unsuccessfully sue Berkeley for alienation of affection (an all but outdated legal action brought by a deserted spouse against a third party alleged to be responsible for the failure of the marriage). Shortly after the suit, Landis and Berkeley split and her contract with Warners wasn't renewed after her first year.

Her career became little more than a huge display of cheesecake publicity shots and a handful of bit parts until 1940, when she signed with producer Hal Roach, who cast her in his prehistoric fantasy, *One Million B.C.* Landis played beautiful cave girl Loana, a role reprised by Raquel Welch in the 1966 remake. The scantily clad actress hit pay dirt and became known as the Ping Girl, "because she makes you purr." In June, *Life* magazine proclaimed that Landis "should be a star within a year." If her career was gaining steam, Carole's personal life was as unstable as ever. On July 4, 1940, she eloped to Las Vegas with yacht broker Willis Hunt, Jr., but by Thanksgiving the couple had divorced.

The up and coming starlet rang in 1941 with a contract at Twentieth Century-Fox and an ongoing relationship with the head of the studio, Darryl F. Zanuck. According to Fox producer and Zanuck associate Milton Sperling, the boss had a daily routine of halting business every afternoon at four o'clock, when "some girl on the lot would visit Zanuck in his office." Zanuck biographer Leonard Mosley claimed, "the only one who ever seems to have been called in more than once was a Fox contract feature player named Carole Landis, who was casually referred to by personnel as 'the studio hooker.'" Despite how she may or may not have landed it, her Fox debut was a bright one as the second lead in the Betty Grable musical *Moon Over Miami* (1941). Next up was yet another second lead in a Grable picture, the dramatic thriller *I Wake Up Screaming*, for which producer Sperling was ordered by Zanuck "to find a role for Carole Landis." When she eventually stopped the four o'clock trysts with Zanuck, Landis found herself relegated to the B-movie brigade at Fox.

In 1942, as a contribution to the war effort abroad, she joined comedienne Martha Raye, dancer Mitzi Mayfair and actress Kay Francis to tour with the USO in England and North Africa. Their travels became the basis of a book called *Four Jills in a Jeep*, penned by Landis and serialized in *The Saturday Evening Post*. It was produced, rather unsuccessfully, as a movie in 1944 starring Raye, Mayfair, Francis and Landis. Part of her USO run included marriage to United States Army Air Forces Captain Thomas Wallace, with whom she became acquainted while in London. The couple married in a much-heralded ceremony in early 1943, with Mitzi Mayfair serving as her maid-of-honor. Ten days after the nuptials, the bride was with her female tour mates in Algiers and the groom back with his squadron. Though not quite as short-lived as her earlier unions, the marriage ended in divorce in the summer of 1945, with Wallace stating he was tired of being "the guy Carole Landis married."

Not one to be single for very long, the actress walked down the aisle yet again in December 1945, this time to wealthy Broadway producer W. Horace Schmidlapp. Carole's gal pal Jacqueline Susann had introduced the pair earlier in the year. The relationship was to be short-lived and the couple separated in 1947 with Landis filing for divorce the following year, claiming extreme mental cruelty. Her career fared no better during this period. Her Fox contract ended in 1946 with the ironically titled programmer, *It Shouldn't Happen to a Dog*.

With her marriage to Schmidlapp on shaky ground, Landis began an affair with Rex Harrison in 1947. Married to German-born actress Lilli Palmer, Harrison had the reputation of being a notorious womanizer, garnering the moniker "Sexy Rexy." He was under contract to Carole's former studio, Twentieth Century-Fox and had started his Hollywood career with such hits as *Anna and the King of Siam* and *The Ghost and Mrs. Muir*. According to Harrison, he first met Carole in Palm Springs in the summer of 1947, an introduction which he described in his 1974 autobiography:

"I was sitting in the bar of the Racquet Club with Charlie Farrell and Lucille Ball, when Carole came in with a group of people. We were introduced and started talking. Carole was a warm, attractive girl, and soon we were swapping funny stories and limericks, sitting up late in the electric desert air."

The relationship soon became an open secret in Hollywood, with the two even working on simultaneous film projects in England in early 1948. Once the couple returned stateside the affair continued hotter than ever, though it was much more emotional for Landis than her paramour. Harrison refused to leave Palmer and was content having Landis on the side. With her career and personal life in shambles, along with chronic health issues (she had suffered from lingering effects of amebic dysentery and malaria contracted while on the USO tour), the actress was extremely depressed. On July 4, 1948, she was found by Harrison and her maid on the bathroom floor of her Pacific Palisades home, victim of suicide from an overdose of Seconal. A note to her mother was found near her that read: "Dearest Mommie, I'm sorry, really sorry, to put you through this but there is no way to avoid it. I love you darling, you have been the most wonderful mom ever. And that applies to all our family. I love each and every one of them dearly. Everything goes to you—look in the files and there is a will which decrees everything. Good bye, my angel. Pray for me, Your Baby." She was twenty-nine years old. Harrison had been with her the evening before and his career in Hollywood was damaged. His contract with Fox was terminated and he went back east to work on the stage.

Landis was laid to rest in Forest Lawn Memorial Park Cemetery in Glendale, California. Among those in attendance at her funeral were Harrison and Palmer. Carole Landis had commented only a few years earlier on the suicide of Mexican actress Lupe Vélez: "I know how Lupe Velez felt. You fight just so long and then you begin to worry about being washed up. You fear there's one way to go and that's down... I have no intention of ending my career in a rooming house, with full scrapbooks and an empty stomach."

Angela Lansbury

An actress whose life and heritage have been richly interwoven with fame, heartbreak and a magnificent career, Angela Lansbury fled London in the wake of Hitler's blitz, married a man she discovered to be a homosexual, and struggled through the adolescent drug addiction of her children. On the other end of her spectrum, she enjoyed a long and loving second marriage, as well as a stellar, award-winning career on the stage, in films and television. Although she is known throughout the world as a leading lady in both the theater and TV, her place during the golden age of Hollywood was as a solid and always dependable character actress and second lead.

Angela Brigid Lansbury was born on October 16, 1925, in central London's Regent's Park, a fact that the actress has been adamant about, contrary to many assertions that her birthplace was in Poplar, East London. Brigid, as she was called during the early years of her life, was the eldest child of Edgar and Moyna (Macgill) Lansbury. The family was upper-middle class and Edgar was both businessman and politician, a member of Britain's Communist Party. His father, in fact, was George Lansbury, leader of the Labour Party in the 1920s. Moyna was an Irish-born actress, active in London's West End theater.

Edgar died of cancer in 1934, when Angela was nine. His passing affected her deeply and she became interested in performing and eventually joined her half-sister, Isolde, (her mother's daughter from an earlier marriage) in acting classes. When war broke out in England, air raids became a regular occurrence during the German Blitz. Lansbury recalled, "We thought bombs would come down then and there." In 1940, just before the heavy bombing began, her mother took her, along with her younger twin brothers, Bruce and Edgar, who had been born in 1930, to the United States. Isolde stayed in England with her husband, actor Peter Ustinov, whom she had just married.

First living in New York, the family moved to Los Angeles and while working at Bullocks Wilshire department store during the 1942 Christmas season, young Lansbury was introduced to John Van Druten, who was co-authoring the script for an upcoming picture at MGM called *Gaslight*. Van Druten recommended Angela to the film's director, George Cukor, for the supporting role of Nancy, a naughty Cockney maid. At seventeen, she got the part, as well as some good notices, including columnist Louella Parsons, who proclaimed the "English refugee girl of 17...shows great promise as an actress." Louella underestimated the "refugee girl" who was nominated for an Academy Award as Best Supporting Actress in her debut film performance.

Lansbury signed a seven-year contract with MGM and was cast next as Edwina Brown, older sister to Elizabeth Taylor's character in *National Velvet* (1944). She then co-starred with Hurd Hatfield and Donna Reed in *The Picture of Dorian Gray* (1945), based on Oscar Wilde's famed novel. As the gentle and tragic Sybil Vane, Lansbury was nominated for her second Best Supporting Actress Oscar at just nineteen years-old. Although she lost the prize to her *National Velvet* co-star, Anne Revere, she did win the Golden Globe for Best Supporting Actress.

In September 1945, Angela eloped with a handsome actor, fifteen years her senior. Richard Cromwell had made a name for himself during the 1930s in films such as *The Lives of the Bengal Lancers* (1935) and *Jezebel* (1938). The marriage lasted less than a year, after the actress came home one day to find Cromwell's car and clothes gone, and a note which read: "I'm sorry darling, I can't go on." Lansbury would later find out that her husband was homosexual, and she filed for divorce in September 1946. "It was a terrible shock," she recalled. "I was devastated. But once I got over the shock, I said, 'all right then, I'm going to take charge of my life and see that I never hurt like this again.'" The two split amicably and remained friends until Cromwell's death in 1960.

She focused on her career, making a striking Technicolor dance hall queen in *The Harvey Girls* (1946), with Judy Garland and John Hodiak. She was cast as bad-girl Em, after Lucille Ball, Eve Arden and Ann Sothern were considered first. Her screen persona began to take shape in shrewish, older women roles. In her early twenties she was often cast as middle-aged characters, bitchy and brittle in nature. During this period, she even received fan mail from people who thought she was in her forties. Her time at MGM did little for her career, though she gave top-notch performances in whatever project she appeared. She recalled how frustrating it could be to petition her boss, Louis Mayer, for better roles. "I visited Mayer in his office on a number of occasions, and that was quite an experience because you had to go down this long corridor which was rather intimidating, to say the least. And you had to go cap in hand, as I often did, saying, 'Please Mr. Mayer, don't make me play the queen of France.' He'd say, 'Yes dear, but I personally think this is a great role for you,' so I'd be sent back to the wardrobe department and I'd end up playing the queen of France [in 1948's *The Three Musketeers*] when I'd rather have been playing Lady de Winter, which was a far more interesting part. But that went to Lana Turner, who was the great glamour puss at that time. I just had to mind my own business and get on with it."

In December 1946, Lansbury met Peter Shaw, a fellow Brit and an aspiring actor. They quickly became a couple but didn't marry until August 1949. Shaw went on to manage his wife's career and the couple became naturalized citizens of the United States in 1951. Besides Peter's son from a previous marriage, the Shaws had two children together, Anthony and Deirdre. Her contract with MGM ended in 1952 and, as she was dissatisfied with the direction of her film work, she turned her attention to the stage and also made several appearances on television in playhouse anthology shows, including *Robert Montgomery Presents*, *General Electric Theater* and *Four Star Playhouse*. She made a handful of movies during the mid and late 1950s, including the fun Danny Kaye vehicle, *The Court Jester* in 1955 and *The Long, Hot Summer* in 1958.

In 1957, she made her first appearance on Broadway in *Hotel Paradiso*, opening the door to one of the most prosperous and gratifying periods of her performing life. Her film performances weren't as rewarding. By the early '60s, she was playing mothers to men only a decade older than her own age. In *Blue Hawaii* (1961), she played the scatterbrained, southern mama to Elvis Presley, who was only nine years younger than Lansbury. The following year she had two very strong roles with the same casting circumstances. In *All Fall Down*, she played Warren Beatty's mother, with only an eleven and a half-year difference in age, and in the Cold War thriller *The Manchurian Candidate*, it was Laurence Harvey, who was only THREE years younger than Lansbury! The latter film offered the actress what was arguably her best and most memorable of her movie roles. As Mrs. Senator John Iselin, she gave a tour de force performance and created one of the most evil and complex characters of the decade (and some would say the decades to come). She was once again nominated for a Best Supporting Actress Oscar, and yet again lost (this time to Patty Duke for *The Miracle Worker*). She did, however, win a Golden Globe and the National Board of Review prizes for the same category.

She continued working in a supporting capacity in pictures throughout the '60s, but on Broadway, she had her greatest stage triumph. In 1966, Lansbury took on the role of Mame Dennis in *Mame*, the musical version of the novel by Patrick Dennis called *Auntie Mame*. Although it was meant for her former MGM co-star, Judy Garland, Lansbury was cast when the grueling schedule was considered too much for Garland. Angela made the role her own and she became as associated with the part on the stage as Rosalind Russell had with the 1958 screen version. *Mame* was a huge success and Lansbury garnered her first Tony for Best Performance by a Leading Actress in a Musical. She followed up the overwhelming hit with *Dear World* and a revival of *Gypsy*, both shows offering her another Tony award each.

Her acting victories didn't come without a price in her personal life. Barely in their teens in the late '60s, her children, Anthony and Deirdre, became involved in drugs, first "with cannabis but moved on to heroin." Her daughter became involved with undesirables in the hills above Malibu, where the Shaws lived. Lansbury recalled: "It pains me to say it but, at one stage, Deidre was in with a crowd led by Charles Manson. She was one of many youngsters who knew him - and they were fascinated." When their home was destroyed by fire in 1970, Shaw and Lansbury decided to move their children to rural County Cork, Ireland, in an attempt to help Anthony recover from his drug addiction, which he eventually did.

Although her film work tapered off in the 1970s, she was discerning in her choices of roles. In 1971, she appeared in the Walt Disney classic, *Bedknobs and Broomsticks*, as Eglentine Price, an apprentice witch who agrees to board three children at her country home as refuge from air raids in World War II London (shades of her own youth). She then retreated from screen work, to focus on the theater, both in London's West End as well as on Broadway. When she returned to movies in the late '70s, it was as colorful characters of classic mystery. In 1978, she played Mrs. Salome Otterbourne, drunken writer of erotica in Agatha Christie's *Death on the Nile*, which featured an all-star cast, including her former brother-in-law Peter Ustinov (he and her half-sister Isolde had divorced in 1950), Mia Farrow and Bette Davis. The following year she appeared as Miss Froy, a part originated on film by Dame May Whitty, in the tepid remake of *The Lady Vanishes*. In 1980, she starred in another Christie based movie, *The Mirror Crack'd*, as a sprightly version of classic sleuth, Miss Jane Marple. In the midst of these two, prim, "old lady" roles, Lansbury took the time to hit the stage as Mrs. Lovett, kooky accomplice in Stephen Sondheim's gory musical *Sweeney Todd* (1979).

Unlike both the movies and the theater, television was an entertainment format that Lansbury had encountered little success; until 1984. With her turn as Miss Marple providing a springboard, the actress took the plunge into episodic television with the weekly mystery series, *Murder, She Wrote* in 1984. She played Jessica Fletcher, English teacher-

155

turned-mystery novelist from Cabot Cove, Maine. Jessica's experience writing potboilers put her in good standing to solve the many murders that seemed to cross her path. The show was wildly successful and ran until 1996, offering periodic TV movies featuring the elegantly down-to-earth amateur detective.

In her post-*Murder, She Wrote* years, Lansbury continued to be active in both television and theater, also making use of her distinctive voice in animated features, most famously as Miss Potts in Disney's *Beauty and the Beast* in 1991, as well as its follow-up video release, *The Enchanted Christmas*. Her husband, Peter Shaw, died in 2003, after fifty-four years of marriage. Her children overcame their demons and Anthony became a television director, overseeing dozens of episodes of *Murder, She Wrote*. Still active at this writing, the ninety-plus year-old actress has enjoyed a long and illustrious career in all aspects of the entertainment industry, and her longevity, as well as gracious personality are shining reminders of the golden age of Hollywood.

Peter Lorre

The memory of actor Peter Lorre often falls somewhere between character and caricature, his roles caustic and creepy yet dripping with pathos on other occasions. He gained fame playing serial killers, sinister psychotics and menacing foreigners. Off-screen the actor had a less than joyous existence, plagued by a typecast career, multiple marriages and chronic pain.

Lorre was born László Löwenstein on June 26, 1904 in Rózsahegy, Austria-Hungary [now Ruzomberok, Slovakia], the eldest child of Jews, Alois and Elvira Löwenstein, who moved to the region when his father gained an appointment as chief bookkeeper at a local textile mill. Lorre's mother died in 1908, leaving Alajos with three very young sons. It wasn't long before he found a new wife, none other than Elvira's best friend, Melanie Klein, a union which produced two more children. However, the fact that Lorre and his stepmother didn't get along, clouded his childhood memories. The Löwenstein family moved to Romania, then to Vienna, and finally to a farm in Austria during World War I before returning to Vienna. It was in the Austrian city that young Lorre was educated in elementary and secondary schools before running away from home at seventeen and joining an improvised theater.

In 1922, he worked as a bank clerk to please his father, but he soon gave it up to devote himself completely to acting, getting bit parts with a company in Breslau Breslau (now Wroclaw, in Poland) in 1924, then securing a part in Galsworthy's *Society* in Zurich. He played in Vienna for two years before going to Berlin in 1928. A product of Berlin's post World War I experimental theatre scene, Lorre honed his craft in plays by Shakespeare, Goethe and Shaw. He was immediately cast in a play, *Pioniere in Ingolstadt* as the village idiot and received rave reviews. At this time, he met his first wife, Celia Lovsky. He also became seriously ill and had to undergo major surgery. The result was lifelong health problems and an addiction to morphine. He adopted the stage name "Lorre" in 1925.

Iconic German director Fritz Lang saw Lorre on the Berlin stage in *Fruhlings Erwachen* (Spring's Awakening) and offered him a part in his upcoming film project. The movie was *M* (1931) and the actor was cast as a sinister child killer. Although he gained international fame for his role in *M*, the actor's follow-up work in German cinema did not live up to the potential he showed in the Lang picture. Like many of his Jewish peers, Lorre left Germany in 1933, as Nazi power was increasing. He moved first to Paris and then London, where he made his English-language film debut for Alfred Hitchcock (who remembered Lorre's powerful portrayal in *M*) in the director's first version of *The Man Who Knew Too Much* in 1934.

Immediately after shooting was completed, Lorre and his wife journeyed to New York, then on to Hollywood where the actor signed a contract with Columbia Studios. Casting the import was difficult, as the studio wasn't sure how to use him, so he was loaned out to MGM to make *Mad Love* (1935). Based on the story *The Hands of Orlac*, *Mad Love* was directed by Karl Freund, a German émigré who had made a name for himself as a stylistic cinematographer on the sets of the silent classic, *Metropolis* (1927) and the iconic horror film, *Dracula* (1931). It was Lorre's American debut and critics praised his performance including the *Hollywood Reporter* who wrote: "Lorre triumphs in a characterization that is sheer horror."

In 1936, the actor would work for Hitchcock again in the spy thriller *Secret Agent,* then, upon his return to Hollywood, Lorre signed on with 20th Century-Fox, where he starred in the Mr. Moto mystery film series between 1937 and 1939. Moto, a Japanese secret agent, was the creation of American author John P. Marquand, whose first novel in the series was published in 1935. The Moto films came to the screen in the wake of the popularity of the Charlie Chan franchise at Fox. Suffering for years with a chronic gallbladder condition, Lorre began taking morphine for pain relief which lead to hardcore addiction. According to many accounts he was battling this addiction during the filming of the Moto movies. With the growing Japanese threat overseas and Lorre's desire to relinquish the role, the Mr. Moto series ended, and the actor left Fox.

In 1940, Lorre signed a two-picture deal with RKO. The first of these was a short B-movie called *Stranger on the Third Floor*, which is cited by film historians as the first film noir in American cinema. Heavily influenced by German Expressionism, the movie featured the actor as yet another deranged maniac, ironically with little screen time and top billing. As witnessed by his role as a disfigured immigrant in *The Face Behind the Mask* (1941), he began to be typecast as strange oddballs, psychopaths and degenerates.

After finishing up at RKO, Lorre moved over to Warner Brothers, where he enjoyed the peak of his movie career. Like Alfred Hitchcock, director John Huston had remembered Lorre's performance in *M* and despite the doubts of Warner Brothers execs, Huston cast the underrated actor in his directorial debut, *The Maltese Falcon* in 1941. According to the director, "Peter could do anything. He had himself such a rich and varied personality that he could incorporate anything into it." As the effeminate villain Joel Cairo, Lorre made a big impression on audiences and became one of Warners' top character actors of the Forties.

He continued his professional attachment with his *Maltese Falcon* co-star Humphrey Bogart, sharing screen time with the actor in many films at Warner Brothers including *Across the Pacific* (1941), *Casablanca*

(1942) and *Passage to Marseilles* (1944). Personally, he advised the macho Bogart to marry his much younger paramour, Lauren Bacall, despite their age difference, telling Bogie: "Five good years are better than none!" Lorre also made several films with his fellow Warners' character counterpart Sydney Greenstreet, including *Three Strangers* (1946), in which they share top billing with Geraldine Fitzgerald. His face, voice and manner became so iconic that he was even caricatured in the studio's popular Looney Tunes cartoons, including "Hair Raising Hare" and "Racketeer Rabbit," both in 1946 and both with Bugs Bunny, of course.

Peter Lorre's career began to decline in the late '40s, as good roles were fewer and far between and his typecasting became more advanced. He went back to Europe to make a psychological thriller called *Der Verlorene* ("The Lost One" 1951), in which he not only starred in but also wrote and directed. The film was a commercial failure and Lorre returned to Hollywood, where he continued working in movies, as well as radio and television. In 1954, CBS produced a one-hour television version of the James Bond adventure novel *Casino Royale*, adapted by Bond creator Ian Fleming. Playing Le Chiffre, Lorre became the first actor to portray a Bond villain.

Lorre's troubled personal life included three marriages, the first two ending in divorce. He had been separated from his third wife for over a year, when on March 23, 1964, the actor passed away, the victim of a stroke. A divorce hearing from his last wife, Annette, had been scheduled for that day.

Marjorie Main

"I always thought of Ma Kettle as a real person. She was someone that I could imagine driving out into the country to see. Ma Kettle was a grand person." That is what Marjorie Main said of the character which made her famous and for which she is best remembered. Like Ma, many would agree that Marjorie was a grand person as well. A veteran character actress, and one of the finest of the breed, Main's brand of brash and cantankerous humor lent itself to many Hollywood classics and enhanced whatever film in which she appeared.

Her first name wasn't Marjorie, nor her last name Main. She was, in fact, born Mary Tomlinson on February 24, 1890, near the small farming community of Acton, in the southeast corner of Marion County,

Indiana. She had the distinction of being delivered by her maternal grandfather, Dr. Samuel McGaughey. Her father, Reverend Samuel Joseph Tomlinson, was a minister in the Church of Christ and heartily disapproved of the theater, though young Mary became interested in dramatics while still in school, reciting pieces for her family. As a teen, she attended nearby Franklin College and after much persistence, was allowed by her strict father to take a three-year course at the Hamilton School of Dramatic Expression in Lexington, Kentucky. Upon graduation in 1909, nineteen-year-old Mary secured a position as drama instructor at Bourbon College in Paris, Kentucky. After teaching for only a year, the young teacher was dismissed for demanding an increase in her salary. No shrinking violet, she. Tomlinson then went on to study drama in Chicago and eventually joined the Chautauqua Theatre Circuit playing Shakespeare and getting paid $18 per week, with an extra $2 thrown in for singing between acts. Although her father grudgingly gave his approval of her choice of earning a living, the young actress took a stage name to save the family any embarrassment: Marjorie Main. She eventually toured in vaudeville, performed with stock companies, and in 1916, made her Broadway debut in a bit part. She also worked with legendary comic W.C. Fields at the famed Palace Theater in New York.

While on the Chautauqua circuit, Marjorie met Dr. Stanley LeFevre Krebs, a former minister turned psychologist-lecturer and the two wed in late 1921. The previously married Krebs was fifty-seven, Marjorie was thirty-one. Her new husband taught courses in applied psychology, with Main organizing her schedule around his lecture tours and giving up her performance career until the couple finally settled in New York City. She began appearing on Broadway and in 1931 made her feature film debut in a small role in the Universal picture, *A House Divided*, starring Walter Huston. Dr. Krebs died in the autumn of 1935 and Marjorie began working regularly again, making several small, uncredited appearances in film shorts as well as features. The month after her husband's passing, the actress opened on Broadway as the mother who withers away in the slums of New York in Sidney Kingsley's play, *Dead End*. She played the same role (powerfully) in the 1937 film version, as well. Her performance did not go unnoticed, with *The Hollywood Reporter* exclaiming in July 1937: "Marjorie Main is superb as the tragic mother, a beautiful bit of character work."

Main signed a contract with MGM, and acted in more than a hundred motion pictures, taking on comedy and drama with equal relish and ease. She played a variety of supporting roles in A-pictures and was cast in starring roles in B's. Appearing in both the 1936 stage production and the 1939 movie version of Clare Booth Luce's major hit, *The Women*, Main more than held her own with the likes of screen queens Norma Shearer, Joan Crawford and Rosalind Russell. Her loud, sloppy, blustering portrayal of Lucy, caretaker of a Reno divorcee ranch, set the tone for her future roles. Metro cast her with its regular roughneck, Wallace Beery, who had lost a female screen partner with the death of cantankerous oldster, Marie Dressler. *Wyoming* (1940) was the first of seven films together, though neither was ecstatic about the other, with Marjorie complaining that Beery refused to speak his lines as written, and he, in turn, bellowed that she could never remember hers. "She's blown her lines already thirteen times on this one take," the actor told a reporter. "If I have to make another picture with her, so help me I'll have a heart attack." Indeed, it was a prophetic statement, as Beery died of a heart attack in 1949, two days after the release of his final movie, *Big Jack*, in which he co-starred with Marjorie Main.

But as popular as her collaborations with Wallace Beery were, they would pale in comparison to her biggest claim to movie fame, playing the character of Ma Kettle opposite Percy Kilbride as Pa in the 1947 comedy, *The Egg and I*. Main was loaned out to Universal to play the part in its bona fide hit, based on a bestselling book by authoress Betty MacDonald and starring Claudette Colbert and Fred MacMurray. As the boisterous, iron-fisted farm matriarch with the heart-of-gold, Main was a high point in what was already a highly entertaining comedy. For her efforts, she was nominated for an Oscar as Best Supporting Actress. It was the role that would shape the rest of her career, as Universal took the success of the Kettle characters and created a low-budget movie series featuring them and their brood (the Kettle children numbered more than a dozen!). The Ma and Pa Kettle franchise included nine films between 1949 and 1957, beginning with the self-titled, *Ma and Pa Kettle*.

After Stanley Krebs' death in 1935, Main never remarried nor had children. It was long rumored that she had a long-lasting romantic relationship with actress Spring Byington, reportedly an active lesbian. Film historian Boze Hadleigh broached the subject of Main's bisexuality in an interview with the actress in her later life. In response to a question about homosexuality with the studio system of the golden age, Main said: "I think the 'different' people should be honest with their relatives, if they want to. That's practical. At work, it's not." Then, when questioned if she would reveal such a thing to a surviving relative, she said: "I wouldn't have to tell 'em. I'd show them. I'd just show up with my lady-friend, and if I had it to do all over, I might live with her. When I was younger, I'd liked to have lived with her," she confessed.

With the release of *The Kettles on Old MacDonald's Farm* in 1957, Marjorie Main, then sixty-seven years old, retired from motion pictures, and with two appearances on the television western, *Wagon Train* in 1958, she ended her five-decade career. In May 1974, she attended the premiere of the musical tribute to MGM's 50th anniversary, *That's Entertainment*. A year later, on April 10, she passed away from cancer at the age of eighty-five, at St. Vincent's Hospital in Los Angeles. She was buried in Forest Lawn Memorial Park, Hollywood Hill, beside her husband.

M i k e   M a z u r k i

"His is an eroded slag heap of a face traversed by gullies. The voice is a kettle drum filled with boulders." That's how UPI Hollywood correspondent Vernon Scott described him. You know his face. You've seen it dozens of times in numerous classic movies. If you're not sure about his name, well, it suits his craggy, battered, sometimes sinister mug. He is Mike Mazurki, and he was born to play strong-arm henchmen, dull-witted gangsters and menacing thugs. With a powerful 6' 5" frame of solid muscle, he started out in films being billed as Tough Sailor, Tough Bill, Thug, Bouncer, Henchman Charlie and Henchman Joe, Japanese Wrestler and Fighter. These roles were played in his career during the first two years alone! As his parts got bigger, the names became less "descriptive" but still representative of his characters: Bruno, Bone, "Little" Joe and "Bigtree" Collins. Two of his most definitive characters during the period were Moose Malloy in the Raymond Chandler story

165

Murder, My Sweet (1944) and Splitface in the comic book inspired film noir, *Dick Tracy* (1945).

Born Mikhail Mazurkiewicz in Tarnopol, Galicia, Austria-Hungary on Christmas Day, 1907, he and his family emigrated to Cohoes, New York while Mike was still a boy. As a youth, he attended the La Salle Institute in Troy, New York, run by the De La Salle Christian Brothers. After graduation, he attended Manhattan College, where he played football and eventually earned a Bachelor of Arts degree in 1930. He was affiliated with a minor league football team in the mid-1930s and became a professional wrestler, known as "Iron Mike" Mazurki. He moved to California, where he was spotted in the wrestling ring by producer Josef von Sternberg, who cast him in a bit part in *The Shanghai Gesture* (1941). Mazurki recounted his discovery in a 1952 Toronto newspaper article.

> "I am wrestling in Los Angeles and while I am in the dressing room later I am getting a note asking if I would be interested in a movie career. I am thinking the boys are playing a joke on me, and I am putting the note in my pocket because I am not going to be laughed at," he explained. "One my way out a guy comes up and asks if I received the note. He says he is Von Sternberg, who discovered Marlene Dietrich. I am asked to report to the studio next morning for an interview. I am still thinking it is a joke, but I decide to play along with the gag."

From that point on he was steadily employed, making well over 200 movies throughout the '40s and beyond, his last film appearance in 1990. He was at home in a variety of genres, being just as comfortable as a brute in a film noir as he did in a slapstick comedy. In addition to Von Sternberg, he also worked with some of Hollywood's most powerful and influential directors including Frank Borzage (*The Spanish Main*, 1945), Cecil B. DeMille (*Unconquered*, 1947) and *Samson and Delilah*, 1949), and William Wellman (*Blood Alley*, 1955). Mazurki later recalled how he began getting regular work with notable director John Ford:

> "I could never work for John Ford while Victor McLaglen was alive, because we were the same type. Soon as Vic died I made six pictures with Ford including *Donovan's Reef, Cheyenne Autumn*

and *Seven Women*. He had his own little company and I took McLaglen's place."

While continuing to get work in feature films during the 1950s, including *Some Like it Hot* (1959), with Tony Curtis and Marilyn Monroe, he also appeared in many popular television shows of the day. *My Friend Flicka, The Adventures of Jim Bowie* and *M-Squad* were just a handful of shows where Mazurki's very recognizable face showed up. His TV work continued with full steam into the '60s and '70s on *Have Gun, Will Travel, Perry Mason, The Munsters, Mister Ed* and numerous other shows, in the comedy, western and drama categories.

As familiar in show business as Mazurki was, one of the largest parts of his personal legacy was a little fraternity known as the Cauliflower Alley Club, a non-profit group of professional wrestlers and boxers. Established in 1965, the club had its roots at the Baron's Castle Buffet Restaurant in Los Angeles, an eatery owned by Mazurki, where he and others in the wrestling and movie industry would meet and eat regularly. The organization is still active today and even uses a photo of Mazurki's ear (swollen and cauliflower-like from all the in-ring abuse through the years) as its logo. He continued his connection with the wrestling profession, throughout his acting career. Twice married, the actor died in Glendale, California on December 11, 1990. He was eighty-two years old. Earlier the same year, he had appeared in *Dick Tracy*, a reworking of the film of the same title from 1945, in which he played the scarred villain, Splitface.

Hattie McDaniel

When being condemned by members of her own race for playing stereotypical domestics in films of the 1930s and 1940s, character great Hattie McDaniel was known for saying, "Why should I complain about making $7,000 a week playing a maid? If I didn't, I'd be making $7 a week being one." True, she played mostly maids, mammies, cooks and housekeepers throughout her career but her personal warmth, humor and natural spark of humanity was consistently displayed, offering more than many who also played the same kind of roles. Despite being cast in the same type of part, McDaniel achieved so much in her interpretation of it, with her career culminating with the distinction of being the first African-American to win an Academy Award.

Born on June 10, 1895, in Wichita, Kansas, Hattie was the youngest of thirteen children. Her father, Henry McDaniel, was a former slave, who fought in the Civil War and later became a Baptist minister and her mother, also born into slavery, was a singer of religious music. In 1900, Henry moved his family to Colorado, first to Fort Collins, then to Denver, where Hattie was enrolled at the 24th Street Elementary School, one of only two black students to do so at the turn of the century. She later attended East Denver High School and began singing at the Central Baptist Church. The actress recalls singing constantly, to the point that her "mother would say, 'Hattie I'll pay you to hush,' and give [her] a dime." She began traveling with her brother Otis McDaniel's minstrel show and later carried her singing over to the radio, where she performed with Professor George Morrison's orchestra, the *Melody Hounds*. When work was slow, Hattie would take a job as a maid to make ends meet. She headlined the Pantages circuit in the mid '20s, where she was called "the colored Sophie Tucker."

With the stock market crash of 1929, McDaniel, like others in her field, was left without a job. She traveled to Milwaukee, hoping to find work at Sam Pick's Club Madrid, where new talent was often hired. Indeed, McDaniel was hired, but instead of being the newest showstopper, she got a job at Club Madrid as a ladies' room attendant for $1.00 a night, plus tips. One night, the manager called for volunteer talent from the staff, when Hattie belted out a rendition of *St. Louis Blues*, garnering herself a job in the floor show, where she stayed until she decided to head west for Hollywood.

Her brother Sam and sisters Etta and Orlena had already moved to California, where Sam and Etta worked at bit parts in the movies and Orlena ran a rooming house for Pullman porters. When Hattie arrived in Hollywood in 1931, she began making the rounds as an entertainer and got a few roles as an extra but not enough to sustain a living at it, so again she took in washing. She eventually landed more and higher profile parts, not huge, but noticeable. After playing over a dozen uncredited bits, she appeared with the very popular humorist Will Rogers in his 1934 movie, *Judas Priest*, even singing with the star. She played numerous roles, always as a domestic, through the mid and late '30s, sometimes causing controversy with various groups. In 1935, she appeared in two different movies, which garnered a negative reaction from opposite spectrums of society. In *The Little Colonel*, which starred Shirley Temple and Lionel Barrymore, the actress played Mom Beck, a black servant, happy in her station in the Old South. Her critics claim that her portrayal made servitude for economic security pleasing. *Alice Adams*, on the other hand, saw certain white audiences in the South unhappy about her portrayal of a disdainful and insolent maid, who steals many scenes from the stars of the picture.

In 1938, Hollywood was buzzing with the casting and preparation of the most anticipated movie of the decade, *Gone with the Wind*. All the hub-bub wasn't limited to the decision of who was going to play the most coveted part of Scarlett O'Hara and a key supporting role of Mammy, the devoted house slave of the O'Hara family was also up for grabs. None other than Elizabeth McDuffie, the White House cook, tested for producer David O. Selznick, who never shied away from publicity of any kind, after First Lady Eleanor Roosevelt suggested the talented member of her staff. A more serious consideration was Louise Beavers. One of, if not the leading African-American movie actresses, Beavers had made a name for herself in the dramatic Universal film, *Imitation of Life* in 1934. Ultimately, McDaniel was chosen to play the role and was awarded an Oscar for her efforts, the first of her race to do so.

Due to Georgia's segregation laws at the time, the actress was not allowed to attend the December 1939 premiere in Atlanta. She did, however, attend the Hollywood premiere, later the same month. In the leap year of 1940, the Academy Award ceremonies for films made in 1939 were held on February 29, at the Cocoanut Grove nightclub in the Ambassador Hotel. Although McDaniel was able to attend the event, being nominated for one of the awards, she was not allowed to sit at the same table with Selznick and her white co-stars, instead relegated with her escort to the rear of the restaurant. The actress was nonetheless overcome with emotion when her name was called as the winner of that year's award for Best Actress in a Supporting Role. Wiping tears from her eyes, she made her acceptance speech.

"Academy of Motion Picture Arts and Sciences, fellow members of the motion picture industry and honored guests, this is one of the happiest moments of my life and I want to thank each one of who had a part in selecting me for one of their awards; for your kindness that has made me feel very, very humble. And I shall always hold it as a beacon for anything that I may be able to do in the future. I sincerely hope I shall always be a credit to my race and to the motion picture industry. My heart is too full to tell you just how I feel, and may I say thank you and God bless you."

After *GWTW*, Hattie appeared in a string of hits at Warner Brothers, where she had signed a contract, including *The Great Lie* (1941) with Bette Davis, *They Died with Their Boots On* (1941) with Errol Flynn and Olivia de Havilland and *In This Our Life* (1942), again with Davis and de Havilland. She worked through the rest of the decade, eventually appearing in less successful movies. Then in the late '40s, she became the star of her own radio program, *Beulah*, yet again playing a maid, but this time the maid was the lead character. She replaced Ethel Waters after the first season of *Beulah* on television but was herself replaced by Louise Beavers, when she fell ill with breast cancer. She was eventually taken to the hospital at the Motion Picture House in Woodland Hills, California, where she died on October 26, 1952, at the age of fifty-seven.

The actress had been wed four times, the first two marriages ending with each husband's death. The two subsequent unions ended in divorce. Throughout her life and career in movies, she was thankful for the good fortune that she received. She was quoted as saying, "My desire for the part of Mammy was not dominated by selfishness, for Hollywood has been good to me and I am grateful." A talented and interesting powerhouse in films, Hattie McDaniel was an example in which to follow.

Una Merkel

It could be said that cute and chirpy character actress Una Merkel owed her career to silent film star Lillian Gish. The uncanny resemblance between the two actresses led to Merkel's being hired as Gish's stand-in for her 1920 silent *Way Down East*, and again in 1928 for *The Wind*. In her heyday, Merkel was best-known for playing the best friend to the film's female star; a pretty wench (but not as pretty as the leading lady by the standards of casting directors) who could deliver a wisecrack with a smart mouth and a tart tongue in a smooth southern drawl.

The drawl was homegrown, as Una was born in Covington, Kentucky, on December 10, 1903, the only child of Arno and Bessie Merkel. Arno was a traveling salesman, who hawked calendars, Lifesavers and a soda called Cherry Smash, which Merkel recalls made her quite "popular with the kids at school." Until she was nine years-old, Una and her mother traveled with Arno throughout the South by horse and buggy while staying in boarding houses. The family then moved to Philadelphia, where a teenaged Una attended school before moving to New York to try her hand at the stage. She studied dance at the Alviene Academy of Theater and Cultural Arts (where Fred and Adele Astaire also tapped toes) and earned money as an extra at D.W. Griffith's Mamaroneck Studios, as well as modeling for *True Story* magazine.

Her first feature film credit was a leading role in the silent melodrama, *The Fifth Horseman* in 1924. Besides her light film work, she continued her attention to the New York stage, with brief parts in brief plays throughout the '20s, gaining little traction until 1927, when she was cast with Helen Hayes in *Coquette*, which ran for twenty-two months. Merkel and Hayes became friends, and it was Una who caught the bouquet at Helen's wedding to playwright and screenwriter Charles MacArthur in 1928.

With the dawn of talking pictures and the new decade, legendary director D. W. Griffith began work on his first sound film, *Abraham Lincoln* (1930). Merkel was cast by Griffith, a fellow Kentuckian, in the part of first lady Mary Todd Lincoln, but when filming began, the director decided instead to give her the part of Abe Lincoln's early love Ann Rutledge. The film was released by United Artists, as was Una's next feature, *The Bat Whispers*, a thriller which co-starred Chester Morris. From then on, she worked steadily throughout the Depression years, including a turn as cute and sexy Effie Perine, secretary to Sam Spade (Ricardo Cortez) in the original, pre-Code version of Dashiell Hammett's mystery classic, *The Maltese Falcon* in 1931. That same year, the actress signed a seven-year contract with Metro-Goldwyn-Mayer, the crème de la crème of Hollywood studios. Her tenure at MGM was as a featured player and it was during this period that Merkel developed the on-screen persona that would be her trademark: perky best friend to the star with a snappy comeback and a knowing wink. In *Red-Headed Woman* (1932), she plays Sally, gal-pal to gold-digger Jean Harlow and tosses out a prime example of the kind of dialogue she would be known for:

Lillian 'Lil' (Harlow): I'm not gonna spend my whole life on the wrong side of the railroad tracks.

Sally: I hope you don't get hit by a train while you're crossing over.

As attractive as Merkel was, she found her distinction as the comic relief in dramas or a fun addition in outright comedies, which offered no competition to her big name, female counterpart. Besides Harlow, she wisecracked alongside film beauties Loretta Young, Carole Lombard and Dorothy Lamour.

Metro loaned their new contract player to Warner Brothers on occasion and one such outing proved to be one of Merkel's best and most remembered films. In Warners' hit musical *42nd Street* (1933), Una and Ginger Rogers are a riot as snappy chorus girls Lorraine and 'Anytime' Annie, both as cute as a button and sharp as a tack. These blonde chorines shine as part of the lively number "Shuffle Off to Buffalo." Back at MGM the gum-chewing kewpie doll appeared in some of the studio's most popular musicals of the period, including *Broadway Melody of 1936* (1935), *Born to Dance* (1936, both with dancer Eleanor Powell) and *The Merry Widow* (1934). She would also appear in the 1952 remake of *The Merry Widow* with Lana Turner.

After leaving MGM in the late '30s, Merkel worked as a free-lance artist as well appearing on the radio in the *Texaco Star Theatre* from 1938 through 1940. The frequency of her film appearances slowed, and the quality of her scripts slacked in the 1940s, though she continued her radio work, as well as going on a USO tour through the South Pacific with Gary Cooper and Phyllis Brooks, a pretty blonde, minor actress and former girlfriend of Cary Grant. Tragedy hit Merkel's family in 1945, when her mother committed suicide in the home they shared together. Una narrowly escaped death when Mrs. Merkel turned on the gas stove in their apartment and slit her own wrists. She tried to shield her daughter from the gas fumes by stuffing a bath towel under the door. The period was a dark one for the comedienne. At the time of the incident, the actress was estranged from her husband of fifteen years, Ronald Burla, an aviation designer who became the assistant to the president of North American Aviation. She filed for divorce in Miami in late 1946 after two and a half years of separation. Then, almost seven years to the day of her mother's suicide, in March 1952, Merkel was rushed to the Santa Monica hospital after being found by the nurse who was attending her for a bout of influenza. The actress had taken an overdose of sleeping pills and was in a coma a full day after her hospitalization.

She recovered, as did her career, with her movement back to the stage in 1953 for *The Remarkable Mr. Pennypacker* on Broadway with Burgess Meredith, which she followed up in 1956 with *The Ponder Heart,* featuring David Wayne and Will Geer. For the latter, Merkel won a Tony award and began a new phase in her movie career, playing middle-aged women, down-to-earth aunts and homespun mothers. Highlights include the Debbie Reynolds comedy *Bundle of Joy* (1956) and Walt Disney's *The Parent Trap* (1961). After a body of film work that covered decades, Merkel was nominated for an Academy Award as Best Supporting Actress in *Summer and Smoke* (1961), which was based on the Tennessee Williams play. Her last movie appearance was in the 1966 Elvis Presley vehicle *Spinout.*

Having no children of her own and never remarrying after her divorce from Burla, Una continued to live with her father in Los Angeles until his death in 1969. Merkel passed away on January 2, 1986 at the age of eighty-two and was buried near her parents in Kentucky. Never one to be self-centered or focus on her looks, the comedienne once told author Richard Lamparski, "I really was kinda cute," adding, "I wish I'd known that then. I always thought I came over like a little hick."

Thomas Mitchell

      To look at the film resume of actor Thomas Mitchell is like looking at a Greatest Films list from the golden age of Hollywood, an impressive, well-crafted body of work of which any motion picture thespian would be envious. In other words, he was a superstar among character players. When delving into biographical retrospectives of Mitchell, the descriptive word that emerges more than any other is: versatile. Despite his great talent, there were no extraordinary physical traits that made him stand out from the pack. He carried his beefy frame with confidence or diffidence, depending on what his role called for. His chubby chipmunk cheeks, which dimpled when he smiled, fell below intense, brooding eyes. As respected and well-received an actor as Mitchell was, his modesty didn't go unnoticed when it presented itself in public. When his name was announced as the winner of the Best Supporting Actor at the 1940

Academy Awards ceremony, Mitchell humbly stated, "I didn't think I was that good. I don't have a speech, I'm too incoherent."

The youngest of seven children, Thomas Mitchell was born in Elizabeth, New Jersey on July 11, 1892, to Irish immigrants James and Mary Mitchell. Following in the footsteps of his father and brother, both newspapermen, Mitchell became a reporter, working for his brother John, the managing editor of the *Newark Journal*, where he earned a whopping twenty-five cents for his first full-length column. He worked in Baltimore, Washington and Pittsburg before eventually realizing that he enjoyed writing theatrical skits more than news items.

In 1913, he began his stage career in earnest, touring extensively with fellow future character actor Charles Coburn, who had formed his own troupe called the Coburn Shakespearean Players in 1905. He made his Broadway debut in 1916, working in a play called *Under Sentence* with Edward G. Robinson and Frank Morgan. He continued working on the New York stage in small roles, as well as writing and directing on some level, into the 1920s. Besides his work on the Great White Way, Mitchell made his film debut in a silent comedy called *Six Cylinder Love* (1923), which also featured the debuts of actors who would make their own mark as character players in Hollywood: Florence Eldridge (Mrs. Fredric March) and Donald Meek.

The next time he graced the screen was sixteen years later, when he moved to California and signed a lucrative three-way contract with Columbia Pictures, as actor, writer and director. It was his acting that got the most attention, however, and before long, it became his career focus. His first movie under his new contract was *Craig's Wife* (1936), starring Rosalind Russell. It was a small role but did receive a very brief mention in Frank Nugent's New York Times review. He finally got noticed for his role in Frank Capra's classic filmization of James Hilton's novel, *Lost Horizon* (1937) and later the same year he was cast in director John Ford's epic *The Hurricane*, for which he was nominated for an Academy Award.

Historically known as Hollywood's golden year, 1939 saw a number of high quality, high profile and extremely popular motion pictures. For Thomas Mitchell, it was certainly one of the most memorable in his career. The actor appeared in five films during 1939. In *Only Angels Have Wings*, he co-starred with two of Hollywood's biggest and most popular stars, Cary Grant and Jean Arthur. He appeared with Arthur again in Frank Capra's *Mr. Smith Goes to Washington*. As Clopin, fifteenth-century peasant, he was one of several well-respected actors in RKO's *The Hunchback of Notre Dame*. Mitchell was cast as Gerald O'Hara, Irish father to southern vixen Scarlett, in the year's (as well as the decade's) biggest hit, *Gone with the Wind* and rounding out his esteemed offerings was his part as alcoholic MD, Doc Boone in John Ford's *Stagecoach*, which was a break-out film for its star, John Wayne. For the last title, Mitchell won the Oscar for Best Supporting Actor, an honor hard-earned, based on his time spent on the set. When Ford, noted for bullying his stars, tried to strong-arm Mitchell over an issue, the actor responded by saying, "That's alright, I've seen *Mary of Scotland*," one of the director's major flops (some versions of the story name *Arrowsmith* as the film in question), flustering the blustering Ford.

The 1940s also proved to be a source of rich characterizations for the multi-talented actor. He starred again with John Wayne in *The Long Voyage Home* (1940) and at Warner Brothers he worked alongside John Garfield in *Out of the Fog* (1941). He was cast in the prestigious RKO production *The Devil and Daniel Webster*, slated to be released in 1941, but when the actor suffered an accident on the set, portly star Edward Arnold replaced him, though some long shots featuring Mitchell were left in the final picture.

True for any talented actor, Thomas (or Tommy as he was known since childhood) could easily move from one character to an extremely different personality. He made the smooth transition from scurvy pirate Tom Blue in the Tyrone Power swashbuckler *The Black Swan* (1942) to atheist doctor Willie Tulloch in the Fox religious drama *The Keys of the Kingdom* (1944). Then, in 1946, in a complete turnabout, Mitchell played what is arguably his most memorable role (with contemporary audiences anyway). Director Frank Capra hired him as one of an ensemble cast of character stars (including Ward Bond, Beulah Bondi, Henry Travers and many more) for *It's a Wonderful Life*. As Uncle Billy Bailey, Mitchell brought to the audience a combination of both pathos and irritation, with his portrayal of the bumbling, weak yet loveable building and loan partner, whose carelessness causes near catastrophe.

Always exploring new career territory, Mitchell moved to television work in the 1950s, even being Emmy-nominated three times during the decade, with a win in 1952. The following year he was back on Broadway, winning a Tony Award as Best Actor for the musical *Hazel Flagg*, making him the first actor to win the "triple crown" of acting awards: An Oscar, Emmy and Tony. Still active on television and films well into older age, Mitchell passed away on Monday, December 17, 1962, from bone cancer. He was seventy years-old.

Frank Morgan

"Pay no attention to that man behind the curtain."

Recognized 'round the world as one of the great lines from classic movie history, it, of course, is from *The Wizard of Oz*, and refers to Frank Morgan, who played the great and powerful Oz, as well as four other roles in the film. On screen, the actor was known as a perpetually absent-mined scatterbrain who fumbled and bumbled through more than fifty films at MGM alone from the early '30s through the late '40s. Morgan had gained such a grand reputation as a fine character actor at Metro-Goldwyn-Mayer that the studio reportedly offered him a lifetime contract.

The baby of a family of eleven children, Morgan was born Francis Phillip Wuppermann in New York City on June 1, 1890. His father, George Diogracia Wuppermann, was, at fifty-two, well into middle age by the time his youngest was born. George was half-Spanish, born in

Venezuela and raised in Hamburg, Germany. Morgan's mother, Josephine Hancox, was born in the United States of English heritage, came from a well-to-do family from the Hudson Bay area and reportedly had relatives on the *Mayflower*. As George was the president of Angostura-Wuppermann, sole agents for Angostura bitters in the U.S., Canada, Mexico and Cuba, he supported his brood in luxurious style.

As a young man, Morgan attended Cornell University for a time, where he was a member of the Phi Kappa Psi Fraternity. He then took on a variety of jobs across the country, including advertising sales for *The Boston Traveler* and cow-punching in Nevada. Not keen on joining the family business, he eventually followed his older brother, Raphael, who had changed his name to Ralph Morgan, to the stage. Ralph would become a noted movie character actor himself and in 1933, the first president of the Screen Actors Guild. He started out in vaudeville, then in late March 1914, young Francis made his Broadway debut in the Lyceum Theatre in a single performance of a show called *A Woman Killed with Kindness*. He went on under the name Frank Morgan, although his next play, *Mr. Wu*, presented later the same year, would see him billed as Frank Wupperman (less one "n" than his birth name) before reverting back to the Morgan surname permanently.

Less than three weeks before making his bow in *A Woman Killed with Kindness*, Frank eloped with nineteen-year-old Alma Muller, whom he had met the previous year. She was the daughter of a wealthy New York real estate tycoon and although the marriage had a rocky start, the couple remained together until Morgan's death and had a son, George, named for Frank's father.

The actor continued throughout the next decade appearing in all manner of theatrical productions including musicals, comedies, farce and dramas, both on and off Broadway. In 1916, he made his film debut in New York and worked steadily in silent movies as well, though at this point in his career he preferred the stage. His reputation grew on Broadway and he easily gravitated to comedy, starring in several shows in the mid and late '20s.

Although he had made several film appearances in New York (when production was still a viable option there in the early part of the twentieth century), he showed disdain for actors who made the move to the west coast and motion pictures. In his 1979 autobiography, *When the*

Smoke Hit the Fan, actor Ralph Bellamy, who also became a popular character actor of the day, recalled his friend Morgan's reaction when he met him en route to Hollywood in 1930: "Frank Morgan . . . came to the Santa Fe station to see me off with the most vituperative language, including calling me a prostitute, selling out for money. Six months later, at the end of the road tour of *Topaze*, Frank was in Hollywood, under contract to MGM."

Although he wouldn't join Metro until 1933, Morgan did begin making pictures in Hollywood in the early '30s at Paramount and RKO. A handsome man in his early '40s, the actor became one of the most esteemed players on the MGM lot and developed the loveable, bumbling on-screen persona which would carry him through the rest of his career. In 1934, he was loaned out to Twentieth Century Pictures (just before they merged with the Fox Film Corporation to form Twentieth Century-Fox) for the Renaissance comedy-drama, *The Affairs of Cellini* with Fredric March and Constance Bennett. As the cuckolded Duke of Florence, Morgan reprised the role he played so well on Broadway in *The Firebrand* in the 1924-25 season. For his characterization of the dithering Duke he was nominated for an Oscar in the Best Actor category, though he lost out to Clark Gable for *It Happened One Night*.

In September 1938, after five years of being a contract player at MGM, the studio cast him in the title role of *The Wizard of Oz*. It was an ambitious picture and Morgan wasn't the first choice for the enviable role. The film's producer, Mervyn LeRoy, wanted vaudeville and radio star Ed Wynn for the part, but the comedian declined, viewing it as too small. W.C. Fields was also considered and offered the enormous sum of $75,000 to play what was virtually a cameo, but the popular comedian requested $100,000 and negotiations ended. MGM's own Wallace Berry was brought up as a possibility, but his stock at the company had fallen in recent years and he was headlining B-pictures by the time *Oz* came along. Morgan wanted the part badly and requested an audition. It was successful, and the studio was impressed enough to cast him not only as the Wizard, but also as Professor Marvel, a rather flustered old charlatan at the beginning of the movie, as well as the Emerald City Gatekeeper, the Carriage Driver and the Guard. The thinking was that Morgan was a big enough name to warrant more screen time than just that required of the Wizard at the end of the picture.

Morgan was a member of the famed Irish Mafia in Hollywood during the early '40s, which included actors James Cagney, Pat O'Brien, Frank McHugh, Ralph Bellamy, Spencer Tracy and Lynne Overman. According to Cagney the group of colorful actors "would get together once a week, have dinner, and make the talk." More than a couple of drinks were downed during their gatherings, as well. Morgan's alcoholism was well-known within the Hollywood colony, though it never hindered his performances or his professionalism. His little black suitcase, containing a miniature bar was a familiar sight on his film sets.

The year after *Oz* was a notable one for the actor, as he appeared in two of his best films. *The Shop Around the Corner* teamed him with two of the year's biggest stars, James Stewart and Margaret Sullavan, and the three reunited later in the year for *The Mortal Storm*, MGM's effort to expose Nazism across the Atlantic. Morgan's performance was one of his finest, a point on which Stewart and Sullavan agreed, with Margaret telling director Frank Borzage: "Frank has played so many dithering idiots and damned fools and dunces and dolts in so many pictures that people forget how wonderful he can be in a straight, serious role."

In the 1940s, Morgan appeared on the radio program *Maxwell House Coffee Time* with comedienne Fanny Brice, who played her famous character Baby Snooks. He also starred in his own program, *The Frank Morgan Show* on NBC in 1944-45. His radio appearances didn't slow his work on the screen, however, and he continued to be a great asset to Metro in some of their biggest hits of the decade, including *Honky Tonk* (1941), *Tortilla Flat* (1942; gaining another Oscar nomination, this time for Best Supporting Actor), *Green Dolphin Street* (1947) and a splashy Technicolor version of *The Three Musketeers* (1948), playing King Louis XIII.

In September 1949, Morgan was in the process of costume tests for his next feature, *Annie Get Your Gun* and just finished filming *Key to the City* with Clark Gable and Loretta Young. A few days later, on Sunday, September 18, both his wife and the housekeeper went into the bedroom at the Morgans' Beverly Hills home to find the actor still sleeping and left the room as not to disturb him. When Mrs. Morgan returned later, she found that her husband wasn't breathing and called for an inhalator squad (an older term for ambulance), but efforts to resuscitate him were fruitless. He died of a heart attack at fifty-nine years-old. Louis Calhern replaced him in *Annie Get Your Gun* and *Key to the City* was released the following year posthumously.

On the following Tuesday, the All Saints Protestant Episcopal Church in Beverly Hills was filled with friends and mourners. Clark Gable and Pat O'Brien were honorary pall bearers and Reginald Owen, Otto Kruger, Frank McHugh, and Ward Bond served as ushers. His friend James Cagney said of Frank Morgan, "What a wonderful man! What fun to be with!" and fans of his movies can also say, what fun to watch.

Agnes Moorehead

Some character actors during the golden age of Hollywood were great because they developed an on-screen persona that didn't deviate too much from one movie to the next. Instead of being boring, this consistency was a clue from their earliest scene in a film that it would be fun because you knew what to expect from them. On the other hand, a great actor, character or otherwise, could handle different types of roles and film genres with equal ease, making their version of a comic cafeteria worker just as believable as their interpretation of a dying duke or duchess. One such actress was Agnes Moorehead.

The first film I saw Moorehead play in wasn't her most famous, not even her fifth most famous, but it was a powerful role nonetheless, despite its brevity. The picture was *Jane Eyre* (1944) and the part in question was Mrs. Reed, Jane's hateful, selfish, aunt, whose overprotectiveness of her spoiled son brought about young Eyre's transfer to the dark and depressing orphanage where she would spend the remainder of her childhood. Like most, I had enjoyed Moorehead's tenure as the wacky and colorful Endora on the '60s sitcom *Bewitched*, but to see her in this very dramatic and very intense capacity in black and white was something to remember.

Agnes was born in Clinton, Massachusetts on December 6, 1900. Her father was a Presbyterian minister and her first public performance was from her father's pulpit where she recited the Lord's Prayer at the age of three. Her family moved to St. Louis, Missouri, where Moorehead would sing in the chorus of the St. Louis Municipal Opera Company. Upon her graduation from Central High School in 1918, her father insisted that Agnes further her education. She attended Muskingum College in New Concord, Ohio where she earned a bachelor's degree in Biology and later to the University of Wisconsin, where she obtained a master's in English literature. Though she taught public school while working on gaining her master's degree, her dreams of the theater continued, and she eventually made the move to New York, where she graduated from the American Academy of Dramatic Art in 1929.

The well-educated, highly intelligent Moorehead married actor Jack G. Lee in June 1930, as she continued searching for acting jobs. Success did not come easy or fast for the actress, who at 30 years-old, was already "mature" for an industry that placed great stock in youth. She eventually began appearing in radio dramas and found steady work in that medium, including the role of Margo Lane opposite Orson Welles as crime-fighter Lamont Cranston in "The Shadow" series. It was her professional involvement with Welles, regarded by many as a genius in his mid-twenties, which turned the tide of her career and allowed her the success she had sought. At Welles' invitation, Agnes joined the newly-formed Mercury Theater, a repertory company founded by the actor and his friend, producer John Houseman in 1937. In 1939, Welles and his troupe moved the Mercury to Hollywood and signed a contract with RKO Studio, where his masterpiece, *Citizen Kane*, would be produced and released in 1941. The eminent actor played Charles Foster Kane, a newspaper tycoon based on real-life newspaperman William Randolph Hearst. Agnes was cast as Kane's mother, Mary, and went on with the other Mercury actors to appear in Welles' *The Magnificent Ambersons* (1942) and *Journey Into Fear* (1943).

Throughout her film, radio and television career, Moorehead built her reputation on versatility. As Violette Shumberg in RKO's *The Big Street* (1942), she displayed light-hearted warmth toward the much put-upon Henry Fonda. In contrast, her character Emily Hawkins in David O. Selznick's *Since You Went Away* (1944) was a nasty, gossipy shrew toward Claudette Colbert and her circle. Her timid, mentally unstable Countess Fosco in Warner Brothers' *The Woman in White* (1948) was a far cry from Aggie MacDonald, the hard-working, no-nonsense aunt of deaf-mute *Johnny Belinda* (also 1948). Highly acclaimed, she was nominated four times for an Oscar as Best Supporting Actress with nary a win, though she did win Golden Globes for the same category in 1945 and 1965. Her accolades also included numerous Emmy nominations for her work in television.

Radio continued to be an important venue for Moorehead and the actress made several appearances on the CBS series *Suspense* throughout the 1940s. Her most famous performance for the show was a 1943 episode of "Sorry, Wrong Number," in which she played a neurotic invalid who overhears her own murder being plotted over the telephone. The radio play was made into a very successful film in 1948 with Barbara Stanwyck in the part of the bedridden victim. With the growing popularity of television, Moorehead gained steady work in the format, finding her largest audience of fans as Endora, flamboyant witch-mother to Elizabeth Montgomery's Samantha in the long-running ABC series *Bewitched*.

Divorced from her first husband in 1952, Agnes married and divorced again before the 1950s ended, living the rest of her life as a single woman. In 1954, Moorehead was cast in *The Conqueror*, released in 1956. Parts of the movie were filmed on location near St. George, Utah, 137 miles downwind of the Yucca Flat Nevada Nuclear test sight. She was one of dozens of actors and crew members who developed cancer after working on the picture, including the film's stars John Wayne and Susan Hayward, as well as producer/director Dick Powell. The extremely talented actress died of uterine cancer on April 30, 1974, leaving behind a wealth of fine performances.

Virginia O'Brien

  Several stars from Hollywood's golden age had a schtick, a trademark to their persona that only they perfected, and with that single gimmick they parlayed success in Tinsel Town. Their niche was an often forgotten (by all but the most loyal of classic movie fans) but revealing slice of pop culture of the day. Charlotte Greenwood used her long lanky limbs to dance all sorts of limber lumbering in musicals throughout the '30s and '40s at Fox. Paramount comedienne Martha Raye was known as "The Big Mouth," due to her oversized kisser and the raucous delivery that spouted from it. Brazilian bombshell Carmen Miranda made a career out of being... Carmen Miranda, the rainbow dressed, fruit-laden tressed, Latin lady who appeared in the biggest and splashiest color-fests produced at 20th Century-Fox in the early 1940s. During the same period,

MGM hired and promoted its own novelty act, a striking brunette who graced numerous comedies and musicals throughout the war years and created her unique yet entertaining trademark: the Deadpan.

Virginia O'Brien was a dark-haired beauty, who, if one only saw her publicity photos, would appear to be one of the studio's sultry, sloe-eyed vamps. Physically reminiscent of glamour girls Joan Bennett and Hedy Lamarr, O'Brien carved her niche as a singer who used a "deadpan" style, warbling out comic, pun-filled ditties with nary a facial movement, even projecting a deer-in-headlights look. The fun and funny Sphinx garnered the nicknames "Miss Deadpan," and "Miss Red Hot Frozen Face," and co-starred with the biggest names at Metro-Goldwyn-Mayer.

Virginia Lee O'Brien was born on April 18, 1919 in Los Angeles. Her father was Thomas O'Brien, the captain of detectives for the Los Angeles Police Department and later in life, LA county deputy district attorney. Her other ancestral claims to fame included General Robert E. Lee on her mother's side and one of her uncles was noted film director Lloyd Bacon, who made a name for himself at Warner Brothers during the Depression-era years. As a youngster, the tall, raven-haired teen studied business and commercial law at North Hollywood High School, where she graduated in 1937, with thoughts of pursuing a legal career, a path encouraged by her law enforcement father. Growing up, however, she was interested in singing and dancing and began taking lessons. With this interest driving her, the young hopeful won a part in a 1939 revue presented by the Los Angeles Assistance League Players entitled *Meet the People*, when fate stepped in and intervened with a career-defining chain of events.

Making her debut in the West Coast production, O'Brien went on stage to sing her number, when she was overcome with fright. Paralyzed with fear, the young singer realized that the show had to go on, and she sung her number, but instead of sashaying around the stage like her idol Ethel Merman, she performed almost motionless and with a "frozen face." The audience didn't know what to make of her at first, then believed the singer's sphinx-like warbling was part of the act and roared with laughter. O'Brien later recalled her angst, saying: "I was so scared the best I could do was move my shoulders. So, I did. Everything else was rigid except my mouth... At the end of my number I ran into the wings and cried. I was awful, but I was the hit of the show." She kept the schtick and the Deadpan Diva was born.

Rumor has it that L.B. Mayer himself caught a performance and scheduled a screen test for the funny brunette, which subsequently led to a contract with MGM, where she made her movie debut in 1940. She had two uncredited bit parts before getting cast in *Hullabaloo*, a musical comedy starring Frank Morgan. Her entire career consisted of nineteen films and of those, all but the last two were made at Metro in the 1940s. The studio wasn't sure how to utilize her particular brand of comedy and she was often featured as a specialty number in many of their top musicals. Also in 1940, she debuted on Broadway with Jimmy Durante and Ray Bolger in the musical revue, *Keep Off the Grass*, increasing her professional exposure even further by recording four of the songs from the show for Columbia Records.

In 1941, O'Brien made an appearance in the Marx Brothers comedy, *The Big Store*, creating an impression with her dead-pan rendition of *Rock-a-Bye-Baby* during the *Sing While You Sell* number. As Flo Foster in the film version of the stage hit, *Panama Hattie* (1942), she sang three numbers, including *"(Did I Get Stinkin') At the Club Savoy,"* a hilarious highlight in the picture. While riding a professional high at MGM, albeit a rather limited one, Virginia got married. On October 11, 1942, she eloped to Yuma, Arizona with actor and radio personality Kirk Alyn, who was famous for being the first actor to play a live-action version of DC comic icon Superman in the 1948 serial. As newlyweds, the couple took an apartment in Beverly Hills and eventually had three children before divorcing in 1955.

The war years proved busy for O'Brien, with appearances in *Lady Be Good* (1941), *Ship Ahoy* (1942) and *DuBarry was a Lady* (1943). One of her best-known roles was as Alma, the man-hungry "plain Jane" in *The Harvey Girls* (1946), with Judy Garland and Ray Bolger. The irony was, as lovely as O'Brien was, she pulled off "ugly duckling" Alma charmingly, particularly with lines like: "I sent my picture into one of those Lonely Hearts Clubs and they sent it back, saying "We're NOT that lonely!" While filming *The Harvey Girls*, the actress committed the unpardonable career sin... she became pregnant. Her condition limited the time she had in front of the camera and when star Judy Garland caused delays on the set,

O'Brien literally disappeared from the second half of the film without any explanation.

In 1947, Virginia filmed *Merton of the Movies* with Red Skelton, a story set during the silent picture years, after which Metro did not renew her contract and she virtually retired from the screen with the exception of *Francis in the Navy* in 1955 and *Gus* in 1976 (ironically both films featuring mules). She did however continue working on the stage and television well into her sixties, even developing her own cabaret act in the 1980s. As for her personal life, after her divorce from Alwyn, the actress married twice more. On January 16, 2001, at the age of eighty-one, Virginia O'Brien died at the Motion Picture and Television Hospital in Woodland Hills, California, with burial at the Forest Lawn Memorial Park in Glendale, California. If given a greater opportunity, it would be interesting to see the entertainer blossom into a bigger star, however, the "Deadpan Diva" took the hand she was dealt and came away a pretty big winner.

U n a   O' C o n n o r

       She perfected her typical role as the supreme busybody, whether it be in the form of local spinster, cook or charwoman, with names like Effie, Maggie or Nora and always sporting her thick and distinctive Irish accent. Una O'Connor was usually found in a film playing a scrawny crone, shuffling along like a sanctimonious bird with a sharp tongue, flailing arms and enormous eyes and much as she may have wanted to break from the mold, here career path as character actor had been set. She took it in stride though, once proclaiming, "There's no such thing as design in an acting career. You just go along with the tide. Nine times out of ten, one successful part will set you in a rut from which only a miracle can pry you." She was almost fifty when she made her first film, worked for world class directors such as Alfred Hitchcock, John Ford, and Jean Renoir and was used to great advantage by James Whale in two of Hollywood's most famous horror movies: *The Invisible Man* (1933) and *The Bride of Frankenstein* (1935).

As with many in her profession, O'Connor came into the world with a different name than the one for which she would later be known. Agnes Teresa McGlade was born on October 23, 1880 in Belfast, Ireland. Her mother died when Una was only two years-old and her father, a "gentleman farmer," moved to Australia. She was raised by an aunt who had eleven children of her own. A staunch Catholic from an early age, O'Connor attended convent schools and was deeply religious throughout her life. She later studied in Paris and eventually graduated from London's South Kensington School of Arts with an M.A. degree in the hopes of becoming a teacher.

Her interest turned instead to acting and she enrolled in the Abbey Players' School in Dublin and changed her name to O'Connor. She made her theatrical debut in the Abbey's production of *The Shewing Up of Blanco Posnet* in 1911 as an American ranch girl and reprised the role on the New York stage later the same year. For the next twenty years the actress would bounce back and forth between London and Broadway with a steady stream of stage roles. She made her film debut in a 1929 British sound picture called *Dark Red Roses*. The following year, director Alfred Hitchcock, not yet the master showman he would become, cast her in his early thriller, *Murder!*

O'Connor's big break, however, came when she was chosen by Noel Coward to appear in his stage extravaganza *Cavalcade* in London. She played Cockney charwoman Ellen Bridges and did such a fine job that when Hollywood planned a film version of the British drama in 1933, that she was asked to repeat the part on the screen. The movie was a grand success, winning three Academy Awards, including Best Picture and Best Director (Frank Lloyd). Una decided to remain in the United States and was in high demand as a prime Hollywood character actress. James Whale, director of the horror classic *Frankenstein* (1931), knew O'Connor from the London stage, and when he began work at Universal Studio on *The Invisible Man* in the summer of 1933, he hired the actress to play what she played best; a landlady and pub proprietress. When the movie hit theaters in November, H.G. Wells, author of the book on which it was based, criticized the production but praised Una's performance.

In 1935, she worked for Whale again in *The Bride of Frankenstein*. Although the film is technically a sequel to the 1931 monster movie, picking up where the former had left off, director Whale chose to take this picture in a different direction. The tone of the film was much less straightforward as a horror film and offered more lighthearted touches of camp comedic relief in the persons of Ernest Thesiger and O'Connor. As Doctor Pretorius, Thesiger plays the prissy mad scientist to the hilt and O'Connor has what is arguably her most famous role as Minnie, the shrieking, googly-eyed servant of Baron Frankenstein's household. As annoying as some found her character, other critics praised her work in the movie, with the *Hollywood Reporter* proclaiming: "Una O'Connor walks away with the feminine honors for as neat a bit of acting as has come to our eyes and ears for some time."

She continued her rich and rewarding film work throughout the '30s, including the high-profile *David Copperfield*, directed by George Cukor at MGM and *The Informer* for John Ford at RKO, proving what acting range she could offer. At Warner Brothers she used her bristling brogue as Bess, the much-married duenna of Olivia de Havilland's Maid Marian in the Technicolor masterpiece, *The Adventures of Robin Hood* (1938). In *Robin Hood*, she had screen time aplenty, even partaking in a bit of romance with Hebert Mundin, her *Cavalcade* co-star, as Much the Miller's Son.

Throughout the 1940s, O'Connor was busy both on stage and screen. She appeared in another Errol Flynn adventure, *The Sea Hawk*, in 1940 and even showed up yet again with Flynn in the costumer *The Adventures of Don Juan* eight years later. She was effective in the British based picture *This Land is Mine* with Charles Laughton in 1943 and had very visible roles in *The Bells of St. Mary's* with Bing Crosby and Ingrid Bergman. She appeared in *Christmas in Connecticut* with Barbara Stanwyck in 1945, as prudish housekeeper Nora, trading quips with fellow character alum "Cuddles" Sakall ("I never flipped in me life... I scoop them," referring to the best method of preparing flapjacks). The mid and late '40s also saw a return to Broadway for the actress, appearing in a handful of New York productions.

In her seventies, during the 1950s, O'Connor concentrated on the stage and television. In 1954, she played a key part in the Broadway production of Agatha Christie's *Witness for the Prosecution*. As the practically deaf witness Janet McKenzie, she offered, yet again, comic relief in an intense courtroom drama. She returned to Hollywood in 1957, after nearly a decade away from the big screen, to reprise the role in the screen version, starring Tyrone Power, Charles Laughton and Marlene Dietrich. Spending her last years in Manhattan, O'Connor died there, at the Mary Manning Walsh home (described in her obituary as "a Carmelite Sisters institution for the aged and infirm"), on February 4, 1959, from heart disease. She was seventy-eight years old. She never married, nor had children, but she left a legacy of fine performances throughout the first half of the twentieth century.

Warner Oland

To many hard-core cinephiles (or just fans of the old-time Sunday Afternoon Mystery Movie), Warner Oland is arguably the definitive Charlie Chan, in a gallery of actors to portray the fictional Chinese detective on film. Chan, the creation of novelist Earl Derr Biggers, was one of the most successful movie series during the classic age in Hollywood, first appearing on American screens in the silent years of cinema and continuing into the 1980s, with the most popular installments hitting theaters during the '30s and early '40s. Although Oland wasn't the first actor to portray the wise and soft-spoken detective, he, along with Sidney Toler after him, made the character a household name for decades after his films were released.

Chan wasn't the first Asian character that Oland played. On the contrary, he was frequently cast as evil Orientals early in his career, beginning in 1919, as a character named Wu Fang in the silent serial, *The Lightning Raider* and in the 1927 film, *Tell It to the Marines*, he plays a rogue simply known as "Chinese Bandit Thief." Two years later he starred as the infamous Oriental film villain, Fu Manchu, a role which he played more than once. For all the parts he played based on characters of Far Eastern descent, Warner Oland was, in fact, from Sweden, of Scandinavian ancestry. His exotic looks helped him create the illusion of being Asian. He told his frequent co-star, Keye Luke, that he owed his Chinese look to a certain amount of Mongolian blood in his heritage. To perfect the countenance, he simply combed his moustache down and his eyebrows up.

The actor was born Johan Verner Ölund outside Umea, in the county of Vasterbotten, Sweden, on October 3, 1879. His parents were Lutheran shopkeepers, thirty-three-year-old Jonas Ölund and Maria Johanna Forsberg, ten years her husband's junior. In October of 1892, when young Johan had just turned thirteen, the Ölunds emigrated to the United States, first to Connecticut, then moving to Massachusetts, Americanizing their name to Oland in the process. From an early age, Oland yearned to be an opera singer, but when he realized the years of dedicated training it would take, he turned to the dramatic stage. While still a teen, the ambitious youngster worked in a machine shop for $6 a week and joined Dr. Curry's School of Expression in Boston, a dramatic institution where "mind, body and voice [were] harmoniously trained for all professions." His first professional stage appearance was in *The Christian,* and in 1906, he began touring with the company led by actress Alla Nazimova.

It was during this period that Oland met artist and playwright Edith Shearn, an artist and sister of Clarence J. Shearn of the New York Supreme Court. The couple married in 1907 and collaborated on a translation of plays by Swedish playwright, August Strindbert, which was published in 1912. At the same time, Oland made his movie debut, getting paid $25 a day, playing John Bunyan in a silent adaption of *Pilgrim's Progress* in 1910. He returned to the stage, not making another picture until 1915 but continued to churn out films throughout the rest of the 1910s, appearing in a total of twenty-four before 1920.

The Twenties saw his bad-guy Asian roles mount up with names like Charley Yong, Fu Shing and Shanghai Dan. He also played villains that weren't necessarily from the Orient, as evidenced in his portrayal of Cesare Borgia in the 1926 silent version of *Don Juan*, with John Barrymore. The following year, Oland had a part in motion picture history, appearing in the first talking movie (though only partial talkie), *The Jazz Singer* with singer Al Jolson. Oland plays Cantor Rabinowitz, who is upset that his son (Jolson) wants to become a "jazz singer." As Jolson belts out "Blue Skies," Oland, as the disapproving Jewish patriarch, cries "Stop!" and that is his contribution to the talkie, as his latter lines are printed along the screen.

His portrayal of Fu Manchu in the films bearing that name made Oland well-known to moviegoers, so when the time came to cast the sage Asian detective, Charlie Chan, in the upcoming Fox Film Corporation mystery, *Charlie Chan Carries On*, the actor was a shoe-in. Although Chan's character doesn't emerge until roughly half-way through the movie, studio research showed it was the driving factor of the picture's success and when the next Chan outing was filmed as *The Black Camel*, later the same year, Oland solidly played the lead. The series was immensely popular, and Oland continued playing the wise and upbeat character in fourteen more films for Fox.

The earlier entries of the Chan series were one of the few sure-fire moneymakers for the Fox Film Corporation (before becoming 20th Century-Fox) before a tiny moppet named Shirley Temple came on the scene and became the top breadwinner for her studio. With his newfound popularity, Oland's salary rose considerably and he and his wife, Edith, lived comfortably. The actor continued making films outside the Chan franchise as well, crossing back and forth into the wickedly exotic roles which had brought him steady work a decade before. He costarred with Marlene Dietrich and Anna May Wong (one of the few true Asians to breakthrough to mainstream films) in Josef von Sternberg's pre-Code classic, *Shanghai Express* (1932) and was equally nasty taking Kay Francis into white slavery in Warner Brothers' glossy potboiler *Mandalay* (1934). He played a werewolf in Hollywood's first mainstream film of the genre, *Werewolf of London*, in 1935.

By all outward appearance, Oland was enjoying a successful career and financial security, but behind the scenes, the actor was suffering from alcoholism and fragile health. His marriage of thirty years was on the skids, with Edith filing for divorce in November 1937. He began filming

Charlie Chan at the Ringside in January 1938 but in less than a week into shooting, the troubled actor walked off the set, rumored to have had a nervous breakdown. The film was abandoned, eventually reworked as *Mr. Moto's Gamble* with Peter Lorre taking the lead as another Oriental based detective character. After a stint in the hospital, Oland signed a new three picture deal with Fox to continue playing Chan. Before starting his next movie, *Charlie Chan in Honolulu,* he took a break and traveled overseas, sailing to Europe and ending up in his native Sweden. He attempted to reconcile with Edith, however, while in his homeland, Oland contracted bronchial pneumonia. Years of heavy smoking had taken their toll with emphysema, which only exacerbated his condition and on August 6, 1938, the actor died in a Stockholm hospital. His body was cremated, and his wife brought his ashes back to the United States and Southborough, Massachusetts, where the couple made their home in a historic farmhouse.

Upon Oland's death, several actors were tested for the role of the famed detective before fellow character actor Sidney Toler was given the part in the planned *Charlie Chan in Honolulu,* released in October of 1938. The series continued for nearly a decade, but with the early '40s, Fox dropped the franchise and it was picked up by the low-budget Monogram Pictures. Whether playing an exotic villain or one of the most popular crime fighters of the Depression years, Warner Oland made the most of each role he undertook.

Edna May Oliver

A brisk and brusque New Englander whose no-nonsense demeanor was well-earned, Edna May Oliver was one of the best-known and most popular character actresses of the entire decade of the 1930s in American cinema. Bluntly put, she was the epitome of the "horse-faced," forthright, tell-it-like-it-is spinster who showed up often throughout movie history, her tenure taking place during and just after the Depression era. The self-admitted plain-Jane discussed her looks and screen persona based on her physicality in the August 1931 issue of *Photoplay* magazine:

> "The first time I ever saw myself on the screen, I was almost nauseated... I never like to see myself on the screen. It hurts my vanity – yes, I've got some left! If other people enjoy seeing me,

that's all right and I'm glad – but I don't enjoy seeing myself! I've found a measure of happiness, and let it go at that, face or no face."

Edna May Nutter hailed from Malden, Massachusetts, born on November 9, 1883, the daughter of Ida May and Charles Edward Nutter and a descendant of president John Quincy Adams. After developing an early interest in acting, she quit school at the age of fourteen to pursue her ambitions on the stage, first in light opera, then as an actress on the Boston stage in 1911.

By 1916 she had made her debut on Broadway in *The Master*, which led to the chance to play what would become her signature persona as the all-knowing spinster aunt, Miss Penelope Budd in the Jerome Kern musical *Oh Boy!* in 1917. The actress worked steadily on the New York stage throughout the 1920s, including being part of the cast of a 1925 comedy called *Cradle Snatchers*, which also included comedienne Mary Boland and a young actor named Humphrey Bogart. Oliver got her biggest break in 1927 as Parthy in Kerns' *Showboat*, starring in both its original run and its revival in the early 1930s. But Edna May wasn't merely strutting her stuff on the boards in New York. She also worked in silent films starting in 1923 with a drama called *Wife in Name Only* and by 1930 had signed a contract with RKO Pictures.

The actress was featured in a variety of films upon her entrée at RKO. She appeared in several comedies headed by funnymen Wheeler & Woolsey, as well as leading the roster in some of the studios routine programmers. She even found herself cast with the likes of Irene Dunne and Richard Dix in the 1931 Oscar-winning Best Picture, *Cimarron* (1931), as Dunne's loyal friend. Then, in 1932, she starred in what many consider to be her most popular film role: Hildegarde Withers, the acerbic spinster sleuth of the Stuart Palmer mystery novels of the period. *Penguin Pool Murder* was the first film in the series, followed by *Murder on the Blackboard* (1934) and *Murder on a Honeymoon* (1935). In each of these installments, she was paired with James Gleason (a superb character actor in his own right) as police Inspector Oscar Piper and together their on-screen chemistry was B-movie mystery gold. However, when Oliver left RKO in 1935, to move to the more prestigious Metro-Goldwyn-Mayer, the series lost steam. The studio tried to make a go of it with actress Helen Broderick and later still with comedienne Zasu Pitts, but the spark ignited by Edna May was no longer there.

Apparently, her face was made for historical films and costume pictures, as she appeared in some of the most expensive and extravagant movie versions of classic literature during the 1930s. Who better could play Aunt March in RKO's 1933 take on *Little Women*? Then on loan-out to Paramount the same year, Oliver was perfect as The Red Queen in the strange yet intriguing interpretation of Lewis Carroll's *Alice in Wonderland*, a celluloid melding of *Wonderland* and *Through the Looking Glass*. After her move to MGM, she was cast in the studio's superb productions of the Dickens' classics, *David Copperfield* (as Aunt Betsey) and *A Tale of Two Cities* (as Miss Pross; both produced by movie impresario David O. Selznick in 1935). After Alcott, Carroll and Dickens, the actress added Shakespeare to her repertoire, filling nicely the Renaissance shoes of the Nurse in Metro's *Romeo and Juliet* (1936).

Over at 20th Century-Fox, Oliver was cast as a tough old bird in the pioneer saga, *Drums Along the Mohawk* (1939), which starred Claudette Colbert and Henry Fonda. As the crotchety but caring Revolutionary-era widow, the veteran character player was finally nominated for an Academy Award as Best Supporting Actress. The recognition could be attributed partly to the film's director. In *Searching for John Ford: A Life*, biographer Joseph McBride notes Ford's difficulty with star Colbert and states that the director "seemed to invest far more sympathy in the character of the hard-boiled old widow Sarah McKlennar, magnificently played by Edna May Oliver..." Critics agreed that her performance was top notch including Frank S. Nugent, who summed her up in his review of the movie in the New York Times: "Miss Oliver could not have been bettered as the warlike Widow McKlennar, with a tongue sharper than a tomahawk and a soft spot in her heart for a handsome man." She, of course, played contemporary prudes and prunes with the likes of Shirley Temple in *Little Miss Broadway* (1938) and Merle Oberon in *Lydia* (1941), though still continuing her run of classics as the haughty and domineering Lady Catherine de Bourgh in MGM's big-budget *Pride and Prejudice* (1940) with Laurence Olivier and Greer Garson.

Although Oliver played the eternal spinster on the silver screen, she was not one in real-life. While working in *Show Boat* in 1928, she married stockbroker David Welford Pratt, ten years her junior. The marriage was short-lived, however, and they divorced after only a few years. In 1942, the actress developed an intestinal disorder that worsened as the year progressed. On November 9, 1942, she died in Malibu, California. It was her fifty-ninth birthday. According to her obituary, Oliver knew she didn't have long to live and asked her dear friend, actress Virginia Hammond (with whom she appeared in *Romeo and Juliet*) to arrange a simple funeral. She was interred in the Forest Lawn Memorial Park Cemetery in Glendale, California. As an actress, Edna May Oliver was tops. Her characters had character, something all actors in her position couldn't claim.

Reginald Owen

You may think you don't know who Reginald Owen is, but you most likely do, if given just one role for which he is most recognizable: Ebenezer Scrooge. Owen's overblown incantation of the cantankerous curmudgeon in the MGM version of the Dickens' classic *A Christmas Carol* is seen by thousands every year. In addition to Scrooge, the prolific actor appeared as both Sherlock Holmes and his loyal sidekick Dr. Watson, though in different films. Owen was a very busy, very British character actor who appeared in eighty feature films, which included historic biopics as well as modern melodramas with a few comedies and musicals thrown in for good measure, usually at his home studio, Metro-Goldwyn-Mayer.

John Reginald Owen was born on August 5, 1887 in the village of Wheathampstead, Hertfordshire, England. He first developed an interest in acting while attending the City of London School, then studied at Sir Herbert Tree's prestigious Royal Academy of Dramatic Art. He made his professional stage debut in 1905 in a production of *The Tempest* and was active on the London stage through the 1910s, including *Peter Pan* (as Mr. Darling) and *Ben-Hur* (as Messala). In the mid-1920s, Owen traveled to the United States to replace actor Philip Merivale as Prince Albert in *The Swan*, which had been a popular show on Broadway and was ready for its U.S. tour. Reginald took the role in the Chicago production and gained much praise, with one local critic writing:

> "*The Swan* was held here too long by at least three weeks. It had a better performance here than in New York, thanks to the management having replaced Philip Merivale with Reginald Owen, a fine comedian, and Miss Hilda Spong with Miss Henrietta Watson"

Once in America, the talented Brit decided to stay, appearing consistently on Broadway throughout the 1920s and the early 1930s, including a part as Cardinal Richelieu in Florenz Ziegfeld's original musical Broadway production of *The Three Musketeers* in 1928.

Owen had made a handful of films while still in England, though nothing of major significance, and in 1929 he made his American movie debut in the silent melodrama, *The Letter*, as cuckolded husband Robert Crosbie. The picture was made at Paramount's east coast studio and the following year, Owen made his way to California. It was the beginning of a long and very prosperous career in Hollywood, with the actor making twelve films in 1934 alone. In 1932, he played Dr. Watson, sidekick, assistant and sometimes foil to detective Sherlock Holmes (played by Clive Brook) in the film of the same name at Fox Film Corporation (before its merger with 20th Century studio). The following year he played Holmes in *A Study in Scarlet*, giving him the distinction of being only one of four actors who played both the detective and the doctor during his career.

By 1935 he was under contract to MGM, which would be home to his numerous characterizations for more than a decade. He appeared in some of Metro's most elaborate productions of the mid '30s, including *Anna Karenina, A Tale of Two Cities* (both 1935) and *The Great Ziegfeld* (1936). His most memorable role, Ebenezer Scrooge in the studio's lavish 1938 version of *A Christmas Carol*, came about by accident. The role had been played on the radio every holiday since 1934 by studio stalwart Lionel Barrymore and the filmed version was planned with the famed actor in mind. Barrymore suffered a broken hip, as well as crippling arthritis, and was unable to work on the production but suggested his fellow Metro actor, Owen, take over in his stead. The Englishman also performed the role in the 1938 Christmas radio broadcast in an effort to promote the film.

Throughout the 1940s he continued to make vast character contributions, playing middle-aged aristocrats, as well as hen-pecked husbands, his British-ness seeping into every role. He, along with Connie Gilchrist and Donald Meek, was one of a band of criminals cavorting with Joan Crawford in the top-notch drama *A Woman's Face* (1941). He was fun as the feeble and doddering Duke of Malmunster on loan-out to Paramount for the historical romance *Kitty* (1945) with Paulette Goddard, whom he co-starred yet again in the following year's *Diary of a Chambermaid*, directed by French filmmaker Jean Renoir. Twenty years after he tromped the stage as Richelieu in *The Three Musketeers,* he played Monsieur de Treville in MGM's lush Technicolor version with Gene Kelly and Lana Turner.

In 1950, at the age of sixty-three, Owen was back on Broadway, loaned out by Metro to star with Celeste Holm in the farce *Affairs of State.* The decade also saw his entry, like many of his contemporaries, into television, which he continued into the 1960s. Back on the film front, Owen made appearances in two Disney films, *Mary Poppins* (as an Admiral) and *Bedknobs and Broomsticks* (as a General). During this period, his claim to popular culture of the day involved none other than The Beatles. The pop music sensation rented Owen's two-acre Bel Air estate, while on their US tour in 1964, when their reservation at the Ambassador Hotel was cancelled due to the establishment's fear of being mobbed by frenzied fans.

The thrice-married actor worked into his eighties, when he said, "I'm surprised I'm still alive. But I'll never retire. I plan to be around for a while, and I shall always be doing something." On November 5, 1972,

Owen died of a heart attack, at the age of eighty-five, in Boise, Idaho, where he was recuperating from a stroke at his stepson's home.

Eugene Pallette

Although he started his acting career as a slim, handsome and athletic leading man in silent pictures, Eugene Pallette will always be remembered for his deep, gruff, frog-like voice and his rotund girth in character parts during Hollywood's heyday. Barking out orders to those around him in an irritated, gravelly rasp, usually in a screwball comedy, is where Pallette was in his element. With well over two hundred films to his credit, his face (and big belly) is recognizable in some of Tinsel Town's most famous movies.

He was born in Winfield, Kansas on July 8, 1889. His parents, William Baird Pallette and Elnora "Ella" Jackson, were an acting couple, who toured from city to city during his youth. After attending the Culver Military Academy in Culver, Indiana, he followed in their footsteps with his own acting career on the stage in stock company roles. Around 1910 he began doing extra work in films, appearing both in one-reelers and features. *The Fugitive*, made in 1913, was his first credited film work. The short film was directed by Wallace Reid, who would go on to be a silent film star and a friend of Pallette's. When Reid died in 1923 of morphine addiction, Pallette was one of the pallbearers at the matinee idol's funeral.

After serving in World War I, Eugene jumped back into show business. Although his early career saw the actor in a state of youthful handsomeness with a fit body (even portraying Aramis in the silent version of *The Three Musketeers* in 1921), he gained a tremendous amount of weight by the late 1920s and began to enter into character role status in comedies. In 1927, he signed as a regular for Hal Roach Studios and was a reliable comic foil in several early Laurel and Hardy movies. This transition was complemented by his distinctive and impressionable voice, which became an asset to a new phase of his career as sound movies began to emerge.

He moved over to Paramount with the new decade and among other roles appeared as Detective Heath in a string of mysteries opposite William Powell as sleuth Philo Vance. He later moved to Warner Brothers and began what would be his peak years in Hollywood, creating memorable characters in many classic films. In 1936 he played Alexander Bullock, Carole Lombard's rotund, exasperated father, in *My Man Godfrey* (reuniting with Powell in 1936). Warners cast him in a huge ensemble of their colorful talent pool as Friar Tuck in *The Adventures of Robin Hood* (1938) starring Errol Flynn. Pallette's portly Friar is undoubtedly the definitive screen portrayal of the classic character and he more than holds his own among the studio's top supporting players. He played an almost identical role as Fray Felipe in *The Mark of Zorro* (1940) at Twentieth Century-Fox, only in black and white this time instead of rainbow Technicolor.

Top-notch roles continued in the 1940s, with Pallette taking a turn as Henry Fonda's wealthy father in the classic comedy *The Lady Eve* (1941). The same year he again played a funny father with millions, this time to Bette Davis in *The Bride Came C.O.D.* Among his numerous films made in 1942 was *The Big Street* at RKO. As Nicely Nicely Johnson, Pallette brought to life one of the many characters created by Damon

Runyon, who existed in the streets of New York's Broadway district. He fit perfectly with the collection of off-beat characters in an off-beat film for the era in which it was produced.

In 1944 Pallette was cast as Henry Preston, the father of Jeanne Crain's character in a Twentieth Century-Fox production called *Army Wives*, which would be released under the title *In the Meantime, Darling*. In his autobiography, Fox director Otto Preminger recalled an incident with Pallette which led to the actor's dismissal from the film. According to Preminger, Pallette was "an admirer of Hitler and convinced that Germany would win the war." The trouble on the set began, however, when the actor refused to sit at the same table as African-American actor Clarence Muse. When instructed to enter the scene and take a seat at the kitchen table beside Muse, Pallette reportedly proclaimed to Preminger: "You're out of your mind. I won't sit next to a nigger." The director went to the studio head, Darryl F. Zanuck and had Pallette fired and his remaining scenes removed from the picture. The actor's career did indeed end only a couple of years after the release of *In the Meantime, Darling* but oddly, in 1953, Palette was one of the guests of a banquet honoring Madame Sul-Te-Wan, an elderly African-American actress with whom he had appeared in the silent classic *The Birth of a Nation* in 1915.

In August of 1937, Pallette purchased over 3000 acres near Imnaha, Oregon, in rural Wallowa County. In 1946, after being diagnosed with a "throat problem," and convinced of an inevitable atomic bomb attack, the corpulent actor left Hollywood and developed a wilderness fortress on the ranch along the Imnaha River, as a hideaway from universal catastrophe. The compound reportedly contained several dwellings, including a main house, guest houses and bunkhouses for work crews and was stocked with a sizable herd of prize cattle, huge quantities of food, and a lumber mill. While at his ranch, Pallette played host to several of his Hollywood friends, including Clark Gable. After a couple of years in Oregon and no nuclear attack on the horizon, Pallette began selling off portions of his ranch and returned to Hollywood, although he didn't resume his film career.

Eugene Pallette died at age sixty-five in 1954 from throat cancer at his Wilshire Boulevard apartment in Los Angeles. His third wife, Marjorie, and his sister, Beulah Phelps, were at his side. His cremated remains were buried in his native Kansas beside his mother and father.

When it came to his longevity in the picture business and his flexibility transitioning from a slim leading man to a large character player, the actor once said: "It sure hurt my vanity to think I was becoming a fat man. But after trying vainly to work off the poundage, I decided to put the poundage to work." And make it work, he did.

Franklin Pangborn

You have seen him before in black and white films of the 1930s and 1940s. You know his face, his manner, his raised eyebrow, but you may not know his name. Franklin Pangborn was, to audiences of comedies in Hollywood's golden age, the quintessential manager, whether it be of a department store, hotel, restaurant or apartment building. This kind of role always put him smack dab in the middle of some insane and inane situation in which his fussy, prissy, nervous persona was used to its comic best. Always perfectly tailored and elegantly suited, with posture perfect and pencil thin moustache trimmed to a tee, Pangborn's effete and haughty demeanor made him the epitome of the service industry snob, a fussbudget who was very easily annoyed and made no secret of it. The actor made a career of these small yet very memorable roles and enhanced dozens of movies.

Born on January 28, 1889 in Newark, New Jersey, Pangborn began appearing on Broadway in the early part of the 20th century, notably in the romantic role of Armand Duvall in *Camille* (1911), a far cry from the film roles for which he would become well-known. He served in the Army during the First World War and on his draft registration form he lists his employer at the time as Jessie Bonstelle, a famed theatrical director and stock company manager in Detroit. After the war, it was more stage work and one more appearance on Broadway in *Parasites*, a comedy that ran for fifty-four performances in late 1924. The actor then switched career gears to silent films, making his debut in 1926. As talkies came into play, Pangborn transitioned well and in the early 1930s, worked for Mack Sennett and Hal Roach making short subjects, playing a particularly memorable role as the flustered photographer trying to capture the youthful essence of "Spanky" McFarland on film in the hilarious "Our Gang" short, *Wild Poses*.

For the first half of the Thirties, his work was primarily in short comedies, but these began to be replaced by bit parts and character roles in "A" level pictures. In these he continued his run as smug store clerks, bartenders and even a Fuller Brush man, often uncredited but consistently funny. So funny, in fact, that his performances usually outshone those who shared a scene with him and was so noted by the media. For his contributions in the W.C. Fields classic *Never Give a Sucker an Even Break*, the Hollywood Reporter said, "Franklin Pangborn gets away with some of his very best scene stealing."

Always persnickety and punctilious, his characters were "sissified" and often typified the gay stereotype of the time. Due to the restrictions of the movie production code of the day, such personifications could only be slightly hinted at and only in the most lightweight and humorous manner. Though he practically owned this persona in the classic era of Hollywood (Edward Everett Horton and Eric Blore played variations, but their eyes weren't as narrowed when suspicious, nor their manner as affected), his finesse in portraying characters kept them from being boring or repetitious. In the Forties, he became part of the Preston Sturges' stock company appearing in six of the director's best-known movies including *Sullivan's Travels* (1941), *The Palm Beach Story* (1942) and *Hail the Conquering Hero* (1944).

One of Pangborn's more substantial roles was as bank examiner J. Pinkerton Snoopington in another of W.C. Fields' comedies, *The Bank Dick* (1940) (The actor also appeared in Fields' pre-Code classic *International House* (1933)). The name was a perfect fictional moniker for all the nosey parkers he had played and would play. He occasionally showed up in more dramatic fare, though not necessarily in a heavy dramatic part. In the Bette Davis soaper *Now, Voyager* (1942), he played a cruise director whose frazzled nerves were in a tizzy when the Davis character is late for shipboard activities.

Like many in his generation of actors, Pangborn did some television work in the 1950s and was briefly an announcer on Jack Paar's *Tonight Show*. He lived in Laguna Beach, California with his mother and, according to author William Mann, his "occasional boyfriend." He died in 1958, after surgery to remove a cancerous tumor.

C l a u d e   R a i n s

If one looks up "Brilliant Character Actor" in the encyclopedia (or Googles it in the 21st century), a photo of Claude Rains should be included with the definition. Although only occasionally the lead in films, his characters were pivotal to the story and always unforgettable. His smile could be sardonic or sadistic, his tears heartbreaking, his performances sublime. Unlike many stars who specialized in a certain type of characterization, Rains had the dramatic range to play a Southern rogue with the same intensity that he could portray a sinister medieval prince.

London-born and stage trained, Claude Rains was an exceptional actor, equally adept at whimsical roles as he was in heavy drama. He made his mark in his very first Hollywood film, *The Invisible Man* (1933), his unmistakable voice doing most of the work. He was, however, not the first choice for the role. Boris Karloff was slated to star, and the script crafted with him in mind, but a dispute in his salary failed to be resolved and Colin Clive, Karloff's fellow Frankenstein alumnus, was then considered. When Clive's participation also fell through, director James Whale immediately thought of Rains. Since the actor who played the role wouldn't be seen for the vast majority of screen time, voice was a major factor in casting, and Whale believed "Rains' soothing voice" would counter the violent nature of the main character.

The actor then signed on with Warner Brothers studio where his performances graced many of Hollywood's greatest and best-known classics. Warners cast him alongside its biggest stars at the peak of their careers and in many of their definitive films; *Anthony Adverse* (1936) with Fredric March, *The Adventures of Robin Hood* (1938) with Errol Flynn, *Now, Voyager* (1942) with Bette Davis and *Casablanca* (1942) with Humphrey Bogart; an exemplary resume in less than a decade.

As Prince John in Flynn's *Robin Hood*, he created one of the screen's great villains. Wearing a heavily banged pageboy bob, Rains' preening prince planned and plotted only to be foiled in the end by the Prince of Thieves. It was the first of nine films he made with noted Warner Brothers director Michael Curtiz, whom Rains gave credit for showing him how to act in front of the camera. Along with his role as the wise and knowing Dr. Jackwith in *Now, Voyager*, he also starred with Davis in *Mr. Skeffington* (1944) and *Deception* (1946). The two actors complemented one another perfectly and Rains was one of the actress' favorite co-stars. The grande dame of the Warners' lot even went as far as to say "he was a pip! The best!" In her autobiography, *The Lonely Life*, she said of the actor: "*Juarez* was the first time I ever met Claude or worked with him. This was the third time I was in awe of an actor... By this time, it must be clear that I was a meek and obscure young actress. Still he scared the life out of me... We have laughed about it many times since. Claude and I made four pictures together in the process of which I am proud to say he considers me a friend."

The actor gave a powerful performance as a corrupt senator opposite James Stewart in Frank Capra's *Mr. Smith Goes to Washington* (1939) and yet another as a sinister Fascist leader in Alfred Hitchcock's *Notorious* (1946), although it's debatable whether he or his character's mother (played by Austrian actress Leopoldine Konstantin) is more evil in the latter. Both performances garnered Rains an Oscar nomination for Best Supporting Actor, an honor he also earned for his roles in *Casablanca* and *Mr. Skeffington*, though he never won the coveted prize.

Though occasionally called on to play the lead, the actor was relegated in most cases to strong supporting parts. Although he claimed the title role in the 1943 version of *The Phantom of the Opera*, with the meatiest part by far, he was third billed to Nelson Eddy and Susannah Foster. Having come to films in middle age, with none of the traditional looks and stature of leading men of the period, Rains settled into his character status comfortably and very successfully. He continued working into the 1960s, and also continued his stage work, winning a Tony Award in 1951. Well respected by his peers, critics and audiences alike, Claude Rains was a consummate actor whose distinguished career firmly established his place in Hollywood history.

Basil Rathbone

When a classic movie fan hears the name Basil Rathbone, the immediate thought conjured up is the definitive characterization of famed detective Sherlock Holmes in a series of films beginning at Twentieth Century-Fox in the late '30s, and later moving to Universal throughout the duration of the war. For many fans of the mystery series, Rathbone IS Sherlock Holmes, complete with meerschaum pipe and deerstalker hat, but those who have followed the actor's complete career know he created some of the greatest villains in the history of classic film. Black-hearted, icily suave and sadistically ruthless, the incomparable Rathbone's pre-Holmes characterizations were anything but forgettable. (Rumor has it that author Margaret Mitchell wanted him to play Rhett Butler in the film version of her novel *Gone with the Wind*!)

Tall and distinguished, Rathbone's sculpted facial features and deep, commanding voice was unmistakable, whether he was portraying an urbane gentleman or a sophisticated cad. Born in Johannesburg, South Africa, in 1892, he was raised in England, where at school he excelled at sports and became interested in the theater. Trained as a Shakespearean actor, his theater career was interrupted during World War I. He served as an intelligence officer and in 1918 was awarded the Military Cross, as a result of daytime enemy scouting missions, which were extremely dangerous.

Rathbone came to the United States in the mid-1920s to perform on the New York stage, but it was his reputation as a polished villain in Hollywood films that made him famous. Although wonderfully sinister in several classics of the mid and late '30s, including *Anna Karenina* (1935) and *Tower of London* (1939), three of his best roles were in *Captain Blood* (1935), *The Adventures of Robin Hood* (1938) and *The Mark of Zorro* (1940). An accomplished swordsman in real life, he fought impressive duels in each of these films with the lead actor (Errol Flynn in the first two and Tyrone Power in the latter) only to lose dramatically in the end. In *Captain Blood*, Rathbone portrayed a French pirate who first joins forces with then defies Flynn. In *The Mark of Zorro*, the distinctively profiled actor played the cool and cruel Captain Pasquale, who acted as nemesis to Tyrone Power's masked avenger. But it's as one of filmdom's greatest scoundrels, Sir Guy of Gisbourne in Warner Brothers' Technicolor masterpiece, *The Adventures of Robin Hood*, which ingrains in the memory Basil Rathbone's vision of menacing rogue.

In 1939, Rathbone portrayed two characters that were both classic from both a literary and motion picture standpoint. He took over the part of Dr. Frankenstein from Colin Clive in *Son of Frankenstein* at Universal and was cast as the definitive detective, Sherlock Holmes, in Twentieth Century-Fox's version of Arthur Conan Doyle's *The Hound of the Baskervilles*. With Nigel Bruce by his side as Dr. Watson, the iconic duo found themselves in the middle of an unforeseen hit. Rathbone's popularity as Holmes was such a surprise, he wasn't even top billed, instead taking the second spot to Fox contract player Richard Greene. The studio quickly developed *The Adventures of Sherlock Holmes* to cash in on the success of *Baskervilles*. Both films were set in Victorian England as reflected in the Conan Doyle stories, but when the burgeoning franchise was acquired by Universal in 1942, the setting was changed to the present and many of the storylines revolved around World War II-based intrigue. All told, Rathbone and Nigel Bruce would make fourteen Holmes films between 1939 and 1946 and appear as their film characters in a long-running Holmes radio program. Quite an offering for what started out as a quaint little period picture.

After leaving Holmes behind in 1946, the actor wanted to put more of his career focus back into the theater. He headed back to Broadway where he was offered the role of Dr. Austin Sloper in the stage version of *The Heiress* in 1947, a performance for which he won a Tony Award in 1948 as Best Actor in a Play (Rathbone shared the award with Henry Fonda for his role in *Mister Roberts* and Paul Kelly for *Command Decision*). Great was his disappointment when he lost the role to Sir Ralph Richardson for the movie adaption the following year. His success in *The Heiress* was followed by less auspicious roles in the 1950s. His films included a couple of parodies of his earlier movie bad guys in the Bob Hope comedy *Casanova's Big Night* (1954) and *The Court Jester* (1956) with Danny Kaye. He made numerous television appearances throughout the decade.

Still, he had become synonymous with his Sherlock Holmes character and even reflected on the fact when he said, "When you become the character you portray, it's the end of your career as an actor." Though Holmes may be the role for which he is most remembered, Rathbone appeared in over seventy films and created some of the best remembered members of movie villainy. He died of a heart attack in 1967 at the age of seventy-five.

Thelma Ritter

Wise-cracking, working class, world-weary characters were Thelma Ritter's specialty. Whenever she was on the screen there was never a dull moment and, though she was fortunate to be provided with some of the brightest dialogue written in Hollywood, it was her razor-sharp delivery that lingers in the memory. A consummate character actress, Ritter was nominated six times for an Academy Award during her career, including four consecutive nods, without winning a single trophy. She is tied with Deborah Kerr for the most nominations for a female actor without winning.

Ritter was born in Brooklyn, New York, on St. Valentine's Day, 1902. After appearing in high school plays, she appeared mostly in stock and repertory companies, and trained for a time at the American

Academy of Dramatic Arts. She made her Broadway debut in a small role in a comedy called *The Shelf*, which ran for only 32 performances in early autumn, 1926. She married a fellow actor, Joseph Moran, who eventually became an advertising executive at Young & Rubicam and took some time away from acting to raise their two children. Later, she continued her stage work and began appearing on the radio.

Ritter was already forty-five years old when she made her movie debut in a small but very memorable role as the Christmas shopping weary mother in *Miracle on 34th Street* (1947) for 20th Century-Fox. A family friend of the film's director, George Seaton, Ritter impressed Fox boss Darryl F. Zanuck enough to expand her tiny part and cast her in other pictures. In *A Letter to Three Wives* (1949), she was again unbilled but unforgettable in a rather meaty part as tart-tongued maid, Sadie Duggan for director Joseph L. Mankiewicz, who remembered her when it came time to cast his next film, *All About Eve* (1950). It was as street-wise maid Birdie Coonan in that movie classic that the actress made her mark so impressively. For *Eve* she received her first of six Academy Award nominations. She would later be nominated for *The Mating Season* (1951), *With a Song in My Heart* (1952), *Pickup on South Street* (1953), *Pillow Talk* (1959) and *The Birdman of Alcatraz* (1962), all in the Best Supporting Actress category.

To share her opinion or give unsolicited advice was a regular characteristic of Ritter's roles. It was the sole theme of one of her most underrated films, *The Model and the Marriage Broker* (1951). Ritter plays Mae Swasey, an emissary of the romantically deficient, a mentor of the lonelyhearts coalition. Although Jeanne Crain, the model of the title, has top billing, it is Ritter's marriage broker who is the real star of the picture. In fact, after *All About Eve*, the tough-talking actress was cast in secondary leads or strong supporting roles for the rest of her career, never lacking for quality work.

Ritter was as popular with her co-stars as with her movie public (and with critics alike for that fact). Celeste Holm called her *All About Eve* compadre, "one of my favorite people in the whole world," and *Eve* director Joseph L. Mankiewicz "adored her," and confirmed that the part of Birdie Coonan was written especially for her. Raving over the actress, playwright Paddy Chayefsky wrote about the 1955 television play, *The Catered Affair* which they worked on together. "*The Catered Affair*,

[was] an unfocused piece in which the first act was farce and the second was character-comedy, and the third was abruptly drama. There aren't a dozen actresses who could make one piece out of all that; Miss Ritter, of course, did."

She appeared in the 1953 version of *Titanic* with Barbara Stanwyck, then director Alfred Hitchcock hired her as James Stewart's caregiver in his suspense classic, *Rear Window* in 1954. After being away for twenty-six years, the actress returned to Broadway in 1957 in the hit musical *New Girl in Town*, for which she won a Tony (in a tie with Gwen Verdon) in 1958. The following year she would support Doris Day and Rock Hudson in the lively *Pillow Talk*, where she would toss her usual quips such as to Day's eternal virgin: "If there's anything worse than a woman living alone, it's a woman saying she likes it."

The 1960s saw even more successes for Ritter, in the films *How the West Was Won* (1962) and again with Doris Day in *Move Over, Darling* in 1963. Like many in her field, she became a regular contributor on television, appearing in *General Electric Theater* in 1960 and the popular western *Wagon Train* in 1962. Thelma Ritter died of a heart attack in New York City, just nine days before her 67th birthday.

Ann Rutherford

As the proverbial girl-next-door Polly Benedict, Ann Rutherford had to compete with MGM starlets of the late '30s and early '40s to keep her man, aka Andy Hardy, in the string of *Hardy* family motion pictures, popular during the era. Lana Turner, Donna Reed, Kathryn Grayson, Esther Williams and others who had just copped a contract with the all-powerful Metro-Goldwyn-Mayer either pursued or were pursued by Mickey Rooney's precocious Andy in the studio's homespun box-office success, while Rutherford waited around for Andy to get the co-ed cutie of the moment out of his system. Although she made her mark as pretty-yet-prickly Polly, the pert and perky actress is also known for her contribution (albeit small one) to David O. Selznick's epic *Gone with the Wind*, in which she played Scarlett O'Hara's sweet younger sister, Carreen.

Born in Vancouver on November 2, 1917, Ann was the daughter of John Dufferin Rutherford, a former operatic tenor who sang under the name Juan Guilberti, and Lucille Mansfield, a silent-screen actress. Shortly after her birth, the family, which included her older sister Judith, moved to San Francisco. Her parents separated when Ann was five and her mother eventually took her and Judith to live in Los Angeles. Although some official biographies state that she appeared in plays as a child, Rutherford once confessed: "That was poppy-cock. Studio publicity. I did do plays as a kid—but just school plays like everybody else." While attending Virgil Junior High School, young Rutherford would roller skate past a local radio station where she would settle into the viewing room and watch the actors perform. After being criticized by her English teacher, a perturbed Ann declared that if she got a job on the radio, she wouldn't have to listen to the offensive instructor. The underage youngster created an acting resume and was offered a job at station KFAC. Her sister had become a minor actress in films under the name Judith Arlen and suggested Ann go for a casting call at MGM for a movie called *Student Tour* in 1934. Sixteen-year-old Rutherford won the role. After a couple of years playing a variety of radio roles, the actress was contacted about a contract with Mascot Studios, a small outfit that would become Republic Pictures.

Rutherford was hired to replace actress Anne Darling in a picture that Darling had quit to get married. The movie was *Waterfront Lady* (1935) and Rutherford, as a complete newcomer, was top-billed. She continued at Mascot in a serial called *The Fighting Marines*, also in 1935, and became leading lady to the likes of Western legends Gene Autry and John Wayne, during his tenure in B-western quickies of the mid-1930s. Of these early days, Ann would later joke, "I was Gene Autry's first leading lady and the only one he ever kissed — after that he kissed his horse." After two years, Rutherford had appeared in a dozen films, and in 1937, she signed a seven-year contract with MGM. Going from a bare bones organization like Republic Pictures to the cream of the Hollywood crop at Metro was a huge boost to her burgeoning career. "I started at MGM at $350 a week, and always got my raises!" she said. Her success at regular pay increases with boss Louis B. Mayer, notorious for keeping contract salaries down, was calculated. According to the star, when she went in for her appointment with Mayer she would bring along her bankbook and explain that she was saving money to buy a house for her mother. "He got misty-eyed; Anything to do with mothers made him emotional," she said.

One of her first assignments at MGM was taking over the role of Polly Benedict in the second installment of the *Andy Hardy* series, *You're Only Young Once* (1937). The role had previously been played by Margaret Marquis, who, like Rutherford, had done her time in B-westerns of the period. The series became a staple in American theaters and Rutherford appeared in twelve *Hardy* films between 1937 and 1942. In 1938, she would don a blonde wig and play The Ghost of Christmas Past in Metro's atmospheric, *A Christmas Carol* alongside Reginald Owen as Ebenezer Scrooge.

That same year, producer David O. Selznick was casting his Civil War epic *Gone with the Wind*. For the role of Carreen, youngest of the O'Hara daughters, Selznick had considered teenaged Judy Garland, but her light was becoming too bright for such a small role. When he approached Louis Mayer (who was his father-in-law) about using Rutherford, the head of MGM said it was a "nothing part" and refused to allow his young contract player to participate. According to the determined starlet, she "begged and beseeched Mayer. Nagged and wept and carried on" until he finally relented. In later years, Rutherford was fond of telling the story of how she explained to Mr. Selznick that all the young women of the day were trying to let their eyebrows grow, an attempt to copy the new Swedish sensation Ingrid Bergman (who Selznick just happened to have under contract). In his infamous "memos," the producer mentions taking Rutherford's suggestion and using it as publicity. Ann was among the cast members who trekked to Atlanta, Georgia for the film's gala premiere.

In 1940, she played Lydia, one of the Bennett sisters in the studio's grand literary spectacle *Pride and Prejudice*, which starred Greer Garson and Laurence Olivier. After that she appeared with comedian Red Skelton in a trio of comedies: *Whistling in the Dark* (1941), *Whistling in Dixie* (1942) and *Whistling in Brooklyn* (1943), before leaving MGM for Twentieth Century-Fox in 1942. The departure from Metro wasn't her choice. According to Rutherford, she complained about her proposed role in the upcoming production *Seven Sweethearts* at MGM, claiming it to be miniscule in comparison to her featured parts in the past. Just as filming was to begin, she discovered she had contracted German measles while entertaining troops early in 1942. Boss Mayer thought she was "sick" as rebellion and sold her contract to Fox with the stipulation that she could be borrowed if they needed her for one of the *Hardy* or *Whistling* pictures.

Her first film at Fox was *Orchestra Wives* (1942), a follow-up to *Sun Valley Serenade*, which had been a box-office success the previous year. Her time at the studio was brief and she wasn't happy there. "It was just as cold as a fish," Rutherford remembered. "MGM had a warmth to it. It was a family, and you felt almost related to everyone there." As unsettled as she felt with her career, Ann's personal life was just the opposite, with the actress marrying for the first time in December 1942. Her new husband was David May, heir to the May department store chain, and though the marriage ended in divorce a decade later, the couple did adopt a daughter, Gloria. After her divorce from May in 1953, Ann married producer William Dozier, who created the *Batman* TV series in the mid-1960s.

Rutherford's career lost steam after leaving Twentieth Century-Fox and her roles diminished in quality, with the exception of *The Secret Life of Walter Mitty*, opposite Danny Kaye in 1947, and *The Adventures of Don Juan* with Errol Flynn in 1948. After making the low-budget *Operation Haylift* in 1950, the actress retired from the big screen, focusing on her child. "When my baby preferred the nanny's company to mine," she said, "I fired the nanny and stayed home with my daughter." She did continue to work steadily on television throughout the 1950s and played the mother of Suzanne Pleshette's character, Emily, on *The Bob Newhart Show* in the 1970s.

As her acting jobs faded, Rutherford found a second career of sorts attending events and functions relating to her participation in *Gone with the Wind*. A regular guest at anniversary galas for the epic film, she was a favorite with fans as one of the few surviving cast members. In the late 1990s, she was approached about playing the elderly Rose in James Cameron's *Titanic* (1997) but declined, allowing Gloria Stuart the opportunity for an Oscar nomination in the role. After spending many years in happy retirement, Ann Rutherford died at the age of 94 on June 11, 2012 at her home in Beverly Hills, California (where she had lived since 1943), following declining health due to heart problems. Her longtime friend, actress Anne Jeffreys was reportedly by her side. She is buried by her husband, William Dozier, at Holy Cross Cemetery in Culver City, California.

Margaret Rutherford

At an age when many female stars were either finishing up their film careers or transitioning to character roles, England's Margaret Rutherford was just getting started. No beauty queen she, the actress had to endure much when it came to her physical appearance and unique persona. One critic went as far as to say that "if you hung the face of Margaret Rutherford on the side of the Notre Dame Cathedral she would make all the other gargoyles look like Audrey Hepburn. It is quite the ugliest old ragbag of a face you have ever seen" and theatre critic Kenneth Tynan declared that "the unique thing about Ms. Rutherford is that she can act with her chins alone." Nonetheless, she endeared herself to her fans with her quirky mannerisms and kooky characterizations in a career which culminated in her portrayal of Miss Marple, Agatha Christie's geriatric female sleuth in a series of British-made comedy-mysteries during the early 1960s.

Her life began under circumstances that were as unconventional as the characters she played on stage and screen. Her father, William Rutherford Benn, was a poet and journalist, who in December 1882 married Florence Nicholson at the All Saints Church, Wandsworth. A month after the nuptials Benn, who was twenty-seven at the time, had a mental breakdown (brought on, it has been suggested, by his inability to consummate his marriage) and he was admitted to the Bethnal House Lunatic Asylum, where his malady was described as "...depression alternating with unusual excitement and irritability." Within a matter of weeks, his condition had improved to the point that he was released under the supervision of his father, Reverend Julius Benn, a Congregational Church minister. In late February, Reverend Benn took his son to convalesce at the spa town of Matlock in Derbyshire, where they took rooms kept by a Mrs. Marchant.

On Sunday morning, March 4, William was found in his bloody nightshirt and his father bludgeoned to death with an earthenware chamber pot, his head split completely open. After murdering his father, William attempted to slit his own throat, though his wounds were not fatal. He was arrested and charged with murder, with a jury declaring unanimously that Reverend Benn had been "wilfully murdered by his son, William Rutherford Benn." Death by hanging was an option open to the judge for sentencing, but as the convicted man saw even further deterioration in his mental state, the murder charges were dropped on the basis of insanity, and Benn was confined to the Broadmoor Criminal Lunatic Asylum.

In July 1890, after seven years as an inmate at Broadmoor, William was released to the care of his wife. With notoriety hanging a black cloud over his head, he dropped his surname and took his middle name, Rutherford, instead. At some point upon his reunion with Florence, their marriage was unquestionably consummated, and on May 11, 1892, Margaret Taylor Rutherford was born in the Borough of Wandsworth. Looking to start afresh with his family, William moved them to India, where he obtained a job as a shipping clerk. While in Asia,

Florence became pregnant once again and soon became increasingly depressed. As signs of an impending mental breakdown occurred, William made plans for the family to return to England, but not before his wife committed suicide, found hanging from a tree. Back in England, three-year-old Margaret was sent to live with her maternal aunt, Bessie Nicholson in Wimbledon, London, and William was eventually readmitted to Broadmoor, following a series of severe breakdowns. Having been told by her aunt that both her parents had died, young Margaret finally discovered the truth about her father at the age of twelve, which caused extreme depression, a condition that haunted her throughout her life. William died at Broadmoor in 1921.

After being educated at Wimbledon High School, Margaret attended Raven's Croft boarding school, where she became interested in the dramatic arts. When Aunt Bessie died in 1923, she left her niece enough money to allow her to enter the Old Vic School, where she made her stage debut in 1925 at the age of thirty-three. Of her time at the Old Vic, Rutherford described it as "a hard school, but a just one. There was no question as to whether you thought that a part was right for you – the actors had to play any part that was given to them." In 1926, she won a students' competition and appeared as Lady Capulet in *Romeo and Juliet*, alongside Edith Evans as the Nurse. She continued appearing in amateur productions throughout the '20s and made her debut in London's West End in 1933 and her film debut in 1936, at the age of forty-four.

She didn't really get recognition for her acting until 1939, when she played Miss Prism in *The Importance of Being Earnest* at the Globe Theater. Then, in 1941, she appeared in Noel Coward's *Blithe Spirit* at the Piccadilly Theatre in London, with the playwright himself directing. She played eccentric clairvoyant, Madame Arcati and it would become one of the two parts with which she would be most recognized throughout her career. She recreated the role in 1945, when Coward adapted the play for the screen.

Also, in 1945, Rutherford, at the age of fifty-three, married for the first time. Stringer Davis was an aspiring actor, seven years Margaret's junior. It has been widely reported that Davis was a homosexual and a hopeless mama's boy, waiting fifteen years, until his mother's death to pop the question to the actress, whom he adored. He remained devoted to the actress, rarely leaving her side, until her death. Another strange "family" relation was that of Gordon Langley Hall, a writer, well into his twenties when Rutherford unofficially "adopted" him. He later went on to have gender reassignment surgery (for which Rutherford paid) in 1968, then going by the name Dawn Langley Simmons. Simmons then went on to marry an African-American man, the first interracial marriage in South Carolina. Margaret Rutherford's reported response to all this was: "I am delighted that Gordon has become a woman, and I am delighted that Dawn is to marry a man of another race, and I am delighted that Dawn is to marry a man of a lower station, but I understand the man is a Baptist!"

After *Blithe Spirit*, Rutherford's career improved greatly, though she still was not in leading lady territory. She had a fun supporting role as eccentric (what else?) Nurse Carey, in the mermaid tale, *Miranda* (1948), and then another as Professor Hatton-Jones in the Ealing comedy, *Passport to Pimlico* (1949). She continued to strengthen her comedic skills throughout the 1950s in film after film and even took on the BBC with various roles on British television.

In 1961, the actress was offered a part that would increase her audience exposure and change her career. Mystery author Agatha Christie had created the character of Miss Marple, an amateur sleuth of the senior citizen set, decades before, but none of the Marple works had ever been translated to the big screen. In the early '60s, Metro-Goldwyn-Mayer bought the rights to most of Christie's stories, with the idea of creating a television show. Although that endeavor never reached fruition, the studio did embark on a feature film, based on the book *4:50 from Paddington* and tentatively titled *Meet Miss Marple*. Director George Pollock saw in Rutherford the perfect candidate to play the role. The actress was not keen on the project at first, stating in her 1972 autobiography: "Murder, you see, is not the sort of thing I could get close to. I never found it amusing. I don't like anything that tends to lower or debase or degrade." One wonders what impact the incidents born from her family tree played in her comment. When Pollock sent her the script and explained that the role was more about "a game of solving problems, rather than of murder," the actress was persuaded.

At Margaret's request, a role was written in for her husband. The name of the film was changed to *Murder, She Said* and Rutherford became to Marple what Basil Rathbone had to Sherlock Holmes two decades earlier. Her light and whimsical interpretation was not as the character was written in Christie's stories, and the author was not pleased with the motion picture outcome. The year after *Murder, She Said* was released, Dame Agatha did, however, dedicate her newest novel, *The Mirror Crack'd from Side to Side*, to Margaret Rutherford. The film's popularity sparked three successive Marple movies, all with Rutherford and Stringer in tow.

With the success of *Murder, She Said*, the actress was cast in the all-star drama-fest, *The V.I.P.s* in 1963. As the dotty and impoverished Duchess of Brighton, Rutherford scored a personal and professional victory by winning both the Best Supporting Actress Oscar and Golden Globe. The cast included Elizabeth Taylor, Richard Burton, Maggie Smith, Rod Taylor and other A-list movie stars. The film allowed Rutherford to utilize her comedic skills along with her more dramatic ones for truly poignant scenes about losing her character's home.

Only a handful of film and television appearances came during the remainder of the decade. The actress was appointed Officer of the Order of the British Empire (OBE) in 1961, and a Dame Commander (DBE) in 1967. On May 22, 1972, at the age of eighty, Dame Margaret Rutherford died at the Buckinghamshire home she shared with her husband. Davis had cared for his wife devotedly, particularly during her last years, when she suffered from Alzheimer's disease. He died the following year, and both were interred in the graveyard of St. James's Church, Gerrards Cross, Buckinghamshire. "A Blithe Spirit" is engraved at the base of her memorial stone.

S. Z. "Cuddles" Sakall

If only for his role as bubbly Uncle Felix in the perennial Yuletide favorite *Christmas in Connecticut* (1945), S.Z. "Cuddles" Sakall would be remembered as a great supporting player, with lines like, "Everything is hunky dunky!" guaranteeing him a spot in movie history during the 1940s. This chubby cherub, with the thick as goulash Hungarian accent, hit the mark in many classics of the period, mainly comedies and musicals. Even if audiences couldn't understand what he was saying, his facial reactions to the situation going on around him, especially when unnerved or befuddled, would cause riotous hilarity every time.

Born Gerő Jenő in Budapest, Hungary, of Jewish parentage, Sakall's father was a stonecutter who specialized in tombstones. Young Gerő began writing vaudeville and comedy sketches while still a teenager in Budapest, taking the pen name Szőke Szakáll, which translated to "blond beard," grown to make him appear older. He transitioned from writing to acting, first on the Hungarian stage then moving to Vienna in the 1920s. He decided he wanted to try his hand at film acting after visiting his childhood friend, director Michael Curtiz, on the set of *Sodom and Gomorrah* in 1922. When directing *Casablanca* in 1942, Curtiz cast Sakall as Carl, the headwaiter, when German comedian Felix Bressart turned down the part.

After finding success in Berlin, the actor returned back to his Hungarian homeland when the Nazis rose to power in 1933. A New York Times review in October 1936 noted Sakall's, border crossing career, as well as his popularity in Europe. "Since that excellent Hungarian comedian, Szoeke Szakall, once so familiar a sight in German films, is barred from working in Nazi Germany under Hitler's racial dispensation, Budapest producers are profiting by the situation." Sakall and his wife fled Europe in spring of 1939 in the wake of the war and made their way to the United States via movie producer Joe Pasternak, who happened to be a relative by marriage. The influence of the Third Reich touched the actor personally when all three of his sisters perished in concentration camps.

Settling in California, Sakall made his American film debut in the Deanna Durbin vehicle *It's a Date* at Universal Studio in 1940. Sakall recounted in his autobiography how his trademark "jowl shake" and "face slap" came into being. On the set at Universal, he said a line and quickly jerked his head, which caused his chubby jowls to shake vigorously. The funny-looking movement caused the uproarious laughter of the director and crew, which only increased as he buried his face in his hands. A fellow Hungarian on the set told him that he would now have to shake his jowls for the remainder of his career and according to Sakall, he was right.

"Everything happened as he had foretold it – with the difference that later they weren't satisfied with the trembling of my jowls," Sakall wrote. "They demanded that they should quiver and shake in a bigger and better way . . . Later the writers made no attempt to put any humour or wit into my roles. They merely added a piece of business: 'Here Sakall shakes his jowls and slaps his own face!'"

He then signed with Warner Brothers, where he appeared in *Casablanca* and other classics. Studio boss Jack Warner is the one who tagged Sakall with the nickname "Cuddles" and insisted, much to the actor's chagrin, that he use it as part of his screen billing. As much as he begrudged the moniker, however, Sakall used the appellation as part of his autobiography, *The Story of Cuddles, My Life Under the Emperor Francis Joseph, Adolf Hitler and the Warner Brothers*, in 1954. At Warners he would shine as uncles, restaurateurs, chefs and befuddled business owners. Metro Goldwyn Mayer borrowed the loveable curmudgeon to play Otto Oberkugen in its production of *In the Good Old Summertime* (1949), a remake of *The Shop Around the Corner* (1940). With his jiggling jowls, Sakall could have been pulled from any number of period cartoons of the day, a colorful comedy caricature.

Arguably his most recognizable role among modern classic movie fans is as "Uncle" Felix Bassenak, cuddly and charming friend and behind-the-scenes chef for faux homemaking maven Barbara Stanwyck in *Christmas in Connecticut*. With fellow Warner Brothers heavyweight Sydney Greenstreet, Sakall formed a corpulent clique. The Hungarian actor's verbal massacre of the English language is matched only by his deadpan delivery of it. When he is informed of the definition of the word *catastrophe*, he pronounces it "CAT'e stroph" ~ no final "e" ~ in the thickest accent imaginable and used often at the most opportune times, with hilarious results.

His final film was the MGM musical *The Student Prince* (1954). The much-loved actor died of a heart attack on February 12, 1955 in Hollywood. Within a month of his passing, Sakall's beloved German shepherd, which he adopted as a puppy while making *Casablanca*, died of a heart attack as well.

George Sanders

Egomaniac. Heel. Rotter. Villain. Scoundrel. George Sanders' film persona (and arguably his off-screen personality as well) encompasses all of these character descriptions and then some, and he took no offense. In fact, his 1960 autobiography is called *Memoirs of a Professional Cad*. Never was there a more decadent, delicious, deliberate bad egg in all filmdom than George Sanders. His voice, a deep, silky British intonation, would carry lusciously to the ear, languid in its delivery, biting in its intent, any number of cynicisms and indignities to the target he chose. Male, female, rich or poor, his verbal affronts knew no bounds. Oh, but his verbal assaults were always carried out with style. His characters were always impeccably dressed, always slightly (and sometimes not so slightly) menacing, snobbish with a droll wit. These intrinsic elements of his persona were used to their peak in his best-known roles but none so perfectly than his portrayal of acid-tongued critic

237

Addison DeWitt in the film masterpiece *All About Eve* (1950). The actor described his screen presence best when he said: "I was beastly but never coarse. A high-class sort of heel," and of his off-screen self he was even more candid. ""I am always rude to people," he once said. "I am not a sweet person. I am a disagreeable person. I am a hateful person."

Sanders was born in St. Petersburg, Russia in 1906 to English parents. His elder brother was actor Tom Conway (born 1904) and the two had a younger sister, Margaret. In 1917, when George was eleven years-old, the Russian Revolution was in full swing and the family moved back to England. His early adulthood included scenes which could have been pulled from one of his future movies, with his employment at an Argentine tobacco company being cut short due to an incident with "a very charming widow" which resulted in his fighting a duel! While working in a British advertising agency, a company secretary suggested he take up acting, which he decided to do. The secretary's name? Greer Garson.

Entering the American cinema in the mid-1930s, Sanders signed a contract with 20th Century-Fox, and later in the decade with RKO, where the actor took over for Louis Hayward lead role as *The Saint* and later took the helm in *The Falcon* franchise, both low-budget but popular detective film series. Brother Conway replaced George after *The Falcon's Brother* (1942), in which the siblings appeared together. The actor didn't hit his stride until 1940 when Alfred Hitchcock cast him as the obnoxious and despicable Jack Favell in his classic romantic suspenser *Rebecca*. Hitchcock used him again that same year in *Foreign Correspondent*. A string of Nazis, narcissists and other nasty nellies followed, including an unrecognizable turn as a red headed pirate (?) in the Tyrone Power swashbuckler *The Black Swan* (1942). On occasion, he would play the hero and do so convincingly but eventually Sanders began to find his groove, as an incomparable heel in *Summer Storm* (1944), *The Picture of Dorian Gray* (1945; as Sir Henry, a role he seemed born to play), *The Ghost and Mrs. Muir* (1947) and *The Fan* (1949). He was also a lot of fun as an incorrigible King Charles II in the historical bed hopper *Forever Amber* (1947), in which he plays the monarch with a bored cynicism most likely used by the real king in his decadent court.

Then in 1950 came his pinnacle role, the one for which he is most closely identified, Addison DeWitt. For his performance as the theater critic with the poison pen, Sanders won an Academy Award as Best Supporting Actor in the much-nominated *All About Eve*. Among so many grand personalities and egos, he more than held his own, introducing Marilyn Monroe's buxom sexpot character, Miss Caswell, as "a graduate of the Copacabana School of Dramatic Art." Classic Sanders. He even tried his hand at television, hosting *The George Sanders Mystery Theater* on NBC in 1957.

Of course, there were his many marriages, including one to super celeb Zsa Zsa Gabor and later to Gabor's sister, Magda, but all ended in divorce except his third union with actress Benita Hume. Hume was the widow of film star Ronald Colman and was married to Sanders from 1959 to 1967, when she died from cancer. The same year, Sanders lost both his mother and his brother, Tom Conway. At this point the actor went into decline. Plagued with health problems of his own, as well as fits of rage, he became weary of life itself. Finally, in April 1972, he was found dead in a hotel room in Barcelona, Spain. Also found were five empty bottles of the barbiturate Nembutal and an infamous suicide note, which read: "Dear World, I am leaving because I am bored. I feel I have lived long enough. I am leaving you with your worries in this sweet cesspool. Good luck." The urbane cynic who sneered in the face of convention remained unrepentant to the very end. Bored perhaps but boring, never.

Gale Sondergaard

On Thursday evening, March 4, 1937, in front of fifteen hundred Academy members and guests at the Biltmore Hotel in Los Angeles, strikingly attractive actress Gale Sondergaard was presented the very first Oscar for Best Supporting Actress in a Film. The physical encasement of the honor was a small plaque, as full-sized statuettes were not awarded to supporting actors until the 1943 awards year. Sondergaard won her plaque for the role of Faith Paleologus in the epic costume drama, *Anthony Adverse*. It was her film debut and such an honor wouldn't be repeated for a decade (when World War II veteran Harold Russell was recognized for his part in *The Best Years of Our Lives*). As prestigious and historic as her achievements were at the time, Gale Sondergaard's career became noteworthy for much more and her film persona as a dark mystery woman or sinister female villain in the films in which she appeared, marked her place in Hollywood's golden age.

Her dark, exotic looks would suggest Spanish or Latin heritage but, in fact, the actress came into the world with solid Danish ancestry in the center of the Scandinavian-American heartland. She was born Edith Holm Søndergaard in Litchfield, Minnesota on February 15, 1899. Her parents, Hans and Kirstine (Holm), immigrated from Denmark separately, marrying in 1894 and bearing their first child, Ragni, three years before Edith. A third daughter, Hester, would join the family in 1903. Hans, a butter maker at the Litchfield Creamery at the turn of the century, eventually became a professor of Agriculture at the University of Wisconsin-Madison. Young Edith would later recount her parents influence on her life:

> "My parents were both progressive people learning much from Henrik Ibsen. My mother believed that a woman should not be tied down to family with nothing else in her life. They were also progressive politically. My father, we thought, voted the Democratic ticket, but actually he voted the Socialist ticket; my mother was a suffragette and I marched in parades with her."

Sondergaard attended the Minneapolis School of Dramatic Art before moving on to the University of Minnesota, where she earned her undergraduate degree. While in school, she was actively involved with the Studio Players, then joining the Chautauqua circuit playing the ingénue, before acting with the John Keller Shakespeare Company in 1921. She toured the USA and Canada with various stock companies, with these years of dramatic experience culminating in her debut on Broadway as a witch in *Faust* in 1928. Along the way, she joined the Theater Guild and married fellow actor Neill O'Malley, but the marriage ended in 1930, when she married her second husband, Herbert J. Biberman. A young Jewish actor from Philadelphia, Biberman had been part of the *Faust* production with Sondergaard and an active participant in the Guild, where he sometimes wrote and directed.

In 1935, the Bibermans traveled West to Hollywood, when Herbert accepted a contract to write and direct for Columbia Pictures. Though Gale had no acting prospects, she auditioned for director Mervyn LeRoy, who was casting for his latest project, *Anthony Adverse*, a lavish costume drama based on a bestselling novel of the same name. She won the part and the Oscar, as well as being offered other movie roles. She was featured in Paramount's *Maid of Salem* (1937), a tale of the seventeenth century witch trials and *The Life of Emile Zola* (also 1937), the Oscar-winning biopic about the famed French writer. She then signed a one-year contract with MGM, where she starred with other female contract players, including Luise Rainer, Lana Turner and Paulette Goddard (borrowed from David O. Selznick) in *Dramatic School* (1938), a forgettable copy-cat of *Stage Door.*

Her friend, LeRoy, had also made his way to Metro and was working on the studio's big Technicolor musical, *The Wizard of Oz*, when Sondergaard began her contract. The imaginative director saw Gale as a sexy, slinky, sinister Wicked Witch of the West in the *Oz* picture. Interest was shown in casting character veteran actress Edna May Oliver, but LeRoy was firm. He wanted Sondergaard to play a glamorous witch, "a fallen woman wearing green eyeshadow and a witch's hat made out of black sequins." Costume tests were done with the sequins and the eyeshadow, and even some photographic stills remain with Sondergaard in "ugly" garb but in the end, evil and ugly won out over evil and sexy and LeRoy and Sondergaard mutually agreed that someone else would be best suited to the part under those circumstances. That someone would become an icon among villains: Margaret Hamilton.

The same year as *Oz*, Sondergaard was back at Paramount as one of a supporting ensemble in the mystery-comedy *The Cat and the Canary*, starring Bob Hope and Paulette Goddard, with whom she had worked the previous year in *Dramatic School*. 1940 was a busy and prosperous year, first appearing as Tylette, a sinister cat come to life in the Shirley Temple vehicle, *The Blue Bird*. As 20th Century-Fox's answer to *The Wizard of Oz*, *The Blue Bird* was a huge Technicolor flop, though Sondergaard was her usual glossy, wicked villainess. The year also brought the actress roles in Fox's *The Mark of Zorro* and *The Letter* at Warner Brothers. The latter film cast Sondergaard as Mrs. Hammond, the scorned Eurasian wife. The actress had such commanding presence, without speaking a word of English in her role, that many have suggested she overshadowed the star of the picture, Bette Davis. She continued making movies, of all genres, throughout the '40s, even copping another Oscar nomination as Best Supporting Actress for her role in *Anna and the King of Siam* (1946).

In 1947, the United States House Un-American Activities Committee (HUAC) began investigations throughout the film colony for those with ties to the Communist party. Herbert Biberman, along with

242

other Hollywood writers and directors who were suspected of Communist activity, became infamously known as the Hollywood Ten, when they refused to testify in front of the committee. They were cited for contempt for Congress, imprisoned and blacklisted from working within the industry. Sondergaard's career was also cut short, her last film appearance for two decades being 1949's *East Side, West Side*, directed by her old friend, Mervyn LeRoy. In 1951, the actress was subpoenaed and ordered to testify before HUAC. "Deeply tanned and wearing a black and white checked suit," the New York Times reported, she "agreed that congressional committees should investigate subversive activities but said 'this committee is doing incriminating work.'" She took the Fifth Amendment and "refused to disclose her political affiliations," ultimately ending her career.

With movie and television work unavailable to her, Sondergaard created a one-woman stage show called appropriately, *Woman*, which she performed in the mid-1950s. In 1969, she returned to films, taking a small role in *Slaves*, her husband's first directorial effort in fifteen years and his last movie before he succumbed to bone cancer in 1971. Gale made a few more pictures, her last appearance in the psychological suspenser, *Echoes* in 1983. Two years later, at the age of eighty-six, the actress died from cerebrovascular thrombosis in Woodland Hills, California. The Biberman's had adopted two children, both of whom predeceased their mother.

Conrad Veidt

Cruel irony is not lost on the fact that suave cinema heavy Conrad Veidt, a staunch anti-Nazi, emigrated from Germany, first to England in the mid '30s, then to the United States (with his Jewish wife) at the onset of America's involvement in World War II, only to be cast as numerous nasty Nazis in several Hollywood productions. An actor of masterful performances spanning three decades and several countries, his career witnessed distinct periods, each offering Veidt the opportunity to display his talent. In a 1942 article for *Hollywood* magazine, writer Connie Curtis summed up the actor's sinister film persona of the 1940s when she said: "When Conrad Veidt takes a movie heroine in his arms, every woman in the audience knows that he is just as likely to choke her as kiss her. Yet there's probably not a woman in the audience who wouldn't gladly change places with the imperiled heroine."

Hans Walter Conrad Veidt came into the world on January 22, 1893, in the Berlin suburb of Potsdam, Bradenburg, Germany. According to Veidt, his father was "affectionately autocratic in his home life, strict, idealistic. He was almost fanatically conservative. It was one of the greatest sorrows of his life when I became an actor." On the opposite end of the spectrum, Veidt recalls that his mother, Amalie, was nurturing and his affection for her great.

As a youth, he gained a keen interest in acting, and spent many evenings at the Deutsches Theatre in Berlin, a well-known dramatic venue run by legendary director Max Reinhardt. These outings were paid for with money out of his mother's household account. Years later, Veidt recalled those early days: "I saw every sort of play and opera... Afterwards I would walk home the two miles from the west end to our suburb, because I had no money for the tram, and I would see myself playing all those parts, thrilling the world." He was introduced to Reinhardt who signed him to a contract as an extra at the Deutsches Theatre, where he slowly progressed to small speaking roles.

His burgeoning acting career was stalled in 1914, when he was drafted into the German Army and the following year sent to the Eastern Front, where he fought in the Battle of Warsaw and fell ill with jaundice and pneumonia. After a long convalescence, Veidt was reexamined in 1916 and found unfit to continue his service. After being given a full discharge, the actor resumed his career on the boards in Berlin, reapplying and being accepted at the Reinhardt Deutsches Theatre, where film scouts frequently attended performances. With his handsome, angular face, 6' 3" lean frame and graceful and dignified carriage, Conrad Veidt soon began acting in motion pictures, appearing in over a dozen in 1919 alone. Two of his early movies would be groundbreaking and launch the actor into one of the most successful careers in German cinema of the day.

Different From The Others (*Anders als die Andern*) was one of the first, if not *the* first, sympathetic portrayals of homosexuals on film. Veidt played a gay musician who is threatened with blackmail over his sexual identity, at a time when such issues were against the law in Germany. The plot was reworked in England in 1961 as *Victim*, starring Dirk Bogarde. In 1920, Veidt appeared in one of his best-known pictures and the one which made him an international movie star, *The Cabinet of Dr. Caligari*, in which he played a murderous somnambulist (sleepwalker) in one of the earliest entries of the horror film genre. It was a masterpiece of the

German Expressionism movement, with extreme sets, makeup and lighting, creating a surreal silent screen experience. Critics were mixed, though the reviews were aplenty across the globe, making Veidt famous, as he later acknowledged: "No matter what roles I play, I can't get Caligari out of my system."

As the 1920s progressed, Conrad became one of the highest-paid actors in Germany and in 1926 he was summoned to Hollywood by none other than actor John Barrymore who invited him to work in his next film project, *The Beloved Rogue*. That summer, Veidt received a telegram which read:

> "I saw your picture, *Waxworks*. You must play in my next picture. You must play King Louis XI. You know you are one of the most talented men in the film world. You don't know me, but I want you to come. I cannot make the picture without you. Yours sincerely, John Barrymore."

With his successful appearance in *The Beloved Rogue* came a contract with Universal Studio, where Veidt made his most famous American film to date, *The Man Who Laughs* (1928). Directed by the German Expressionist Paul Leni, the movie featured Veidt as Gwynplaine, a man whose face is mutilated by having a hideous grin carved from ear to ear. *Batman* creator Bob Kane acknowledged that Veidt's Gwynplaine inspired his visualization of the infamous comic book villain, the Joker, immortalized in the super hero series. As well-received as his performance in *The Man Who Laughs* was, long-term stardom in America was not to be. With the advent of sound films, the actor's poor grasp of English and his heavy accent, influenced him to move back to Germany in 1929.

Upon his return to his homeland, Veidt continued acting in films until the rise of the Nazi party caused the vehement anti-Nazi to make the decision to leave for good and relocate to England, where he had made a few pictures after his stint in Hollywood. In April 1933, a week after the actor's marriage to Ilona "Lily" Prager, who was Jewish, Veidt emigrated, despite efforts by Joseph Goebbels, right hand to Adolf Hitler in the Third Reich, to convince him to make only pro-Aryan films. As the Nazi movement continued to grow, Veidt was eventually able to get his former wife, Felicitas, and their young daughter Viola, out of Germany and into Switzerland before the start of World War II (Thrice married, Veidt was first wed in 1918, to German cabaret singer Augusta "Gussy" Holl, then Felicitas Radke in 1923 and finally Lily Prager).

After settling in London, Conrad Veidt worked on his English and made films, mostly in the spy thriller genre, often set during World War I. At the end of the decade, he and Lily became British citizens and the actor made three films for famed English director Michael Powell, including *The Spy in Black* (1939), *Contraband* (1940) and *The Thief of Bagdad* (1940). The last of these three was filmed in vivid Technicolor and cast Veidt as the evil Jaffar, bringing his screen persona closer to the kind of roles he would frequent during the next phase of his career.

While in New York promoting his British spy yarn, *Contraband*, the actor was contacted by Louis B. Mayer, head of MGM, Hollywood's most prestigious studio, offering him a juicy part in an upcoming production, *Escape*, which would feature two of the studio's biggest stars, Norma Shearer and Robert Taylor. Veidt accepted and subsequently remained in the United States working steadily in A-level pictures at both MGM and Warner Brothers. Aware that many if not most of the roles he would play would be Nazis, Veidt had it written into his contract that they be villainous, part of his contribution to the war effort. He wanted no trace of sympathetic representation for the group on film. A more tangible contribution was financial assistance, as the actor sent large portions of his salary back to Britain to support the Allies.

His smooth, menacing characters were played seamlessly and elegantly, first with Joan Crawford in Metro's *A Woman's Face*, then opposite Red Skelton in the comedy *Whistling in the Dark* (both 1941). In 1942, Warner Brothers contacted MGM to request Veidt's services for their upcoming production of the wartime romance, *Casablanca*. Warners' originally wanted to cast actor/director Otto Preminger, who was under contract to 20th Century-Fox, in the part of villainous Nazi, Major Heinrich Strasser. However, Preminger's boss, Darryl F. Zanuck, demanded $7,000 for the Austrian actor's services and Warners balked. With shooting slated to begin and desperate to cast the part, the studio paid the $5,000 requested by Louis Mayer for Veidt, the next obvious choice, according to Warners honcho Hal Wallis. "This role epitomizes the cruelty and the criminal instincts and murderous trickery of the typical Nazi," Veidt said of Strasser. "I know this man well. He is the reason I gave up Germany many years ago. He is a man who turned fanatic and betrayed his friends, his homeland, and himself in his lust to be somebody and to get something for nothing."

Back at MGM there was more irony, as Veidt was cast as a leader of the German resistance, a heroic part, in the glossy wartime suspenser, *Above Suspicion* with Joan Crawford in 1943. It would be his last role. On April 3, 1943, the actor collapsed at the Riviera Country Club in Los Angeles, the victim of a massive heart attack. He was taken to the Santa Monica Hospital where he was pronounced dead. As character actors go, Conrad Veidt could play suave and sinister with equal ease and often portraying them in the same role. A kind man, his talent was as large as his generosity.

L u c i l e   W a t s o n

"Of course not, but we women are so much more sensible. When we tire of ourselves, we change the way we do our hair, or hire a new cook, or... or decorate the house. I suppose a man could do over his office, but he never thinks of anything so simple. No, dear, a man has only one escape from his old self: to see a different self in the mirror of some woman's eyes." Wise words from the no-nonsense Mrs. Morehead, mother of soon-to-be-divorced Mary Haines (Norma Shearer), in MGM's classic comedy, *The Women* (1939). Perfectly portrayed (as most every character was in the all-female cast) by the stately and distinguished Lucile Watson, it was exactly the kind of role in which the elderly actress excelled: a quintessential dowager, both moneyed and mannered, blue-blooded and haughty, yet with a certain degree of warmth that transferred through her character.

A daughter of Canada, Watson was born in Quebec on May 27, 1879. Her father, Thomas Charles Watson, was a major with the Royal Sherwood Foresters. As a girl, she was educated at the local Ursuline Convent, then, determined to be an actress, she came to the United States and trained for two years at the American Academy of Dramatic Arts in New York City. In 1902, she was on Broadway, at the Empire Theater, in a show called *The Wisdom of the Wise* and in subsequent shows, usually played mothers or aunts, much older than her actual age. Her next play was *The Girl with Green Eyes*, written by Clyde Fitch, an extremely popular playwright at the turn of the 20th-century. She appeared in several other Fitch plays before his death in 1909. She was a very active stage actress for decades after, gaining accolades and fine reviews, with a 1934 issue of *Theatre Arts* claiming: "When she comes on stage, everyone else might as well go off."

In the autumn of 1928, at the age of forty-nine, Watson married playwright Louis E(van) Shipman, a fellow Canadian who was ten years her senior. It wasn't her first marriage, however, having wed actor Rockliffe Fellowes very briefly around 1910. Upon her marriage to Shipman, she left the stage except for a short appearance in *That's the Woman* in 1930. The couple moved to France and Watson remained married to the playwright until his death in 1933.

The actress had a small, uncredited role in the short silent film version of *The Girl with Green Eyes*, and another in 1930. In 1934, after the death of her husband, she returned to work, both on stage and screen. She appeared as Mrs. Fanny Townsend on Broadway in *No More Ladies*, a role that was recreated in the 1935 Joan Crawford movie by Edna May Oliver. On the screen, Watson played her first substantial role, at the age of fifty-five, in the MGM romantic comedy, *What Every Woman Knows*, starring Helen Hayes. The late '30s offered the beginning of many rich characterizations by the actress including aristocrats, a nun and disapproving mothers, parts that filled her arsenal of screen personas.

1939 brought the role of wise and knowing Mrs. Morehead in *The Women*, directed by George Cukor. It became one of her best-known parts, in a cast of Hollywood's most stalwart movie actresses of the day (though not a man to be seen). She was then considered for the part, along with fellow character stars Laura Hope Crews, Mary Boland, Cora Witherspoon and Alice Brady, of Edythe Van Hopper, the wealthy

American snob in Alfred Hitchcock's *Rebecca* (1940). The part went to newcomer Florence Bates, but Watson got her chance to work with the talented director the following year in his screwball comedy, *Mr. and Mrs. Smith* with Carole Lombard and Robert Montgomery.

She continued working in the theater during this period, garnering a good role as Fanny Farrelly in the drama, *Watch on the Rhine*, a part she reprised for the 1943 film version starring Paul Lukas (who also played his character in both stage and screen versions) and Bette Davis. She was nominated for an Oscar for her efforts and *Variety* praised her performance as "a gem in the original play, [and] is even more striking in the expanded part on the screen." Time on the set wasn't all sunshine and roses, however, as she and the film's star, Davis, butting heads over their respective political views, Watson being a staunch Republican and Bette fiercely Democratic. According to Davis biographer, Charles Higham, Bette "found her [Lucile] tiresome and made no bones about showing it."

The actress appeared in many golden era classics in significant roles, as well as co-starring with Hollywood's biggest stars. In *The Thin Man Goes Home* (1944), she played detective Nick Charles' mother (with Harry Davenport as his father). In 1946, she portrayed the grandmother in Walt Disney's *Song of the South* and was a perfect, if not cantankerous Aunt March in MGM's *Little Women* (1949). Except for three film roles, Watson's professional time during the 1950s was spent in television work, with her last appearance being in 1954. The respected actress died in New York on June 25, 1962, at the age of eighty-three, the victim of a heart attack.

Dame May Whitty

When the Order of the British Empire was established in 1917 to honor those who had "rendered valuable service to the State," it was decided that distinguished women who had made notable contributions to the arts and sciences or offered themselves to public service would receive a rank comparable to men's knighthood. The title bestowed on them was Dame. Throughout the twentieth century and early part of the twenty-first, numerous actresses from the stage and screen have been the recipient of the prestigious honor, among them Edith Evans, Elizabeth Taylor, Maggie Smith and others. The very first of this exclusive group, however, bears the name that many have forgotten, if they ever knew of her to begin with: May Whitty.

She was born Mary Louise Whitty in Liverpool, England in the summer of 1865. Her father, William, was a journalist and her paternal grandfather, Michael James Whitty, was the Chief Constable in Liverpool, as well as the founder and editor of the *Liverpool Daily Post*. She made her first appearance on the stage in 1881, at the age of sixteen, in the chorus of *The Mountain Sylph* at the Liverpool Court Theatre. The following year she made her London debut in a comic opera, *Boccaccio*. She then went to work under the Hare and Kendal management at the prestigious St. James's Theatre.

In 1892, Whitty married Ben Webster, a barrister with dramatic ambitions who gave up his law career for the stage. The couple had a son, Benjamin Webster IV, who died in infancy. They traveled to America in 1895 and Whitty appeared on Broadway and played rather colorless characters. In 1905, the actress bore a daughter in New York City, and named the child, Margaret (as an adult she would become a well-known stage producer and director). Whitty eventually returned to England, where she was "in constant demand in the West End." In London, the Websters lived in a flat in Covent Garden, overlooking St. Paul's. Their home served as a meeting place for actors, both English and American alike. According to one source, "the Barrymores might just as easily be there as some unknown player." They were so involved in seeking the best interest of those in their profession that the British Actor's Equity was founded in their home.

During the First World War, the actress divided her time between the stage and patriotic war work. Among her contributions for the British cause was the raising of $1,000,000 for a disabled soldier's and sailor's home. It was for this civic commitment, and not her stage work, that she was made a Dame Commander of the Order of the British Empire by King George V in 1918.

She continued to work on the stage, transitioning to middle-aged and elderly characters. In 1935, she played one such part on the London stage which would become her breakout role. As Mrs. Bramson, an irascible old lady who holds court in her ever-present wheelchair, Whitty was one of the central characters in the thriller, *Night Must Fall*. She played the part again on Broadway in the fall of 1936, and the following year recreated Mrs. Bramson in the film version, making her Hollywood motion picture debut at the age of seventy-two. Her tour de force performance garnered her an Oscar nomination as Best Supporting Actress and led to a string of quality roles in A-list pictures, in which she played elderly aunts, maiden ladies and wealthy dowagers. Her most memorable film was arguably *The Lady Vanishes*, a 1938 mystery-thriller directed by Alfred Hitchcock. She is the *Lady* of the title, Miss Froy, who mysteriously disappears from a moving train. One story goes that the famed director told the cameraman not to put film in the camera during a screen test of an actress auditioning for Miss Froy, as he had already secretly committed Whitty to the role.

In 1938, she and Webster moved to Hollywood permanently, though retaining their British citizenship. She hit Broadway again in 1940 as the Nurse in the revival of *Romeo and Juliet*, which starred Laurence Olivier and Vivien Leigh, who would marry shortly after the show ended its run. Her husband would play Montague, a role which would be his last. For Dame May, the 1940s saw many fine roles, usually as aristocrats and upper-crusts. She was nominated for a second time as Best Supporting Actress in the wartime melodrama, *Mrs. Miniver* (1942), and had a fun part in another British based American classic, *Gaslight* (1944), starring Charles Boyer and Ingrid Bergman. She appeared once again with her *Mrs. Miniver* co-star, Greer Garson in the biopic, *Madame Curie* and with Irene Dunne in *The White Cliffs of Dover*.

In 1945, at the age of eighty, she again appeared on Broadway, in a play called *Therese*, which was staged by her daughter, Margaret Webster. A year and a half later, in February 1947, her husband of more than fifty years, died at the age of the age of eighty-two in Hollywood. She would follow a year later, also at the age of eighty-two, of cancer. Always popular and respected in the British colony in Hollywood, her funeral was attended by several of that community's elite, including, C. Aubrey Smith, Edmund Gwenn, Herbert Marshall, Boris Karloff and Brian Aherne. At her request, in lieu of flowers, packages were sent to the England's needy through Co-Operative for American Remittances to Europe (CARE).

Oh, What a Character!

The people and their respective lives featured above are only a partial representation of those who populated the world of the classic Hollywood character actor. Their talent and energy lit up hundreds of classic Hollywood movies. During their heyday, they helped ease the harsh realities of the Great Depression during the Thirties and World War II in the Forties. They were funny, heartwarming, inspiring, while others were conniving, sinister or downright evil. They covered all genres that Tinsel Town felt like producing. It was with their undeniably essential support that classic movies became just that; classic.

Audiences who originally saw performances by their favorite supporting players enjoyed them in first run, but contemporary movie buffs can appreciate them over and over again with modern technology. DVD collections abound with Eve Arden, Eugene Pallette and Ward Bond. They have become and continue to be old, dear and trusted friends, who make us feel good, scared and always involved in the story in which they are a part. They represent a time when movies had a unique quality, vintage if you will. They produce in the viewer a safe and comfortable feeling of familiarity and satisfaction. They are a vital part of Hollywood history and we wouldn't have it any other way.

Nostalgia is a powerful thing and these nostalgic personalities remind us of another time when the magic of the silver screen could make us laugh, cry or gasp in suspense. For that we are truly thankful. They instill in the viewer a feeling of warmth and comfort because even if the audience hasn't seen the picture yet, if a classic movie character actor was a part of it, they know that they are in for quite a treat. Fasten your seat belts....

A Note to Loyal Readers & Classic Movie Fans

If you enjoyed this book (and I truly hope you did as I thoroughly enjoyed writing it), I hope you will consider leaving a positive and favorable comment/review on Amazon. A positive review is important to independent authors and only takes a moment.

Also, if you'd like to read more about classic Hollywood and the movies it produced, feel free to check out my other books and e-Magazines at my Amazon author page or check out a sampling of the titles listed below. I thank you for your interest in my work and genuinely appreciate your support.

Other books on Classic Movies by Rupert Alistair

Girl Next Door: The Life and Career of Jeanne Crain

The Search for Scarlett O'Hara: Gone with the Wind and Hollywood's Most Famous Casting Call

Sin and Vice in Black & White: 15 Classic Pre-Code Movies

Hollywood and the Home Front: 25 Fabulous Films from the Forties

Classic Movies: 14 Films You May Not Have Seen, But Should

Bibliography

Aberth, John. *A Knight at the Movies: Medieval History on Film*. Psychology Press, 2003

Bainter, Fay. "Only 26 – But on the Stage 21 Years." *The American Magazine*, Vol 89, Crowell-Collier Publishing Company, 1920

Bickford, Charles. *Bulls Balls Bicycles & Actors*. Paul S. Eriksson, Inc., 1965

Bolino, August C. Men of Massachusetts: Bay State Contributors to American Society.

Bonanno, Margaret Wander. *Angela Lansbury: A Biography*. New York: St. Martin's Press, 1987

Brotherton, Jamie and Ted Okuda. *Dorothy Lee: The Life and Films of the Wheeler and Woolsey Girl*. McFarland, 2013

Burke, Billie, with Cameron Shipp. *With a Feather on My Nose*. Appleton-Century-Crofts, Inc., 1949

Button, Simon. "Dame Angela Lansbury: 'I run a real British household.'" *Sunday Express*, March 2, 2014

Callow, Simon. *Charles Laughton: A Difficult Actor*. Mt Prospect, Illinois: Fromm International, 1987

Canton, Rolf J. *Minnesotans in the Movies*. Nodin Press, 2006

Carradine, David. *Endless Highway*. Journey Editions, 1995

Christensen, Lawrence O., William E. Foley, Gary Kemer. *Dictionary of Missouri Biography*. University of Missouri Press, 1999

Curtis, James. *James Whale: A New World of Gods and Monsters*. Boston, Faber and Faber. 1998

Current Biography Yearbook 1979. H.W. Wilson Company, 1980

Current Biography: *Charles Coburn*. H.W. Wilson Company, 1944

Current Biography, 1946. *Sydney Greenstreet*. Hw Wilson Co. 1946

Current Biography, 1943. *Edmund Gwenn*. Hw Wilson Co. 1943

Current Biography, 1946. *Edward Everett Horton*. Hw Wilson Co. 1946

Current Biography, *1950. Elsa Lanchester*. Hw Wilson Co. January 1950

Current Biography: Volume 10. *Walter Huston*. H.W. Wilson Company, 1949

Current Biography, 1940. *Hattie McDaniel*. Hw Wilson Co. 1940

Current Biography, 1953. *Lucile Watson*. Hw Wilson Co. 1953

Disability Studies, Temple U Blog; article on Edith Lanchester (1871-1966)

Davis, Ronald L. *The Glamour Factory: Inside Hollywood's Big Studio System*. Southern Methodist University Press. 1993

Davis, Ronald L. *John Ford: Hollywood's Old Master*. University of Oklahoma Press, 2014

Dumont, Hervé. *Frank Borzage: The Life and Films of a Hollywood Romantic*. McFarland, 2006

Emden, Richard Van and Vic Piuk. *Famous: 1914-1918*. Pen and Sword, 2010

Fay, Robin. "Charles Coburn (1877-1961)." *New Georgia Encyclopedia*. 28 August 2013

Fitzgerald, Michael G. and Boyd Magers. *Ladies of the Western: Interviews with Fifty-One More Actresses from the Silent Era to the Television Westerns of the 1950s and 1960s*. MacFarland, 2006

Foster, Charles. *Once Upon a Time in Paradise: Canadians in the Golden Age of Hollywood*. Dundurn, 2003

Freeman, Nicholas. *1895: Drama, Disaster and Disgrace in Late Victorian Britain*. Oxford University Press, 2011

Garraty, John Arthur and Mark Christopher Carnes. *American National Biography, Volume 8*. (Gladys George) Oxford University Press, 1999

Gordon, Ruth. *Myself Among Others*. Atheneum, 1971

Grobel, Lawrence. *The Hustons: The Life and Times of a Hollywood Dynasty*. Skyhorse Publishing, Inc., 2014

Hanke, Ken. *Charlie Chan at the Movies: History, Filmography, and Criticism*. McFarland, 1990

Harrison, Rex. *Rex: An Autobiography*. William Morrow & Company, 1975

Harvard College Class of 1900 Second Report. University Press, 1906

Harmetz, Aljean. *The Making of the Wizard of Oz*. Chicago Review Press, 2013

Harmetz, Aljean. *Round Up the Usual Suspects: The Making of "Casablanca" – Bogart, Bergman, and World War II*. Hyperion. 1992

Higham, Charles. *The Life of Bette Davis*. New York: Macmillan, 1981

Hollywood Magazine. "Magnificent Menace." May 1942

Jackson, Carlton. *Hattie: The Life of Hattie McDaniel*. Madison Books, 1993

Johns, Eric. *Dames of the Theatre*. Arlington House, 1975

Johnson, Briscoe. *The actors' birthday book: First -third series. An authoritative insight into the lives of the men and women of the stage born between January first and December thirty-first, Volume 2*. Moffat, Yard and Company, 1908

Lanchester, Elsa. *Elsa Lanchester, Myself*. New York: St. Martin's Press, 1983

Leff, Leonard J. *Hitchcock and Selznick: The Rich and Strange Collaboration of Alfred Hitchcock and David O. Selznick in Hollywood*. University of California Press. 1999

Leve, Ariel. Angela Lansbury: "I'm never left behind. I'm the bionic woman." *The Telegraph*, May 21, 2012

Mank, Gregory W. *The Hollywood Hissables*. Scarecrow Press, 1989

Mank, Gregory William. *Women in Horror Films, 1930s*. MacFarland, 2005

Mann, William J. *Behind the Screen: How Gays and Lesbians Shaped Hollywood, 1910-1969*. Viking. 2001

Mantle, Burns. *The Best Plays of 1924-25*. Dodd Mead, 1924

Matzen, Robert. *Fireball: Carole Lombard and the Mystery of Flight 3*. Paladin Communications, 2013

McBride, Joseph. *Searching for John Ford: A Life*. St. Martin's Press, 2001

McClure, Arthur F., Alfred E. Twomey and Ken D. Jones. *More Character People*. Secaucus, New Jersey, Citadel Press. 1984

Merriman, Andy. *Margaret Rutherford: Dreadnought with Good Manners.* Aurum Press, 2011

Monush, Barry. *Encyclopedia of Hollywood Film Actors, Vol. 1: From the Silent Era to 1965.* Applause. 2003

Morgan, Michelle. *The Mammoth Book of Hollywood Scandals.* Little Brown Book Group, 2013

Mosley, Leonard. *Zanuck: The Rise and Fall of Hollywood's Last Tycoon.* McGraw-Hill, 1984

New England Vintage Film Society, Inc. *Playbills to Photoplays: Stage Performers Who Pioneered the Talkies.* Xlibris Corporation, 2010

The New York Times Film Reviews, Volume 2. *Boss Tweed,* page 974

Nissen, Axel. *Mothers, Mammies and Old Maids: Twenty-Five Character Actresses of Golden Age Hollywood.* McFarland, 2012

Parish, James Robert, and Robert L. Bowers. *The MGM Stock Company: The Golden Age.* Arlington House, 1973

Picture-Play Magazine, March 1917

Pollock, Christopher. *Reel San Francisco Stories: An Annotated Filmography of the Bay Area.* Lulu.com, 2013

Preminger, Otto. *Preminger: An Autobiography.* Doubleday & Co., 1977, page 84

Rathbone, Basil. *In and Out of Character.* Limelight Editions (Reprint), 2004

Regester, Charlene B. *African American Actresses: The Struggle for Visibility, 1900-1960.* 2010

Reid, John Howard. *Movie Westerns: Hollywood Films the Wild, Wild West.* Lulu.com, 2005

Rutherford, Margaret and Gwen Robyns. *Margaret Rutherford: An Autobiography.* W.H. Allen, 1972

Seaman, Barbara. *Lovely Me: The Life of Jacqueline Susann.* Seven Stories Press, 1996

Shields Family Archive. 1907-1974. James Hardiman Library, NUIG

Schlossheimer, Michael. *Gunmen and Gangsters: Profiles of Nine Actors Who Portrayed Memorable Screen Tough Guys.* McFarland, 2001

Schmidt, Karl. A Star of To-morrow. *Everybody's Magazine*, Vol 39, 1918

Soister, John T. *Conrad Veidt on Screen: A Comprehensive Illustrated Filmography.* MacFarland, 2002

Tornabene, Lyn. *Long Live The King: A Biography of Clark Gable.* Putnam, 1976

Tucker, David C. *Eve Arden: A Chronicle of All Film, Television, Radio and Stage Performances.* MacFarland. 2011

Vogel, Michelle. *Marjorie Main: The Life and Films of Hollywood's "Ma Kettle."* McFarland, 2011

Wallis, Hal and Charles Higham. *Starmaker: The Autobiography of Hal Wallis.* MacMillan, 1980

Who's Who at Metro Goldwyn Mayer. Loew's, 1940

Newspaper & Magazine Articles; Websites

Texas State Historical Website. Jacoby, Florence Rabe

"The Girl Nobody Knows." *Silver Screen Magazine*, October 1941

"She Flouted Rules in Winning Career." *Philadelphia Inquirer*, June 9, 1942

"Edward Arnold Seeking Divorce." *St. Petersburg Independent*, May 15, 1948, pg. 3

Photoplay Magazine. "From Pauper to Prince." May 1936, pg. 79

"Those Old Reliables." *Brooklyn Daily Eagle*, October 15, 1939

"AFRA Won't Support Members Who 'Offend' Via Red Links." *Billboard*, April 7, 1951

"Una Merkel Little Changed by the Years." Ward Morehouse Syndicated Column, February 14, 1960

Una Merkel Obituary. *Los Angeles Times*, January 4, 1986

"Una Merkel in Death Escape." *Lodi News-Sentinel*, March 6, 1945

"Actor Thomas Mitchell Dies of Cancer at 70." *Pittsburgh Post-Gazette*, Dec. 18, 1962

"Two Bits a Column." *The Deseret News*, June 15, 1945

Theatre: Tour. *Time Magazine*, July 22, 1940

"All Feminine Except the 'Billie'." *Photoplay Magazine*, Dec. 1917

"Marjorie Main Got Her Start in Chautauqua." *St. Petersburg Times*, October 14, 1941

"Warner Oland Dies in Sweden." *Associated Press* (*The Tuscaloosa News*), August 7, 1938

"A Highbrow Villain from the Arctic Circle." *Photoplay Magazine*, February 1918

"Born at Studio." *Associated Press*, May 30, 1948

"Hardworking Actress Virginia Grey Dies at 87." *Washington Post*, August 5, 2004

"Once Was Never Enough." *Vanity Fair*, January 2000.

"Carole Landis Does Not Want to Be 'Ping Girl.'" *Life*, June 17, 1940, page 94

"Carole Landis Sues Fourth Husband for Divorce." *Lewiston Evening Journal*. March 23, 1948, p 9

"The Biggest Stars in the WOW Country Firmament." *Wallowa County Chieftain*, May 30, 2008

"Film's Heavyweight Champ Chops (Puff) Wood (Puff)." *Pittsburg Press*, August 3, 1944

"Notes on a Cockney Accent." *New York Times*, September 1, 1940

"Heart Attack Fatal to Actor Walter Huston." *Los Angeles Times*, April 8, 1950

http://www.atsu.edu/museum/subscription/pdfs/1st_school_of_medicine.pdf

"Classic Hollywood: Ann Rutherford relives growing up in the movies." *Los Angeles Times*, August 18, 2010

John Carradine Obituary. *New York Times*. November 29, 1988

"Gladys George Dies of a Brain Hemorrhage." *Nashua Telegraph* (N.H.). December 10, 1954, page 1

"Expert Laird Tells How to Lose Weight." *The Pittsburg Press*, December 3, 1944

Laird Cregar, Obituary. *New York Times*, December 10, 1944

American National Biography Online: *Charles Douville Coburn*

"Famed Actor Charles Coburn Dies in New York City at 84." *Lawrence Journal-World* (AP report), August 31, 1961

The March of Time and the American Century. ProQuest, 2007

"Charles Coburn Celebrates 60-Year Theatrical Career" *Reading Eagle*, March 8, 1950

"A Murder Mystery Even Miss Marple Couldn't Exorcise." *UK Daily Mail Online*, November 5, 2009

"Dawn Langley Simmons, Flamboyant Writer, Dies at 77." *New York Times*, September 24, 2000

"Miss Marple's torment". *Express: Home of the Daily and Sunday Express*, September 25, 2009

wwwthepeerage.com

The Daily Times from New Philadelphia, Ohio. September 6, 1929, page 5

"Kentucky Beauty in 'Syncopating Sue.'" *Ottawa Citizen*, November 20, 1926

US Census Record, 1930, Los Angeles (Districts 0001-0250), Los Angeles County, California

Voices of Oklahoma: Ed Dumit Transcript

"Things are Happening to Patric Knowles." *St. Petersburg Times*, February 17, 1946

"Ingram Meets Olympic." *New York Times.* September 29, 1964, page 43

"Charles Bickford Dies; Jennifer Jones Found Near Death." *Ocala Star-Banner*, November 10, 1967

"Charles Bickford Dies on Coast." *New York Times*, November 10, 1967

"Charles Bickford's Battle with Lion Caused Him a Seven Year Wait for Job." *The Milwaukee Journal*, June 24, 1943

"Clara Blandick Dies." *Bridgeport Post.* April 16, 1962, page 44

The Pittsburgh Press, June 12, 1932, Page 34

"Dame May Whitty Acts at 80." *Life*, October 22, 1945, page 57

Dame May Whitty Obituary. *Billboard*, June 12, 1948, page 47

"Percy Kilbride, Film Actor, Dies." *New York Times*, December 12, 1964

"Sounds Just Like an Old Rusty Gate." *Pittsburgh Post-Gazette*, July 3, 1944

"The Story of Conrad Veidt." *Sunday Dispatch*, October 1934

Frank Morgan, Actor in Movies, Dies at Age 59. *The Springfield Union*, September 19, 1949

Frank Morgan – Of Morgan-Ameche-Langford Show. *The Coaticook Observer* (Sherbrooke, Quebec),

October 10, 1947, page 7

"Fitzgerald Meets Fame — and He Frowns." *New York Times*. January 14, 1945

Manufactured by Amazon.com.au
Sydney, New South Wales, Australia

13248784R00156